DEVELOPMENT WITH A HUMAN FACE

DEVELOPMENT WITH A HUMAN FACE

Poverty Eradication and Globalisation

G P Isser

GYAN PUBLISHING HOUSE
NEW DELHI-110002

Development With A Human Face : Poverty Eradication and Globalisation

Rs. 720

ISBN: 81-212-0956-0

Published In 2007 in India by
Gyan Publishing House
5, Ansari Road, Darya Ganj,
New Delhi-110002
Phones : 23282060, 23261060
Fax : 011-23285914
E-mail: books@gyanbooks.com
Website: www.gyanbooks.com

Lasser Type Setting by: Rudra Computer Graphics, Delhi
Printed at : Salasar Imaging System, Delhi

Dedication

Ganesh Prasad Isser passed away on 27 December 2006 in New Delhi just after completing the manuscript of this book. As per his wish, this book is dedicated to all those individuals and groups who dedicate their time and lives to the eradication of poverty

Contents

List of Annexures

List of Tables

Preface

Globalization has been widely perceived as a road to economic development. Progressive integration of developing countries with the global economy combined with technological advances has yielded rich dividends in the form of rapid economic growth across the globe. As more and more countries have integrated with the global economy, it has given rise to new concerns and challenges. It has been strongly debated whether economic growth propelled by globalization has promoted welfare to the society. In the current literature on globalization, perceptions widely differ on the human face of globalization. This issue has been a subject of intensive debate among economists and policy makers. Some argue that since the invisible hand of the market distributes the benefits of economic growth, globalization has no human face. On the other hand, the argument runs that the social outcome of globalization depends on the choices of the policies through an appropriate development strategy, and economic growth can be combined with human welfare. In other words, the proponents of globalization argue that there is no contradiction between development with a human face and globalization.

Globalization is irreversible and it generates economic growth, which is an indispensable condition to wipe out poverty and deprivation from the developing world. The world has witnessed massive increase in resources, which can be harnessed to shape appropriate and adequate response to the challenges that emerge from the play of market forces in promoting equity and justice along with rapid development. It is true that globalization is driven by market forces and these determine the beneficiaries of the dividends generated.

This study addresses this concern and brings to focus the imbalances that persist among nations and within nations in economic and social capabilities. It is through the eradication of poverty from the developing world that globalization will acquire a human face. The study analyses the development experience of some countries that succeeded in combining high rates of economic growth and eradication of poverty. The development path chosen by these countries enabled all to participate in the dividends of a growing economy, which was spurred by the forces of globalization. In all these cases, it shows that welfare oriented public policies played an important role in giving human face to development.

The book incorporates a detailed study of the process of India's integration with a global economy and it brings to light the challenges that policy makers are facing in combining rapid economic growth with equitable development. India has endeavored to meet this challenge by choosing a development pattern which has made a dent in poverty. The development strategy shows that along with progressive integration of a developing economy with the global economy, positive social outcomes can also be reaped.

G.P. Isser

Acknowledgement

The analysis in this book centers around two basic themes viz. poverty and globalization. With a fast changing development scenario and speeding globalization, it was not possible to capture the changing economic parameters without the cooperation and assistance given to me by several organizations and institutes that I drew on for material and information. In this regard, I must acknowledge with grateful thanks the help and assistance rendered to me by the Director, (library) Ministry of External Affairs; Librarian, National Council of Applied Economics Research (NCAER); Librarian, Research and Information System for the non-alignment and other developing countries (RIS); Librarian, World Bank Documentation Center; Librarian, United Nations Information Center (UNIC); and Librarian, United Nations Development Programme (UNDP). They extended excellent cooperation to me in my present work.

To understand the multi-faceted dimension of poverty in its totality, an endeavour has been made to project the poverty-profile of the "poorest of the poor" in the developing world. Writing on these aspects required a mass of up to date material and statistics related to the dynamics of development of the "The Least Developed Countries". This was facilitated by the study of the LDC Reports and TDRs of UNCTAD which incorporate very comprehensive analysis of development scenario of LDCs.

In facilitating my task of collecting statistics related to poverty profiles of developing countries, the functionaries of World Bank, UNIC and UNDP gave valuable support. I extend my grateful thanks to them.

In the process of completing the book, Shri BP Garg, Managing Director, Gyan Publishing House made valuable suggestions. I owe words of gratitude to him. I had commendable help from Shri Amit Garg, Director (Production) Gyan Publishing House in organising various aspects of publication such as design etc. Shri Pritam Giri from editorial staff provided much needed assistance in completing the book. I extend my grateful thanks to Shri Amit Garg and to his colleagues.

My heartfelt gratitude to my most loyal and steadfast support, my wife Godavari, who stood by me always despite the innumerable demands on her time and effort.

Introduction

The book is organized in seven chapters which cover the themes and sub-themes developed during the study.

Chapter-I. Through the analysis of the concepts expounded by many economists, the chapter brings to focus the emphasis that has been given to trade in the process of economic growth. It traces out the various stages through which the concepts of economists on the subject have undergone significant changes. It also brings out the slowly emerging institutional support to the role of trade in development during the last five decades. After analysis of the theoretical aspects the study shifts to empirical aspects of growth and trade relationships. While on this subject, the development experience of developing economies since the first development decade is analysed.

The chapter builds up empirical support to the thesis that trade is a crucial factor in economic growth. It also shows how the growth of trade among developing countries can contribute to trade expansion. The study of the role of exports in Indian economic development up to the 1980s gives a comparative evaluation and brings out constraints that the economy faced because of weak export performance and limited import capacity. The study analyses the effects of adverse balance of payments on Indian economy in 1991 which led to the economic crisis.

Chapter-II. The second chapter brings out the main features of economic globalization; capturing it through expanding international trade, increased accessibility to global finance for economic development, revolution in information technology and advent of a knowledge economy. It throws light on the positive impact of globalization which has led to an enormous increase in the creation of wealth in the global economy. The chapter brings to focus the extraordinary speed with which globalization is progressing and, in this context, identifies new forces such as revolution in information technology and technological advances in production and business organization. These new forces have led to increasing economic activities at international level, which were earlier conducted at the national level.

Chapter –III. The third chapter analyses the catalytic role of globalization in accelerating economic growth of developing countries in East and South East Asia. The case studies of selected developing countries such as the Republic of Korea, Malaysia, Thailand, Indonesia, China etc. adds to the empirical evidence of dividends in terms of economic growth while highlighting the benefits of globalization. The chapter draws attention to the concerns and challenges that have surfaced during the era of globalization. In this context, three major concerns are brought to focus. First, progressive integration of developing countries with the global economy makes them vulnerable to financial instability. Second, it brings to focus the stagnation in the Least Developed Countries mostly located in sub-Saharan Africa. The contrast in growth scenarios presents a key developmental challenge for globalization in the 21st century. Apart from the development gap, other imbalances have surfaced which need to be removed for globalization to effectively impact the process of economic development. For developing countries, integrating with the global economy can be fruitful only when they are able to reap dividends from their comparative advantages in expanding international trade. Globalization should be all-inclusive rather than selective.

Finally, the study brings out the areas of importance for developing countries such as Agriculture and Services, which have not been adequately covered by globalization. Unless these sectors are liberalized, the benefits of globalization will continue to be asymmetrical.

Chapter IV. This chapter presents an analysis of the impact of globalization on South Asian economic developments. The study brings to focus the regional dimensions of globalization and shows the divergence among the developing countries in sharing the dividends. It also shows the progress made by South Asia in adapting it's economic and trade policies to the forces of globalization. The increasing trade and investment in the post-reforms era underlines the importance of integration of the regional economies. It also analyses the prospects for South Asian integration with the global economy, which will depend on national and regional policy initiatives. The chapter brings to focus the need for adequate global response to enable these economies to realize comparative advantages in international trade.

Chapter V. This section brings out the changing landscape of poverty in the developing world. It presents empirical evidence of developing countries in East and South East Asia who succeeded in combining high rates of economic growth with significant reduction in poverty. The chapter brings to focus the role of choice of policies, which enable economies to combine economic growth with a human face. The era of globalization has witnessed a decline in the incidence of poverty and rise in the living standards of people in a number of countries. The chapter highlights the challenges that globalization faces in the 21st century. In this context, it contrasts the persistence of poverty among the Least Developed Countries (LDCs) where poverty instead of declining shows an increasing trend. The commitments made by the international community in achieving the Millennium Development Goals

(MDGs) are also examined. The study finds a huge gap between the targets for reducing poverty, both income and non-income, and the progress in the fulfillment of these goals. Unless the interaction between globalization and economic growth redresses this imbalance in the global economy, development with a human face will continue to remain an unfinished agenda of global development.

Chapter VI. This section identifies that in the emerging global economy, India has a special role to play. It has made progress towards integrating with the global economy and has improved its capabilities to play an important role in the world economy. In the new millennium, it has witnessed a sustained high rate of economic growth, a strong and healthy external profile with foreign exchange reserves at dollar 170 billion, increasing foreign trade etc. The country has also achieved a revolution in information technology, which has brought it on the global information technology scene. The chapter examines the growing economic strength and analyses how it can progressively integrate with the global economy and emerge as a global economic player.

While India has progressed towards integration with the global economy, it faces serious challenges in achieving high levels of human and social development. In this context, chapter-V brings out the progress made by India in four important areas of human and social development viz. **i.** Poverty alleviation **ii.** Employment **iii.** Education **iv.** Health. The chapter also traces out the progress made by India in the fulfillment of the Millennium Development Goals. The issue of energy to fuel growth along with growing environmental concerns is also explored.

Chapter VII. The concluding chapter takes into account some of the critiques of globalization by the UN, NGOs and others. These are relevant to developing countries in avoiding the pitfalls experienced by some while 'opening up' too rapidly to global forces.

The issue of an equitable trade regime is also deliberated upon. Due cognizance is taken of the conceptual critique viz. the battle of the individual versus the MNCs. The chapter ends with some general prescriptive ideas for India to serve as a role model of growth in the new global paradigm.

1

Role of Trade in Development

TRACKING THE EVOLUTIONARY THOUGHT PROCESS

The role of trade in development has been a subject that has been exposed to considerable controversies. Classical economists held that foreign trade could make an impressive contribution to a country's development. Trade was considered to be not simply a device for achieving productive efficiency; it was also an "engine of growth". When a country specialises according to its comparative advantage, it gains an increase in real income. This gain is tantamount to an outward shift in the country's production frontier, which increases the domestic resource potential for capital formation. In classical economic thought, there was clear-cut recognition of growth transmitting aspects of trade. The classicists held that the gains from trade were entirely consistent with the gains from growth. An over-riding issue in the relations between trade and development is the ultimate question whether there is a conflict between the gains from trade and growth. The orthodox interpretation as expounded by classical and neoclassical economists is that foreign trade can be a propelling force in development.

Adam Smith's model of foreign trade postulates the existence of idle land and labour before a country is opened to world markets.

The excess resources are used to produce a surplus of goods for export, and trade thereby "vents" surplus productive capacity that would otherwise be unused. In Smith's concept of trade and development relationship, trade contributes to development also through extension of market. In his book, 'An Inquiry into the Nature and Causes of the Wealth of Nations,' he stated, "By means of it, the narrowness of the home market does not hinder the division of labour in any particular branch of art or manufacture being carried to the highest perfection. By opening a more extensive market for whatever part of the produce of their labour may exceed the home consumption, it encourages them to improve its productive powers and to augment its annual produce to the utmost and thereby to increase the real revenue and wealth of the Society." Thus, Adam Smith clearly envisaged a process in which foreign trade plays vital role in extending the market and hence leads to increase in productivity through the scope given for greater specialization.

In Ricardian economic thought, trade and development was integrally related. The key initiator of growth in the model is the capitalist class, which rather than consuming most of its profits, invests these funds to hire additional labour and thereby expand production. While this action bids up the wage-rate for a given size of labour force, it also has the effect of increasing the supply of labour as the wage rises above its natural level and death rates are reduced. Increasing the use of labour in the manufacturing sector always increases output in the same proportion, but the application of labour to agricultural production is subject to diminishing marginal productivity because of the fixed supply of high quality land. Consequently, as capital accumulation takes place mainly in the form of larger wage-fund, the prices of agricultural products rise relative to manufactured goods and competition for better quality land causes an increasing proportion of the output of a given amount of labour employed on high quality land to be transferred to the land owner in the form of rent. Increasing amount of output is absorbed by the landlord. In the manufacturing sector, the relative cost of subsistence-wages squeezes the profit rate earned by capitalists. Consequently capital accumulation and population growth tend to decline until a stationary state is reached.

Through trade, an economy can postpone the stationary state. In Ricardian thought, comparative differences among countries in the labour required to produce agricultural and manufactured goods are based on differences in land/labour ratio or in the technological knowledge. This serves as the basis of trade at any point of time. For England, as Ricardo realised, the comparative cost situation favoured exports of manufactured goods and imports of agricultural products.

John Stuart Mill was exceptionally clear on the role of trade as propelling force for development. Trade, according to comparative advantage, results in a more efficient employment of factors of production and this may be considered the direct advantage of foreign trade. According to Mill, there are some dynamic benefits of trade, one of which is the tendency of every extension of the market to improve the process of production. A country which produces for a large market than its own, can introduce a more extended division of labour, can make greater use of machinery and is more likely to make inventions and improvements in the process of production.

In his book, 'Principles of Political Economy', Mill stated, " Another important consideration principally applicable to an early stage of industrial advancement is that a people may be in a quiescent, indolent, uncultivated state, with all their tastes either fully satisfied or entirely undeveloped, and they may fail to put forth the whole of their productive energies for want of any sufficient object of desire. The opening of foreign trade, by making them acquainted with new objects, or tempting them by the easier acquisition of things which they had not previously thought attainable, sometimes works a sort of industrial revolution in a country where resources were previously undeveloped for want of energy and ambition in the people inducing those who were satisfied with scanty comforts and little work, to work harder for the gratification of their new tastes and even to save and accumulate capital, for the still more complete satisfaction of these tastes at a future time."

The classical economists thus perceived trade as a crucial factor for growth in three ways: as a vent for surplus; maximisation of gains through comparative cost advantage; through widening the extent of market; and the scope of the division of labour. In classical economic thought, trade was conceived as a dynamic force which by widening the extent of the market and the scope of the division of labour, permits a greater use of machinery, stimulates innovations, overcome technical invisibilities, raises the productivity of labour and generally enables the trading country to enjoy increasing returns and economic development. Trade gives a developing country opportunity to remove domestic shortages and to overcome the diseconomies of the small size of its domestic market. It offers opportunity for the exchange of goods with less growth potential for goods with more growth potential, thereby achieving the progress that results from a given effort on the savings side.

Classical economists also noted the effects of trade on domestic factor supply, especially on capital accumulation. The capacity to save increases and real income rises through the more efficient resource allocation associated with International Trade and the stimulus to investment is strengthened by the realisation of increasing returns in the wider markets that overseas trade provides. Further, by allowing economies of large scale production, the access to foreign markets makes it profitable to adopt more advanced techniques of production which require more capital; the opportunities for the productive investment of capital are greater than they would be if the market were limited to the small size of the home market.

In the neo-classical approach, International Trade propels development through efficiency in the allocation of scarce resources. The central proposition of neo-classical trade theory is that given certain assumptions, free trade is superior in economic efficiency. The equilibrium production according to comparative advantage maximises global production. For internationally traded goods and services, the efficient allocation of resources is determined according to their marginal productivities at international prices. This will be achieved through the unfettered operation of the market mechanism with market prices serving to allocate resources efficiently according to comparative advantage. The basic policy prescription which flows form the neo-classical analysis is the need to get the price right. To achieve these ends, two complementary policy prescriptions are invariably advocated: the removal of domestic market distortion; and the liberalization of international trade and exchange markets by the removal of trade and exchange controls, so as to allow the economy to function as near as possible within a free trade regime. The central proposition of neo-classical trade theory is that, given certain assumptions, free trade is superior in efficiency-terms both to autarky and various forms of trade restrictions. The neo-classical theory emphasises the gains from free trade which will lead each country to specialise in the production for exports that are in line with its relatively abundant factor of production.

From the early nineteenth century until the late 1950s, international trade theory was dominated almost entirely by the concept of comparative advantage. According to this concept, countries trade to take advantage of the differences in the cost of production which primarily arise from differences in factor endowments. In the formal models incorporating these concepts, economies were assumed to be characterised by constant returns to scale and perfect competition. On the empirical evidence of the actual international trading relations in the Post-War era, economists perceived that several factors such as increasing returns, imperfect competition, endogenous technical change, consumer's demand, intra-industry trade, influence and determine the flow and pattern of trade. The new theories of international trade analysed relationship between these factors and international trade. One of the new trade theories focused on the influence of technology on the pattern of international trade. Technological Gap Theories emphasise that innovating firms enjoy a temporary monopoly at home and in foreign markets. Innovation determines export mix rather than capital-labour ratio which was emphasised in neo-classical theory. The location of innovative activity is not random; Innovation, improvements in new product and marketing require highly skilled labour. So the new goods are produced in the most skill abundant country. As the product matures, its demands for skilled labour in production and marketing become less pronounced until the product becomes standardised.

In 1966, R. Vernon developed the idea of a product cycle in which trade patterns depend upon country's relative skilled endowment and the age of each product. According to the Theory of Product Cycle, when the new product is first produced in the skill abundant countries, exports from the innovating country to other developed countries begin. Over time the importing countries begin to produce the goods domestically reducing their demand from original exporter. With increasing product maturity, demand in lower income countries develops and is supplied first by the original innovator and then by imitators. Eventually, the second generation producers become net exporters of the by now mature product and the innovating country becomes net importers. Later still, the less developed countries may become net exporters if the standardised product is unskilled labour intensive. Many examples of the product-cycle determining the pattern of trade during post-war era can be documented and these include automobile, semiconductor, synthetics and chemicals.

The other important factor which called for the re-examination of the assumptions underlying the neo-classical theory of international trade was the effect of intra-industry trade on the pattern of international trade flow. In the neo-classical theory, international variations in production-functions determine in which goods, country's comparative advantage and comparative disadvantage lie and trade patterns follow in which exports come from the former group and imports from the latter group. There is no room for simultaneous import and export of the same good.

In a series of articles collected in their book in 1975, Grubel and Lloyd documented the pervasive importance of intra-industry trade in the trade flows of the major trading nations. They identified over 2000 categories of products in which intra-industry trade flows. According to Grubel and Lloyd, scale economies and product differentiations, were the two crucial factors which restrict the number of varieties which can be produced domestically. As a result, minority interests are satisfied by imports and popular varieties are supplied by exports. The automobile industry provides an example of an imperfectly competitive industry in which economies of scale and product differentiation are important. Thus, Grubel and Lloyd stimulated new thinking about imperfectly competitive markets and international trade. In other words intra-industry trade phenomenon is the result of increased division of labour which is dependent on the size of the market. As countries have grown economically and become more integrated into the world economy, they have faced a larger market which has permeated further division of labour. Vertical specialization i.e. the location of different stages of production in different countries, underlines the growth and current preponderance of intermediate goods in international trade.

Paul Krugman developed the theory that economies of scale lead to arbitrary specialisation by nations on products of industries that operate under monopolistic conditions because they enjoy increasing returns. Countries specialise in trade not only because of underlying differences in factor-endowment, but also because increasing returns are an independent force. Thus, imperfect competition emerged as one of the significant contributing factors to modern international trade.

The neo-classical theory of trade was also challenged by SB Linder who said that the theory of trade based on the notion of relative factor abundance is possible only for an analysis of trade in primary products but not of trade in manufactured goods. He developed an analytical framework which gave an alternative explanation of trade in manufactures. Linder's basic thesis is that demand structures are an important determinant of the pattern of trade. In his concept, the more similar the demand structure of the two countries, the more potentially intensive is the trade between these two countries. According to Linder's theory, the volume of trade between a country and each of her trading partners as a proportion of national income will be higher, the greater the similarity in the demand pattern measured in terms of per capita income levels of the pair of trading countries.

In further theoretical evolution, the classical view of trade as an engine of growth was questioned by development economists. At theoretical level it was contended that the conclusions from the static equilibrium analysis of traditional trade theory are irrelevant for interpreting the problems of development which are inherently dynamic. The continuation and spread of underdevelopment in a number of countries in Asia, Africa and Latin America also did not indicate the classical optimism of trade and development relationship. Critics of the traditional view, that trade will transmit development, denied the relevance of the conclusions of traditional trade theory and secondly they contended that historically the forces of international trade impeded the development of poor countries.

During the post-war decade, the literature on the economic development of less developed countries was dominated by critics of foreign trade. Ragnar Nurkse, one of the pioneers in Development Economics, applied DH Robertson's trade pessimism to developing countries and argued, "The tremendous expansion of Western Europe's and especially Great Britain's demand for food stuff and raw materials, which had provided the basic inducement that caused, especially USA, Canada, Argentina and Australia, to develop could not be expected to function as the engine of growth for the still under developed countries of the third world."

The so-called trade pessimists of fifties were represented by Ragnar Nurkse, Raul Prebisch and Gunnar Myrdal. The classical theory of international trade was rejected as inapplicable to less developed countries. They argued that International Trade far from acting as an engine of growth had been responsible for hindering development.

In a study of "Growth, Disequilibrium, and Disparities : Interpretation of the Process of Economic Development" (1949), Prebisch argued that the "growth of the west had left untouched the vast peripheral area with its enormous capacity for assimilating technical progress so as to raise the very inadequate standard of living of the great masses of its population". He also argued that because of inelastic demand for primary products and a combination of monopolistic pricing of manufactures with competition for primary commodities, "the periphery tends to transfer a part of the benefits accruing from its technical progress to the centres while the latter retain their own benefits for themselves."

Gunnar Myrdal developed a theory of international trade as a mechanism of international inequality. In his view, contrary to what the equilibrium theory of international trade would seem to suggest, the play of market forces does not work towards equality in the remuneration of factors of production and consequently in incomes. On the contrary, Myrdal argued, international trade strengthens the industrial countries while the underdeveloped countries find their traditional industry injured by cheap imports, their skills impoverished. He conceded that international trade stimulated the production of primary products, but these face inelastic demand and excessive price fluctuations. Under these circumstances, the forces in the market in a cumulative way tend to cause even greater international inequalities between countries as to their level of economic development and average per capita income.

Ragnar Nurkse, in his Wicksell Lectures stated, "In a world in which (out side the Soviet Area), over nine-tenths of manufacturing and over four-fifths of the total productive activity are concentrated in the advanced industrial countries, the ideas of symmetry, reciprocity and mutual dependence, which are associated with the traditional theory of international trade are of rather questionable relevance to trade relations between the centre and periphery.

In 1950, HW Singer, a famous development economist, questioned the development effects of trade. In the existing international division of labour the periphery produced and exported raw materials while the centre specialised in producing manufactured goods. According to Singer, the division of labour was an obstacle to the economic development of the periphery; since the under-developed countries producing raw materials were subjected to deteriorating terms of trade vis-à-vis the industrialised countries. Thus the gains from foreign trade were appropriated by the centres and did not raise the welfare in all countries trading with each other as claimed by the neo-classical theory of trade.

The chief policy-inference for the under-developed countries drawn from this analysis was an urgent need for rapid industrialisation based on import-substitution. The "import-substitution, elasticity pessimism" view of the role of trade in development was virtually universal in the 1950s. Two strands of thought led many development economists to advocate protection and import-substituting industrialisation strategy. The first was based on the premise that developed countries had such a head start, that industrialisation would not proceed at a satisfactory rate in the absence of protection. The second was based on the belief that developing countries' comparative advantage lay in highly specialised, primary commodity lines that an open trade regime, would result in each country's continuing specialisation in a few primary commodities lines and that the demand for these commodities was both price and income inelastic. That being the case, it seemed self-evident that developing countries could not hope to attain rates of growth above the world-average through maintaining their specialisation. The income-elasticity of demand for importable goods would exceed unity, and hence the relative price of importables could be expected to rise. The logical solution was therefore "Import substitution" which could become a "leading growth sector". It was also expected that the growth of industries could satisfy upward shifts in demand for importables as incomes rise, thereby simultaneously removing pressures that would otherwise arise in the Balance of Payments. The chief policy inference for the underdeveloped countries drawn from the analysis was an urgent need for rapid industrialisation based on import substitution. Prebisch, in 1949 an ELCA study argued that there is in fact, a dynamic element in industry which is not found to a comparable extent in primary production. The attempt to raise income in the Latin American countries, by means of exports may run into serious difficulties, caused by competition from other countries.

Prebisch traced the path of economic development through protective tariffs. He said, "The attempt to raise income in the Latin American countries by means of exports may run into serious difficulties caused by competition from other countries and technical progress in agriculture which is necessary to raise rural income, inevitably creates surplus of labour. Since there is no other way of absorbing the gainfully employed population and increasing its productivity, the activities which can be developed by protective tariffs, within certain limits, give rise to an increase in real income." Gunnar Myrdal in his book 'The International Economy' argued that import-restrictions afford a means of creating at once the necessary demand for a particular domestic industry. The argument that a major obstacle to Economic Development was insufficiency in demand was also developed by Rosenstein-Rodan and Nurkse.

The accent on industrialisation through import-substitution, which was prescribed by the school of thought, represented by structuralists viz. Prebisch, Nurkse, Singer, Myrdal, resulted in maximising import-requirements of inputs and technology. While protective tariff could enlarge the market for industrialisation, the underdeveloped countries had to import capital equipments and raw materials for expanding their manufacturing sector. A closed economy was thus not the answer to the problems of development.

In Development Economics, since early sixties, the relationship between foreign-trade and development came in for a serious review and trade pessimism which pervaded the thought of most of development economists in 1950s, could not be sustained in terms of development realities of 1950s and sixties. In the process of development, many developing countries experienced 'foreign exchange gaps' in addition to savings-gaps and they also experienced disenchantment with the import-substitution strategy. The notion slowly emerged that International Trade might play a more positive role in economic development by narrowing "dual gaps." The economists engaged themselves in making estimates of LDC import-requirements, usually based on assumed target-rates of economic growth with fixed input coefficients. These studies revealed that foreign exchange gap could be a more serious constraint on economic development. In the theoretical literature, this gave rise to a "two gap analysis". In practical policy dimensions, it led to the slogans "Trade not aid" or "trade and aid". Intellectually the economists by and large agreed that for financing industrial development, the exports of developing countries had to be increased.

In 1957, the GATT, appointed a group of economists under the chairmanship of Professor Haberler to report on "certain trends in international trade, in particular the failure of trade of less developed countries develop as rapidly as that of industrialised countries, excessive short-term fluctuations in prices of primary products, and widespread resort to agricultural protectionism." In the evolution of development theory, 1957 marked a water-shed which set the trend towards linkage of Development and Trade. The development-economists engaged themselves in working out estimates of the capital-requirements of LDCs which revealed major saving-gaps. The estimates of LDC import requirements were based on assumed target rates of economic growth together with fixed import coefficients. Uniformly they revealed the prospects of 'foreign exchange gaps' left by adverse prospects for LDC export and inadequate aid by developed countries. Of the two gaps, the 'foreign exchange gap' appeared to be more serious constraint on economic development as the LDCs with a few exceptions struggled to meet chronic balance of payment difficulties through import and foreign exchange controls. In the theoretical literature, this gave rise to "two gap analysis".

The Haberler Report criticised the tariff and other barriers erected by developed countries, which it described as an important factor contributing to the foreign exchange difficulties of LDC. This led to the appointment of a standing Committee-the famous Committee III, with the task of encouraging policies to help exports. The Report commented adversely on LDC policies of import substitution which had almost been to the disadvantage of the underdeveloped countries themselves.

The other landmark in the evolution of the concept linking 'Trade and Development' was the study of 'Europe and Trade Needs of the Less Developed Countries' by the UN Economic Commission for Europe in which it was argued that since aid and exports of primary products would meet only two-thirds of the import requirements of the third world in 1980s, this would leave the remaining one- third i.e., at least $ 15 billion to be filled by exports of manufactures and on infant-industry ground prepared the first scheme for a generalised system of preference for LDC manufactures.

At the Belgrade Conference in September 1961, President Tito launched the idea of a World Conference on trade and development. In December 1961, the UN General Assembly endorsed President Kennedy's designation of the 1960s as the UN Development Decade and passed resolution 1707, which gave approval in principle to the idea of a Conference on Trade and Development. Subsequently another non-aligned Conference in Cairo in June 1962, gave more precise form to the demand for a Conference on Trade and Development. ECOSOC resolved to convene UNCTAD, known as UNCTAD I, established a preparatory Committee, appointed Prebisch, Secretary General of UNCTAD and invited him to prepare a report on the issue.

Thus, the organisational link-up between Trade and Growth was established and in the report which Prebisch submitted to the Conference was entitled "Towards a New Trade Policy for Development". In this document, policies to increase the trade of developing countries so as to make it a vital instrument of growth were identified. It was emphasised that policy of removal of trade barriers by developed countries should be supplemented by positive policies to assist the trade of developing countries. The main policy innovation of the Prebisch Report was a new emphasis on the need for developing countries to export manufactures. It was also pointed out in the report that the inward looking import substitution policy had generally insulated national markets from external competition, weakening and even destroying the incentive necessary for improving the quality of output and lowering costs under the private enterprises system. It had thus tended to stifle the initiative of enterprises as regards both the internal market and exports.

During the decade 1960-70s, several studies by development economists such as IMD Little and Be La Balassa of the industrialisation experience of a number of developing countries was undertaken with a view to evaluate the effects of import substitution policies on the growth. The studies indicated that industrialisation sheltered by high levels of protection had led to the creation of high cost enterprises. In some cases, it was found out that with high industrial prices, maintained by high tariffs, industrialisation was carried out at a high cost to agriculture. By 1967, the encouraging experience of some of the developing countries in East Asia and South East Asia, further contributed to shift of development thinking away from inward looking strategies and towards an outward looking strategy of trying to export manufactures early in the process of industrial development. The development economists gradually felt that there was a need to search for new engines of economic growth in the international economy and to push the development of export oriented industrial-activity. Hla Myint, one of the pioneers of development economics also endorsed the view that the South East Asian countries should move away from import substitution policies towards a radically different approach to industrialisation.

Thus, while on the one hand it became difficult to retain the validity of Prebisch-Singer concept of trade-development relationship, on the other hand the emergence of NIEs in mid 60s and 70s clearly showed that there was a strong link between export performance and economic growth. The theoretical evolution in the growth theories also strengthened the link between trade and development. The 'dual gap' theory of economic growth which was pioneered by Hollis-Chenery and M. Bruno in 1962, gave a new orientation and focus to the study of relationship between trade and development. Growth requires investment goods which may either be provided domestically or be purchased from abroad. The domestic provision requires savings; the foreign provisions require foreign exchange. For import of investment goods from abroad, a developing economy must earn sufficient foreign exchange to sustain growth process in a situation where there is a limited availability of external finance and the inflow of foreign exchange through external borrowing is beyond the capacity of a developing country.

In developing economies, a salient feature of development is the heavy reliance on imports, particularly the import of capital goods. There is a positive relationship between export performance and economic growth because the increase in exports helps to finance the import of capital goods which in turn gives rise to a more rapid rate of capital formation and hence a higher rate of growth of output. According to 'dual-gap' theory of economic growth, there is a minimum necessary amount of imports required to support a given increase in national output. At a certain projected level of output, imports may exceed exports and the trade gap, if not financed by external resources, inhibits the optimum rate of economic growth. If developing countries can expand their exports rapidly to generate sufficient earnings to finance imports, then there should not be any foreign exchange constraint on development. In many cases where rapid development has failed to take place, one of the major reasons lies in the inward looking policies based on the pessimistic view of export possibilities. So a synthesis between the 'two-gap' analysis of economic growth and the concept of export led growth can provide the basis for a conceptual link between trade and development. The role of export expansion in economic growth lies in its importance in financing capital goods imports which are necessary for rapid economic growth because of its significant effects on domestic investment. This results in economic growth and employment. At current stage of developing thinking, there is no doubt on the positive effects of trade on development. The question that has been debated most in 1970s and 1980s is whether free trade is conductive to economic growth or not. A number of economists have undertaken various studies and the point still have remained open to debate.

The NIEs' spectacular export-led growth since 1970s generated considerable interest among economists for research and study in the relationship between export performance and economic growth of the developing economies. Many empirical studies were conducted to assess the role of exports in economic growth. The recent works on the subject include the studies conducted by Be La Balassa, G. Feder, Hollis Chenery, A Maijels, Anne Krueger, GS Fields etc. They all are in agreement that positive export performance has beneficial effects on economic growth and free trade accelerates the rate of economic development.

Anne Krueger in her book 'Perspectives on Trade and Development' analysed how trade and employment is linked in developing countries. In Heckcher-Ohiln model of international trade, labour abundant countries will have a comparative advantage in net exports of labour intensive goods. Lower wages in labour abundant countries would render production costs for relatively labour using commodities lower than in more capital abundant countries. With appropriate choice of technique of production and with the increase in the production of export, the demand for labour in a developing economy will shift upwards. The choice of trade strategy thus becomes important in a developing economy. If there is outward oriented trade regime, there will be greater impact of trade on economic growth.

The comparative advantage of a country with a relatively large endowment of unskilled labour will lie in exporting labour intensive goods and importing relatively capital intensive goods. In a protectionist trade regime, which restricts the imports, protection could induce positive production levels of more capital intensive goods that would not be produced in a situation of free trade. Hence with protection, for labour abundant countries, capital intensity of protected industries could be greater than that of exportables.

In an open trade regime, commodity composition of output will shift towards more labour using activities and this would shift the demand for labour upwards. Selected studies of commodity and composition of trade before and after shift in trade strategy in the late 1960s showed a marked increase in labour intensity. Between 1967 and 1974, a period during which Brazil liberalised her trade, the workers per unit of output increased from 20-22 at the beginning of the period to 28-29 at the end in the production of exportable items, while at the same time the labour inputs per unit of output in import competing industries remained unchanged.

For Korea too, the shift to an outward oriented strategy had a pronounced impact on the labour market. The labour intensity of Korea's exports rose markedly over the 8 years following the shift to an outward oriented trade strategy from 1960 onward. Non-farm employment rose from 2.15 million in 1960 to 4.63 million in 1970. There is thus, a reasonable amount of evidence that the orientation of trade regime significantly affects the demand for labour and hence has decisive impact on the rate of economic growth in developing economies. The theoretical links between trade and development analysed in this chapter will be further supported by empirical evidence later.

DEVELOPMENT EXPERIENCE: DIVERGENCE IN GROWTH PERFORMANCE

The development story of third world began roughly four decades ago against a background when the old economic order based on the classical doctrines of reliance on 'equilibrating' market mechanisms almost broke down. Between 1929 and 1933, world trade declined and competitive devaluation, heavy deflation, rising unemployment, protectionism, with terrible social and political consequences exposed the fallacies of classical economic theory which relied on market-forces. The belief in classical policies was swept by a new Keynesian consensus on active macro economic management by governments with full employment set as the primary objective.

The war-time experience of industrial countries had demonstrated the potential for macro-economic planning and effective government action to maximise output, mobilise resources and full employment. The consensus slowly grew that the same principles of macro-economic management of the economy by governments and mobilisation of resources based on Keynesian principles were applicable to the developing countries' concerns in the international field too. This principle was extended and the national policies were replaced by international rules of conduct and control by international institutions. The Bretton Woods System comprising of two institutions viz., IMF and World Bank, was the international counter-part of national planning and management.

The decades of 1950s and 1960s were a period of global expansion of production and trade with full employment and little inflation in the industrial countries. The main approach to development during the decade was almost exclusive emphasis on physical capital accumulation. The neo-Keynesian development model, embodied in the Horrod-Domar formula emphasised capital accumulation as the source of growth. National and international initiatives including the UN shared the emphasis on capital-accumulation as the main engine of growth. In the development strategies, this requirement was projected and policies were adopted to provide requisite capital to the developing countries for the desired rate of economic growth. The emphasis on physical capital accumulation was linked with the optimism regarding the domestic capacity of developing countries and their governments to mobilise domestic savings and investment and an equally optimistic belief that this might be supplemented by large foreign aid.

In 1961, designating the ten year period, 1961-70 as the First UN Development Decade, the General Assembly called upon the member States to "intensify their efforts to mobilise and to sustain support for the measures required on the part of both developed and developing countries to accelerate progress towards self-sustaining growth of the economy of the individual nations and their social advancement so as to attain in each underdeveloped country a substantial increase in the rate of growth, with each country setting its own target, taking as the objective a minimum annual rate of growth of aggregate national income of 5 percent at the end of the decade". In the Second UN Development Decade, the General Assembly suggested that the average annual rate of growth in the Gross Domestic Product of the developing countries as a whole during the decade should be at least 6 per cent.

In the 15 year period stretching from 1960 to the' mid-point of the Second UN Development Decade, the developing countries sustained an average rate of increase of 5.1 per cent a year over the first half of the 1960s in GDP The pace quickened to 5.8 percent in the latter half of the decade. Thus, the record of economic growth in the 1960s turned out to be better than had been anticipated in the General Assembly. The pace of expansion achieved over the 15 years period as a whole was remarkable. It compared favourably with what had been achieved by the economically advanced countries when they were in earlier phase of development. The rate of growth also compared favourably with the rate of growth registered by the developed market economies over the same 15 years since 1970.

In the first half of 1960s, per capita income of developing countries increased by 2.5 per cent annually and at about 3 per cent annually over the subsequent 10 years. In absolute figures it increased from $ 169 per annum in 1960 to $ 222 in 1970 and then to $ 260 in 1975 (All figures expressed at exchange rates prevailing in 1970). While the developing countries as a whole registered increase in the GDP over the period under review, the rate of economic growth was not uniform for all developing countries. The economic growth of the developing countries was marked by wide diversity in performance. Out of the total population of developing countries of around 1.6 billion at the outset of seventies, roughly 1.2 billion lived in countries with a per capita GDP in 1970 below the nominal $ 222 average for all developing countries and a slightly smaller number (accounting for seventy per cent of the total population) in countries with a per capita product of less than $ 200. Please see Table 1.1 for growth of world output by country groups in 1960-85.

During this period, the middle income group (the group comprising countries with per capita GDP in 1970 of $200 or more but less than $400) and the developing countries in higher income group registered increase in GDP. The lower income group slowed down in the first half of 1970s to an annual rate of economic growth of 3.6 per cent as against the corresponding rate of 6 per cent and 7.5 per cent respectively for the middle income and higher income group.

The disparate rates of increase in total gross domestic product also reflected in the disparate rates of increase in per capita product for the lower-income countries. The rate of increase in per capita product came to below 2 per cent a year in the 1960s and not much more than 1 per cent a year in the first half of 1970s and (only 0.5 per cent a year if the petroleum exporting countries in this group Indonesia and Nigeria are excluded). Middle Income and higher income groups of developing countries registered 2.7 per cent and 3.5 per cent increase in their per capita income in the

1960s respectively. In the first five years of 1970s, the annual per capita income increase was 3.2 per cent for middle income group in first half of 1970s and 4.6 per cent in the first five years of 1970s for higher income group of developing countries.

The 1980s were further marked by continued divergence in the economic growth of the developing countries. The annual average growth of GDP for developing countries as a whole during 1980-84 fell to little less than 1% from 5.5% during preceding five years. For countries in North Africa, other Africa and West Asia, the rate of growth was negative (Please see Table 1.2). The other striking feature of the growth pattern after 1975 was that the number of developing countries experiencing either low or negative rate of economic growth more than doubled between the periods 1975-79 and 1980-1984. Even for these countries which registered positive growth, the rate of economic growth stagnated at 3.5% per annum. The low growth of GDP was most marked in Africa and Latin America. The table below shows that 46 countries of other Africa experienced growth rate of less than 3.5% between 1980 and 1984; and 24 of the 35 countries experienced growth rate of less than 3.5% during the same period.

An analysis of Table 1.3 demonstrates the growing diversity in growth as well as stagnation suffered by developing economies since 1980.

During 1960-74, there were 42 developing countries which have registered growth of over 5.5%. In 1985, there were only 7 countries within this group. Similarly, during 1960-74, there were 38 countries registering growth rate of 3.5% to 5.4%. The number of countries under this group decreased to 22 in 1985. As against this there were 57 countries falling under very low or negative rate or economic growth. The number of countries growth-rates of 0.5% to 5.4% in 1960-74 was 20, and this number increased to 35 in 1985. Similarly, there were only 5 countries with negative rate of growth in 1960-74. The number of developing countries under this group also increased to 22 in 1985.

Table 1.1: World *Per Capita Growth 1960-85.*
(Average annual percentage change or change over previous year)

Country group 1969	1960-1974	1970-1979	1975-1984	1980	1980	1981	1982	1983	1984	1985
World	5.3	4.9	4.4	1.9	1.9	1.7	0.4	2.1	4.2	2.9
Developed market -economy countries *	5.2	4.3	4.0	1.9	1.3	1.6	-0.2	2.4	4.5	2.8
North America	4.8	4.1	4.7	2.2	-0.2	2.7	-2.3	3.6	6.7	2.5
Western Europe	4.6	4.1	3.2	1.0	1.3	0.0	0.5	1.4	2.2	2.3
Japan	10.2	5.4	5.1	3.7	4.4	3.9	2.8	3.1	5.8	5.0
Others	5.7	5.0	2.2	1.9	3.8	3.9	0.2	0.2	5.3	2.8
Developing Countries and territories **	5.5	6.8	5.6	0.8	3.2	1.3	0.9	-0.5	2.5	2.0
Latin America	5.2	6.6	5.0	-0.4	4.9	0.5	-1.3	-2.4	2.9	2.8
North Africa	5.7	5.4	9.1	1.7	5.0	-0.3	2.3	1.4	3.3	2.3

(Contd.)

(Contd. Table 1.1)

Country group 1969	1960-1974	1970-1979	1975-1984	1980	1980	1981	1982	1983	1984	1985
Other Africa	4.3	5.9	2.7	-1.1	3.4	0.4	0.4	-3.3	-1.5	1.9
West Asia	7.7	10.6	5.4	-1.9	-3.9	-2.8	2.1	-5.8	-1.0	-2.8
South Asia	3.7	1.5	4.0	4.6	6.9	5.1	2.2	6.8	4.2	5.0
East Asia	6.6	8.8	8.9	5.4	5.7	6.9	3.5	6.0	5.8	2.6
China ***	6.6	8.8	8.9	5.4	5.7	6.9	3.5	6.0	5.8	2.6
Socialist countries of Eastern Europe****	6.6	6.4	4.5	3.4	3.1	2.4	3.0	4.2	3.8	3.2

Source : UNCTAD secretariat calculations, based on official national and international sources. * Gross domestic product or grass national product. ** Gross domestic product. *** National income. **** Net material product.

Table 1.2: Per Capita Growth Bracketed Quantitatively (1960-85)

Period 1969	*1960-1974*	*1970-1979*	*1975-1984*	*1984*	*1985 ***
Growth of GDP					
5.5 per cent and above					
Total	42	48	48	15	7
Latin America	10	12	10	-	1
NorthAmerica	1	3	6	1	-
Other Africa	15	18	14	4	3
West Asia	8	5	8	2	-
South Asia	1	-	2	2	2
East Asia	7	10	8	6	1
3.5 Per cent to 5.4 per cent					
Total	38	16	22	17	22
Latin America	13	6	10	1	2
North Africa	3	1	-	2	3
Other Africa	16	7	7	7	9
West Asia	1	1	1	3	1
South Asia	3	1	4	2	3
East Asia	2	-	-	2	4
0.5.per cent to 3.4 per cent					
Total	20	31	19	35	35
Latin America	2	7	2	10	11
North Africa	2	1	-	2	1
Other Africa	11	15	14	17	13
West Asia	-	2	-	-	6
South Asia	3	5	1	3	1
East Asia	2	1	2	3	3

(Contd.)

(Contd. Table 1.2)

Period 1969	*1960-1974*	*1970-1979*	*1975-1984*	*1984*	*1985 ****
0.4 per cent or below					
Total	5	10	16	38	22
Latin America	-	-	3	14	11
North Africa	-	1	-	1	2
Other Africa	4	6	11	18	4
West Asia	1	2	1	5	3
South Asia	-	1	-	-	-
East Asia	-	-	1	-	2

Source: UNCTAD secretariat calculations, based on official national and international sources. *Based on available statistics for 105 countries. **Preliminary, No data available for one country in South Asia, one country in East Asia and 17 countries in other Africa.

Table 1.3: Exports/Imports in Select Developing Countries as Share of GDP

Country	*Exports / GDP(Percentage)*		*Imports / GDP(Percentage)*	
	1979-1981	*1985-1987*	*1979-1981*	*1985-1987*
Argentina	7.3	9.1	8.0	5.1
Bangladesh	5.8	6.3	16.5	17.0
Bolivia	22.7	21.7	20.5	18.4
Brazil	9.3	11.5	11.0	6.9
Chile	21.3	26.5	27.1	19.0
Colombia	15.4	17.0	15.1	12.6
Costa Rica	28.1	27.0	34.4	32.2
Cole d Ivoire	33.0	32.1	38.0	22.9
Ecuador	25.8	29.0	23.9	18.0

(Contd.)

(Contd. Table 1.3)

Country	Exports / GDP(Percentage)		Imports / GDP(Percentage)	
	1979-1981	1985-1987	1979-1981	1985-1987
Ghana	8.8	7.7	8.6	7.0
India	6.4	6.2	10.5	9.8
Indonesia	30.5	21.4	21.9	20.1
Jamaica	50.5	70.5	52.7	78.8
Kenya	27.8	27.6	36.1	23.2
Malaysia	56.8	71.3	53.0	52.4
Mauritius	47.3	56.5	58.4	57.0
Mexico	10.9	16.4	12.7	7.1
Morocco	18.5	19.7	31.3	25.2
Nigeria	22.9	12.1	17.7	8.1
Pakistan	12.4	14.5	22.4	17.6
Peru	22.8	20.3	21.7	15.4
Philipines	19.6	25.4	25.6	22.4
Rep of Korea	33.2	42.4	41.4	39.7
Senegal	29.8	25.2	45.5	34.6
Sierra Leone	20.5	14.6	34.5	12.8
Sri Lanka	32.9	36.6	50.5	56.5
Thailand	24.2	30.1	30.1	26.7
Turkey	80.	20.2	14.6	23.9
Uruguay	15.4	20.4	20.5	16.4
Venezuela	29.7	29.9	22.4	20.6
Yugoslavia	18.0	16.3	22.7	14.8

Source : UNCTAD secretariat calculations, based on data (in constant 1980 prices) in World Bank, World Tables.

Since mid 1970s, the development experience shows widening variation in economic performance of developing countries in various regions. It has been a matter of intensive debate among development economists as to what could be the factors contributing to the diversity of growth experienced among developing countries. The constraints faced by the developing economies included both domestic and external constraints. Several studies were undertaken by UNCTAD with a view to analyse to what extent economic performance in developing countries was influenced by international trade. The export performance of 31 countries and the GDP growth was studied for the period 1980-87. The table above shows that most of these countries whose exports of manufactures registered high rate of growth during this period succeeded in maintaining positive rate of growth in GDP during 1980-87.

The influence of exports on the economic growth can also be studied by comparing the per capita exports of the least developing countries with the per capita exports of developing countries. According to UNCTAD Secretariat calculations in 1980, LDCs per capita output was valued at $ 26 only. This further decreased to 22 dollar in 1987 whereas the value of exports per capita of developing countries in general in 1980 was $ 253 and in 1987 was $ 192. The study of growth pattern of 1980s for developing countries also shows that in sub-Saharan Africa during the first eight years of 1980s, the decline in income was very drastic. Even in West Asia and North Africa, the income gains in 1970s were wiped out during 1980-88. In Latin America, the fall in per capita income was substantial.

The onset of recession in 1980s is perceived as one of the factors responsible for decline in income growth of the developing economies during this period. This, however, does not fully explain the persistent unequal pattern of economic growth in developing countries. Even after recession was over by 1983, the countries having a positive growth rate in recession continued their satisfactory growth performance during 1983-88 period of recovery. Those developing countries who have registered poor growth performance during recession continued to do so even during recovery period. Analysis of this aspect of development experience also leads to a relationship between the export performance and economic growth. The growth pattern of 61 developing countries

Table 1.4: Analysis of Growth of Sixty-One Developing Countries.

(Annual percentage change)	Number of	Average rate *
Countries with negative growth in 1980-1983	37	- 35
of which in 1983-1988		
Growth performance		
- unchanged	20	- 21
- improved	17	14
Countries with poor growth		
performance in 1980-1983 **	3	05
of which in 1983-1988; Growth performance		
- deteriorated	2	- 1.2
- unchanged	1	09
- improved	-	-

(Contd.)

(Contd. Table 1.4)

(Annual percentage change)	*Number of*	*Average rate* *
Countries with moderate growth		
performance in 1980-1983 ***	11	19
of which in 1983-1988;		
Growth performance - deteriorated	7	- 21
- unchanged	2	1.6
- improved	2	4.4
Countries with high growth		
performance in 1980-1983 ****	10	5.8
of which in 1983-1988;		
Growth performance - unchanged	6	5.7
- deteriorated	4	0.5

Source: UNCTAD secretariat calculations, based on national and international sources.

* Arithmetic average of growth rates for respective country groups. ** Per capita growth between 0 and 1 percent per year. *** Per capita growth between 1 and 3 per cent per year. **** Per capita growth over 3 per cent per year.

between 1980 and 1988 is analysed in Table 1.4, showing per capita GDP growth in developing countries, 1980-1988.

Out of 37 countries with negative per capita income growth rate during recession, 20 continued to register declines during the recovery period. Out of 11 countries with moderate rate of growth in 1982-83, nine countries continued the same trend during recovery. Out of 10 high growth performer during recession, six countries maintained the rate of growth during recovery. The analysis shows that most of the countries in Latin America and Africa who continued to register poor and negative growth rate in the GDP, had suffered heavy losses in their export earnings which persisted even during recovery in 1983-88. The strong recovery after 1983 resulted in increase in demand for manufactured goods and those countries with capacity to export manufactures maintained their income growth. On the other hand, countries depending on primary products continued to incur heavy losses in the earnings and that adversely affected the growth. As a result of weak demand for primary products between 1980 and 1984, the loss in the earnings of major primary non-oil commodities exported by the developing countries amounted to as much as $ 55 billion. The external shocks of early 1980s also resulted in the doubling of the major debtor country's external payment. The external payment deficit was at the level of $ 50 billion in 1980.

In the early 1980s and continuing throughout the decade, export performance emerged as one of the major contributory factors in the divergence of rate of growth among developing countries. With a slow growing export market and depressed export prices, the reduction in the earnings of most of the developing countries affected their growth performance through affecting the import capacity adversely. During these difficult years, however, some developing countries in South Asia and East Asia succeeded in maintaining high rate of growth. The East Asian developing economies with their expanding export of manufacture during 1980s registered much better growth performance during the decade than other developing countries.

In early 1980s, the influence of trade on economic development was also evident from the pattern of economic growth followed by developing economies. The successful exporters of manufactures in South and East Asia registered an average growth rate of 5% to 6% during 1989-93 as against continued low growth in developing economies in Africa and Latin America. In Africa, per capita income continued to decline through the first half of 90s. Even in the face of stagnation in the industrialised countries, the developing economies in South and East Asia maintained high rate of economic growth. In the newly industrialised economies, the continued strong export growth determined strong GDP growth. This was also true of second generation of NIEs such as Thailand, Indonesia and Malaysia etc. Because of rapid diversification from commodities to manufactures and from labour intensive consumer goods to capital and skill intensive electric equipment, decline in commodity prices did not adversely affect these economies.

The change in the product composition of exports of newly industrialised economies assured export earnings of these developing economies in South and East Asia. The other important contributing factor for the more effective role of trade in the development in this region was that there was significant increase in intra-developing Asian exports. There was significant increase also in the share of intraregional exports in Asia. As we will see in later paragraphs, South-South trade has played an important role in the effective link between trade and economic growth of some developing countries. It was the increase in intra-regional exports which helped newly industrialised economies in 1980s in maintaining their investment in manufacture for exports in spite of slackening of global demand for their products. The share of total exports from South and East Asia to developed economies declined from 70% in 1980 to 51% in 1992. At the same time the share of exports to developing Asia rose from 25% to 31% during the same period.

The influence of export-performance on the growth of GDP of developing countries is also evident from the table at Appendix

'M'. The table clearly shows that most of the countries who achieved high rates of export-growth had also high rate of economic growth. An analysis shows that a strong export growth during 70s and 80s in developing countries such as Indonesia, Thailand, Korea, Hong Kong, Mexico, China, Morocco and Singapore coincided with relatively high rate of economic growth in those countries. The export performance had also positive impact on industrial production and rate of investment.

TRADE EXPERIENCE OF DEVELOPING COUNTRIES

A study of trends in world trade in 1970s and 80s shows a changing pattern of trade of developing countries. During these two decades, while certain positive and encouraging trends were discernible, developing countries faced new challenges which did not exist in 1950s and 1960s. (Please see table below).

For developed market economy countries, the period 1973-80, saw an annual average rate of growth in volume of exports of 5 per cent. Over the period 1980-85, the growth was substantially less at 3.2 per cent per annum. For developing countries, the period 1973-80, saw an annual average decline in the volume of their exports at the rate of 3.8 per cent per annum. For developed countries, the rate of change in the terms of trade was negative during 1973-80, whereas during 1980-85 the terms of trade were relatively stable. For developing countries, there was significant improvement in the terms of trade for the first period during 1973-80, largely on account of petroleum exports. But during 1980-85, the terms of trade deteriorated. The deterioration in the terms of trade of the developing countries during 1980-85, adversely affected their import-capacity. The positive growth in the purchasing power of exports during 1973-80 (8.1 per cent per annum), turned to negative growth rates in the second period that is 1.9 per cent per annum during 1980-85. The effect of this sharp reversal in the growth of export purchasing power in the period following 1980 was accentuated by an enhanced claim on export-earnings to meet increased payments on foreign debt and by drastic

Table 1.5: Changes in Trade Volumes, Terms of Trade and Purchasing Power of Exports by Regions and Economic Grouping 1973-85

(Percentage change per annum)

Region and Economic grouping	*Period*	*Export volume*	*Terms of trade*	*Purchasing power of exports*	*Import volume*
Developed market-economy countries	1973-80	5.0	-2.8	2.0	3.1
	1980-85	3.2	0.2	3.4	2.7
Developing countries	1973-80	-3.8	12.0	8.1	6.6
	1980-85	-1.0	-1.0	-1.9	0.2
By region :					
Latin America and the Caribbean	1973-80	-0.4	2.9	2.7	3.4
	1980-85	3.5	-2.1	1.0	-5.8
North Africa	1973-80	-5.4	16.6	11.1	8.1
	1980-85	-5.3	-0.4	-5.8	3.0
Sub-Saharan Africa	1973-80	-4.3	8.6	4.0	4.6
	1980-85	-3.9	-1.9	-5.6	-4.1
West Asia	1973-80	-6.4	26.8	18.2	7.2
	1980-85	-11.6	1.0	-10.6	1.4
South & South East Asia	1973-80	3.6	1.8	6.1	5.9
	1980-85	7.9	-1.2	6.5	4.4

(Contd.)

(Contd. Table 1.5)

Region and Economic grouping	*Period*	*Export volume*	*Terms of trade*	*Purchasing power of exports*	*Import volume*
by economic group :					
Major petroleum exporters	1973-80	-4.4	23.4	17.2	14.0
	1980-85	-8.5	0.2	-8.5	-1.2
Non-oil exporting developing countries	1973-80	3.8	-2.6	1.7	3.8
	1980-85	7.7	-2.3	5.4	1.0
Major exporters of manufactures	1973-80	9.5	-6.9	3.2	4.4
	1980-85	9.7	-0.8	8.7	1.2
Least developed countries	1973-80	1.2	-1.2	-0.3	4.6
	1980-85	1.9	-0.6	1.2	1.6
Other developing countries	1973-80	0.6	-1.0	-0.3	2.7
	1980-85	4.6	-3.4	1.2	0.6

Source: UNCTAD, Handbook of International Trade and Development Statistics, supplement 1986 (United Nations publication, Sales No. E/F.86.11.D.4) part two.

curtailment in new borrowings from commercial banks. As a result there was a dramatic decline in the rate of growth of oil imports from 6.6 per cent per annum during period 1973-80 to only 0.2 per cent per annum in the period 1980-85.

As regards decline in the volume of exports, there was great diversity in the performance of developing countries. During the period 1980-85, the volume of exports drastically declined in the case of developing countries of North Africa, Sub-Saharan Africa and West Asia. In some other groups of developing countries there was positive rate of growth in the volume of exports. Latin America and the Caribbean registered 3.5 per cent annual growth rate in export volume. South and South East Asia registered 7.9% per annum.

The experience of the country groupings with respect to their terms of trade and purchasing power of exports is different. The overall impact of these factors was a decline in the growth rate of import volume of the developing countries. There was a rapid decline in the volume of imports in the developing countries. Even the major exporters of manufactures saw a decline from 4.4 to 1.2 per cent in their growth rate of import volume. The fuel exporting countries were most adversely affected by deteriorating terms of trade. As oil prices began to recede from earlier peaks and as export volumes weakened in the face of energy conservation, inter-fuel substitution and the development of alternative sources of supply, the purchasing power of fuel exporting countries, fell sharply.

Initially the large current account surplus registered by these countries in 1979-80 had sheltered domestic spending from the effects of falling revenues. By 1982, however, their current account was in combined deficit by $ 26 Billion after having been in surplus by $ 95 Billion two years earlier. To cope with this, the investment spending was curtailed and the average ratio of investment to GDP declined from 27% per cent in 1981 to 23% per cent in 1985. This also resulted in large import cuts.

Economic activity among the non-fuel exporting countries was much better sustained than those of oil exporting developing countries. Output growth in non-fuel exporters averaged two and half per cent in the years 1981-83 and accelerated to five and half per cent in 1984. A major factor underlying the much stronger performance of these economies was relative stable growth in foreign demand for their export.

It is necessary to clarify at this stage that the group of non-fuel exporting countries covers a diversity of economies each facing rather different external and internal circumstances. When we consider terms of trade losses, the situation in 1985 was that the primary product exporters incurred terms of trade losses not experienced by the exporters of manufacturers. Whereas the terms of trade of the exporters of manufactures were unchanged in 1985, those of the primary product exporters deteriorated by three per cent. The resulting real income losses in primary product exporting countries had depressing effects on domestic demand and supply.

In 1980s, the developing countries emerged as the most dynamic partners in the world exchange of goods as both exporters and importers. The decade of the 1980s also saw yet another encouraging trend in the composition of exports from developing countries. The growth of manufactured exports from developing countries continued to grow. The growth of exports was highly concentrated not only by country of origin but also by country of destination. Some developing countries such as Republic of Korea and Hong Kong provided almost half of the manufactured exports of developing countries in 1986. In terms of markets, the USA accounted for nearly 80 per cent of the increase between 1980 and 1985.

The increasing share of developing countries' trade in International Trade and changing composition of the exports with marked upward shift in the percentage of manufactures in their exports, were encouraging trends in the 1970s and eighties. These two decades also witnessed the struggle of developing countries in coping up with the 'external shocks' and unfavorable international environment since 1973. Most of the developing countries suffered from chronic balance of payments difficulties. Summarising the trade experience of the developing countries in seventies and eighties, in one of the IMF studies Sy Chu & Morrision in 1984 highlighted, "During 1981-82, commodity-prices declined further (25 per cent) and for a larger period (8 quarters) than they have in the last three decades, in 1981, real commodity-prices reached a post war low: and in 1982, they declined a further 11 per cent to a level of 16 per cent below the trough reached in the 1975 recession." The sharp decline in commodity-prices during 1981-82 was a culmination of a trend towards more unstable prices that began in the payment difficulties and the rate of economic growth was retarded for those developing countries that could not absorb those shocks.

In 1970s, developing countries faced a series of external shocks - oil price increase, global price inflation, recession, high interest rates and exchange rate instability and interruption in the supply of external finance. From 1979 onwards, they were hit by the largest and most severe recession since the Second World War and then by an unprecedented increase in the interest rate, appreciation of the US dollar, low price of for their export commodities.

The long term downward trend in real commodity prices from 1972 to 1982 has been more than twice the trend from 1957 to 1971. The study noted that as a consequence of these adverse factors, the economic growth of most developing countries was interrupted and per capita income in many of them declined. According to the IMF the average growth in the output of developing countries, was minimal during 1976-83 period. Please see table below.

Developing countries were also adversely affected by recession in industrialised countries. Between 1979 and 1983, most developing countries found their external circumstances deteriorating in many respects. The relationship between economic growth of developing countries and trade in developed countries has been a key question of debate among economists since 1975 recession. There is a direct trade linkage between growth in the industrialised group of developed countries and developing countries' exports. In 1973, 65 per cent of total exports of non-oil exporting developing countries went to industrialised countries.

The slow-down in world trade volume had depressing effects on both the volume and price of developing country exports. Weak demand in the industrial countries during 1980-82 was the main cause of falling exports prices for developing countries. Prices for industrial raw materials fell and food prices dropped. Overall the prices of primary products in relation to those of manufactures reached a post 1945 low in 1982. In volume terms as well the developing countries' exports of raw materials and fuels fell absolutely during the recession. Exports of manufactures from developing countries, having grown at 10.6 per cent a year between 1973 and 1980, rose at only 6.9 per cent a year between 1980 and 1983.

In their response to external shocks, some of the developing countries showed greater ability to adjust to those shocks and some others suffered significant loss in trade and income. While analysing the factors contributing to the diversity in the impact of external shocks on the developing countries, the World Bank Report 1984, referred to the benefits of outward looking policies in the trade sector adopted by a group of developing countries who could adjust to the shocks without suffering its adverse effects.

The report referred to the study of 22 oil-importing developing countries between 1979 and 1982. It found that the countries with strong export growth had GDP growth at 3.8 per cent a year compared with 2.8 per cent a year where export growth was

Table 1.6: Annual Percentage Change in Output in Developing Countries 1978-1983

Country / region	*Change from preceding year*				
	1979.0	*1980.0*	*1981.0*	*1982.0*	*1983.0*
All developing countries	4.8	3.5	1.2	0.2	0.8
Non-oil developing countries	5.1	5.0	2.8	1.5	1.6
By analytical group					
Net oil exporters	7.6	7.3	6.6	1.1	-1.5
Net oil importers	4.7	4.7	2.2	1.6	2.2
Major exporters of manufacture	6.4	4.5	0.1	0.3	-0.1
Low-income	3.3	6.0	4.3	4.3	6.1
Excluding China and India	2.3	3.4	3.4	3.3	2.6
Other Net oil importers	3.6	3.2	3.1	0.4	1.1
By area (b)					
Africa (excluding South Africa)	2.2	3.0	1.8	1.2	0.1
Asia	4.7	5.4	5.1	4.5	6.5
Western Hemisphere	6.7	6.1	0.2	-1.6	-2.3

Source: IMF, World Economic Outlook, 1984[a], p.170 [a] Arithmetic average of country growth rates weighted by the average united States dollar value of GDPs over the preceding three years. [b] Europe and Middle East not shown.

average and 1.3 per cent a year where it was weak. As a result of strong export growth, the middle-income developing countries of Asia had a much stronger recovery during 1983 than those in Latin America. For low income countries, the deterioration in the terms of trade was more serious than the effects of debt problem.

From the beginning of the 1980-83 recession, oil importing developing countries as a group were forced to start curtailing the volume of their imports. Nevertheless, their combined current account deficit grew from $ 29 billion in 1978 to $ 70 billion in 1980 and $ 82 billion at their peak in 1981. From 1980 to 1983 current account deficits of developing countries as a whole also increased. The international financial relationship was characterized by massive arrears on external payments, necessitating partial or total suspension of debt servicing. Interest-payments on accumulated external debt exceeded net new flow of foreign capital to developing countries.

One of the significant reasons for the increase was the rapid rise in the interest payments. The recession in the industrial economies did not bring down interest rates substantially. Two-thirds of developing country debt was denominated in dollars and much of it at variable interest. The rise in real interest therefore greatly increased the cost of borrowing. In 1982, interest due from all developing countries, including that on short-term debt, was $ 66 billion-more than half of their total current account deficit.

In the early part of recession, the experience of oil-exporting developing countries was different from non-oil exporting developing countries. In 1980, oil-exporters ran current account surpluses and increased the volume of their imports. The higher prices were not sustained and the volume of their oil-exports fell. In 1981 they too slipped into deficit - of $ 26 billion followed by $ 32 billions in 1982. In both years, the oil- exporting developing countries drew down resources. The alarming increase in external debt of developing countries from 1979 to 1982 brought to focus the imperative of external adjustments by developing countries if momentum of growth had to be maintained, resulting from prolonged recession in Industrial countries, the strong dollar and high rates of interest between 1979 and 1982. Ratios of debt to G.N.P. had risen from 19.3 per cent to 24.9 per cent, of debt to exports from 84 to 109 per cent and of debt service to exports from 15 to 20 per cent.

The combined effect of these factors was emerging debt crisis which further led to diminishing availability of private lending to developing countries. The lack of fund further strained balance of payment. In 1982 some of the developing countries reduced strains on the balance of payment by improving their trade balances. The current account deficit of oil-importing developing countries fell from $ 82 billion in 1981 to $ 66 billion in 1982.

In many countries, these declines resulted largely from cutting imports in relation to output. Between 1980 and 1982 the volume of imports fell by 50 per cent in Argentina, 20 per cent in Brazil, imports as a proportion of GDP fell from about 10 to 6 per cent between 1980 and 1983. The import restrictions employed in many indebted countries threatened long term economic growth.

The trade-experience of the developing countries since 1979 shows that two important factors influence the responsiveness of developing countries to the developments in the World Trade environment. These include commodity-composition and the geographic distribution of their exports. The diversity in the pattern of export-performance among developing countries emanating from their level of income, composition of exports and package of policies followed by these countries has emerged as one of the most important features of developing countries' trade experience.

The trade-experience of developing countries during these four decades pointed to the following trends –

- The exports of developing countries as a whole grew slowly and did not keep pace with the expansion of world trade.

This led to balance of payment difficulties and import-compression causing slow growth. This also led to increasing external borrowing of the developing countries precipitating debt crisis in 1980s and 90s.

- Over the decades while there was some diversification in the direction of third world's trade, the developed countries continued to be major markets for exports of developing countries. The result was that the growth of developing countries, suffered from periodical external shocks induced by external factors such as recession, protectionism.

- One of the most significant trends in the trade of the developing countries has been the increasing share of the manufactures in the export of the developing countries. This underlines the fact that the developing countries have reached various stages of development and that the developing countries have acquired new complementarities which have increased the prospects for expansion in trade among developing countries.

The trade experience also showed that expansion of North-South trade had some limitations which reduce the development impact of trade on the growth of developing countries. During these four decades, trade of developing countries had witnessed a very positive trend and that is the evolution of trade among developing countries as a dynamic factor. This leads us to the study of trade among developing countries. In the paragraphs that follow we trace the trends in South-South trade and its prospects as to what extent it can increase the effectiveness of trade and thereby increase the momentum of development.

Historically, before the Second World War, much of the third world exports went to the industrialised countries. The growth of industrialisation in the third world since 1950s has created a favorable environment for the expansion of intra-trade among the developing countries. In contrast to the trend of the 1950s and

1960s, the 1970s witnessed a significant intensification of trade among developing countries. Between 1955 and 1970 the proportion of developing countries' total exports and imports destined for or originating in other developing countries fell from 24.5% to 19.6%. Starting in 1970 the trend was however, reversed and by 1981 the corresponding shares were 27% of exports and 30% of imports.

Several factors contributed to the increasing South-South Trade. One of the contributing factors was the increase in fuel prices which was exported by developing countries. The South-South Trade registered increasing trend even after excluding fuel from trade. Trade among developing countries showed an annual average growth rate of some 25% during the period 1970-80 corresponding to an increase in their share of world non-fuel trade from 2.5% to 4.3% over the same period. One of important factors contributing to reversal of trend lies in the dynamism of developing countries' economic growth during the 1970s compared with that of the developed market economy countries. The growing ability of the more advanced developing countries to supply manufactured goods and machinery and equipment opened up complementarities that had not existed in the 1950s and 1960s. This is reflected in the change between 1960 and 1980 in the commodity structure of trade among developing countries excluding fuels. During this period, there was a gradual decrease in the share of food and agricultural raw materials and a rapid increase in that of manufactured goods within non-fuel trade.

Along with these positive trends in the evolution of South-South Trade, analysis of direction and pattern of trade reveals following disturbing trends :-

- Not all developing countries have participated in the growth of South-South Trade.
- Trade among developing countries has been adversely affected by the serious balance of payment difficulties,

crushing debt service burden, historically low prices that the developing countries receive from export of primary commodities.

- After 1970, the declining trend in South-South trade was reversed as the share of South-South export in world trade grew from 4% in 1970 to 8% in 1980. In current value it went up to US $ 138.7 Billion in 1980 according to 'UNCTAD Hand Book of International Trade and Development Statistics 1981.' In the first years of 1980s the growth in South-South trade continued despite the recession which hit the Northern countries in 1979-80. But soon the South was hit by the debt crisis which resulted in a seriously constrained import capacity and between 1981 and 1984 imports in the South were cut out by 12%. In value terms the total South-South exports declined after reaching the peak in 1981 at US $ 152 Billion towards a minimum at US $ 117 Billion in 1986.

As regards the geographical composition of South-South Trade, South East Asian countries have been the main exporters to other developing countries when all products are included. In 1980, they accounted for almost 35 per cent of South-South Exports. Oil exporters of the Middle East with a share of 33 per cent were the second net important exporters in 1980 followed by Latin America with 23.5 per cent.

The significant role of South East Asian countries in South-South Trade is better illustrated when the regional composition of manufactured exports is examined. In 1980, these countries accounted for 60 per cent of all the intra-South exports of manufactured products and for 64 per cent in 1982. Latin American countries accounted for 23.5 per cent in 1980.south Asian countries decreased their participation dramatically between 1962 and 1982 when their market share was reduced from 24 to 3 per cent. The other important feature of South-South trade is that most of the intra-South trade was trade between neighboring countries. In 1985, 57 per cent of total South-South trade and more than two-thirds of non-fuel trade were between neighboring countries. (Please see table below)

From Table 1.8 it is clear that South-South trade was also concentrated among few major exporter-importer countries. The ten largest South exporters accounted for 62 and 65 per cent of the value of the total South-South exports in 1975 and 1979 respectively. Product-wise Malaysia, Indonesia, Singapore, Brazil were the major exporters of raw materials in 1979 and the four largest exporters of manufactures include Singapore, Brazil, Hong Kong etc. The four largest exporters of fuels in 1979 were Saudi Arabia, Venezuela, Kuwait and Nigeria. It is also interesting to note that the countries which are the largest exporters of manufactures to industrial countries are also the largest exporters of manufactures in trade among developing countries. The ten largest exporters of manufactures in South-South trade include Hong Kong, the Republic of Korea, Taiwan, Singapore, Brazil, India, Mexico, Argentina and Pakistan.

The evolution of South-South trade since 1950s shows a cyclical pattern. The first two decades of expansion in World Trade was less beneficial to the trade among developing countries and to overall trade of developing countries than to the trade among industrial countries and to developed countries total trade. During the 1950s and 1960s the value of world exports increased at 7.1 and 9.4 per cent yearly. During that period, the exports of developing countries increased at rates below average. Consequently the share of non-oil developing countries was reduced from 30 per cent in 1950 to 16 per cent in 1970. The trade of developing countries decreased from 6.2 per cent of world trade in 1955 to 3.5 per cent in 1970.

The share of South-South trade in the total trade of developing countries is yet at low level. The trade-experience of the developing countries shows that the South-South trade reduces the vulnerability of developing countries' exports to external shocks and unfavorable external environment.

Table 1.7: International Trade in South – South Trade: All Exports * 1955 – 1985

REGIONS	*YEARS*				
	1955	*1965*	*1975*	*1980*	*1985*
Developing America	91.1	88.8	83.1	78.3	72.9
Developing Africa	57.4	61.2	38.8	25.5	29.5
Developing West Asia	46.6	41.8	21.4	21.2	31.7
Developing South and S East Asia	77.4	75.9	63.9	65.4	71.9
All Countries					
Intra-regional	76.4	72.7	49.7	48.0	56.6
Inter-regional	23.6	27.3	50.3	52.0	43.4

* Current values. The figures represent the share of intro-regional and inter-regional trade in South – South trade, by region. Source: UNCTAD 1983b, Annex A: UNCTAD 1985b Table A1.

Table 1.8: South-South Trade; Largest Manufactures Exporters

Country of Territories	All Non-fuel Value**		All Manufactures Value**	
	(IN $)	%	(IN $)	%
SINGAPORE	7112.0	11.2	4321.0	12.2
BRAZIL	6136.0	9.6	3620.0	10.2
KOREA. REP. OF	5418.0	8.5	4139.0	11.7
MALAYSIA	3518.0	5.5	820.0	2.3
HONG KONG	2603.0	4.1	2438.0	6.9
ARGENTINA	2324.0	3.6	833.0	2.3
THAILAND	2297.0	3.6	671.0	1.9
INDIA	2097.0	3.3	1208.0	3.4
INDONESIA	2094.0	3.3	319.0	0.9
PAKISTAN	1226.0	1.8	467.0	1.3
TOTAL 10 COUNTRIES	34725.0	54.6	18836.0	53.2
ALL DEVELOPING COUNTRIES	63607.0	100.0	35397.0	100.0

* SITC, sec. 5 to 8, excluding subsections 67 and 68. ** Million US Dollars. Source: UNCTAD data bank.

ROLE OF EXPORTS IN INDIA'S ECONOMIC DEVELOPMENT

We have seen previously that export plays a crucial role in accelerating the rate of economic growth in developing countries. The success of South Korea, Mexico, and Brazil has shown the crucial role of exports in the high rate of economic growth achieved by these countries. The exports from a developing economy finance the imports of necessary inputs required for the industrialisation and also provide employment in the economy to generate income and growth. Through exports domestic industries also develop as in some cases domestic demand is not enough for optimum utilisation of manufactured products. In an economy where exports can pay for foreign exchange requirements to finance inputs and invisibles such as loans and interest-payments and in the process, the economy has a surplus in balance of payment; the development process does not suffer from external constraints. The surplus earned in the external economic sector propels the growth by meeting capital requirements in the beginning of growth process. On the other hand, if indispensable imports are not paid for by the exports, the resulting negative deficit balance of payment adds to the indebtedness of the country and slows the process of economic growth.

As compared with Asian NIEs, ASEAN and some countries in Latin America, export had not been a major factor in the economic development of India. In the early stage, India's development plans gave a key role to capital accumulation and industrialisation in the process of development. As regards trade, the wave of trade pessimism of development economists of 1950s favoured inward oriented trade policy and preponderance of primary products in the export-composition dimmed the prospects of trade playing the effective role in development.

India's export performance had been relatively poor. Throughout 1960s, India's exports stagnated. Exports grew at 3.3 per cent annually in 1960s and 7.5 per cent per annum in the 1970s. India's exports were 5.5 per cent of GDP in 1980-81, which was the same as in 1950-51. The share of exports in the GDP of developing countries as a group, on the other hand increased from 15 per cent of their GDP in 1960 to 22 per cent in 1980-81. India's share of world trade fell from 2.4 per cent at the time of independence to 0.4 per cent in the 1980s. Since Second Five Year Plan 1956-57, slow export growth in relation to import requirements strained the balance of payment. Between 1956 and 1976, low foreign exchange reserves and current account deficit at the level of 1.3 per cent of GDP put enormous constraint on the growth prospects. In 1979-80, India faced the second oil shock. The increase in the oil-price had its adverse effects on trade balance. The trade deficit increased; however, the impact of trade deficit on reserve was not very serious because of continued increase in remittances and net invisible in 1979-80. Since 1980-81, the Indian economy faced serious constraints resulting from increasing deficit in balance of payments. One of the unfortunate developments during this period was decline in contribution from net invisibles in financing the trade deficit. India had to depend more and more on the inflow of external capital to finance trade-deficit.

While the trade deficit widened, the flow of concessional assistance also slowed down. The deficit had to be financed from loans at market rates and with short maturity. After 1984-85 the deficit was financed by substantial inflow of capital by way of commercial borrowings and deposits by non-resident Indians. This led to increase in the external debt of India. Total external debt outstanding increased from $ 18.7 billion in 1980 to $ 26.5 billion in 1984 and to $ 56.3 billion in 1989. The increase as a percentage of GNP was from about 10.8 per cent of GNP in 1980 to 21.5 per cent in 1989. Debt service, as a percentage of exports of goods and services, increased from 9.1 per cent in 1980 to 18.1 per cent in 1984 and further to 26.3 per cent in 1989. In earlier years, the balance of payment was mostly financed by concessional inflow of capital but after 1984-85 recourse to non-concessional loan increased the debt-burden of India.

Industrialisation in a developing economy necessitates increasing import of capital goods and raw materials and other imports which are not domestically provided but are yet essential for development. The developing countries that succeed in building up adequate import capacity through increase in the export-earnings and pay for their essential imports face minimum constraints in the process of development. A strong export base also enables this group of developing countries to absorb external shocks resulting from unfavorable external environment. From the case- study of some of the developing countries in the higher income and middle income group which include, South Korea, Mexico, Brazil etc., as was observed earlier, a very strong export-sector in these countries generated high rate of growth in 1970s and 1980s which was sustained despite periodical ups and downs in world economy. Let us now compare the broad and salient features of external sector of these countries with the variables in India's external sector and examine the ways and means to evolve a growing export sector in Indian economy so as to accelerate the rate or Indian economic growth.

In comparison to most of the developing countries, India's export performance had been poor. Her share of total world exports declined from 0.98 per cent in 1965 to 0.45 per cent in 1988. The stagnation of exports during the period 1979-80 to 1980-86 was one of the important factors which contributed to acute balance of payment crisis in 1980s. Only after 1985-86 up to 1989-90, export growth picked up and it grew 15 per cent per annum. But during second half of the 80s even if export growth was satisfactory, the repayment of loan, decreasing worker's remittances and increasing imports strained the balance of payments situation. Category-wise, Indian export of manufactures decreased in 1980s and even in Textiles which was a major export-growth item, India lost to China, South Korea etc. Please see Table 1.9 which shows the sluggish export growth of India.

As against the modest growth in exports, imports have been increasing at higher rate and played a critical role in the Indian economy. The average rate of growth since 1960s has been 13 per cent. Major share of India's imports consists of bulk imports such as crude oil, fertilizers, steel and non-bulk items such as capital goods, raw materials components etc. Please see the summary of imports at Table 1.10.

Since 1985-86, the first year of Seventh Plan imports increased by 15.4 percent in rupee terms which was significantly higher than 8.5 per cent growth recorded in 1984-85. In 1985-86 there was a rise in the imports of capital goods, iron and steel, pharmaceutical products, and non-ferrous metals. In 1985-86, non- oil imports recorded a growth of 25.6 per cent as compared to the previous year. This was due to greater import of capital goods following liberalization measures. Let us now analyse the composition of merchandise imports from 1974-75 to 1984-85 as given in the tables above and below.

India imported essential inputs which in near future did not have much flexibility except at the cost of loss of momentum of development. In 1984-85, petroleum, oil and lubricants accounted for 25 per cent of total imports; fertilizers accounted for 12.4 per cent, import of metals between 5 to 10 per cent; and chemicals accounted for 5 per cent. It was because of the import inelasticity and sluggish export that the gap between import and export had been widening in seventies and eighties. The gap in value terms between merchandise imports and merchandise exports, which had remained below 25 per cent of imports from 1974-75 to 1978-79 widened after 1979-80. In 1980-81 exports leveled only 52 per cent of merchandise imports and continued to be less than 60 per cent of imports in value terms throughout the Sixth Plan. In 1980-81 the trade-deficit was at a peak of 4.7 per cent of GDP.

The financing of persistent and rising trade deficit had constrained the process of economic growth in the Eighties and Nineties. Since India's export-earnings are not adequate to finance trade deficit, supply of sufficient foreign capital without putting India in debt-trap has been a major challenge for economic development.

Table 1.9: Summary of India's Exports and their Growth

(US million at constant 1978-79 prices)

	19880-81	*1981-82*	*1982-83*	*1983-84*	*1984-85*	*Growth Rate*	
						6th Plan	*7th Plan (Target)*
Primary Exports							
Or which	2611.0	2477.0	2404.0	2322.0	2150.0	-2.7	4.5
Agri Products	2202.0	2063.0	2049.0	1958.0	1766.0	-2.7	4.0
Ores & Minerals	409.0	414.0	355.0	354.0	384.0	3.5	7.1
Manufacture Exports							
of which	5093.0	4928.0	4909.0	5438.0	5752.0	5.08.1	
Chemicals	409.0	529.0	464.0	526.0	537.0	0.0	10.0
Textiles	1078.0	886.0	844.0	811.0	965.0	0.2	4.8
Total Merchandise Exports	7705.0	7405.0	7313.0	7760.0	7902.0	4.5	6.8

Note: Growth rates for the 6th Plan Period are derived from the 1978-79 based constant price sense. While those for the 7th Plan Period are based on 84-85 prices. Exports figures and the 6th Plan growth rates for individual commodities are based on 'custom series' while total export figures and growth rates reflect adjustments for statistical discrepancy.

Table 1.10: Summary of India's Imports and their Growth

(US$ million at constant 1978-79 prices)

	1980-81	*1981-82*	*1982-83*	*1983-84*	*1984-85*	*Growth Rage*	
						6th Plan	*7th Plan (Target)*
Food Grains	110.0	433.0	380.0	751.0	292.0	24.60	-100.0
Edible Oils	1049.0	967.0	564.0	745.0	619.0	5.9	5.4
POL	2677.0	2166.0	1977.0	1672.0	1585.0	-7.2	8.3
Total Fertilizer	910.0	710.0	352.0	475.0	1381.0	13.3	10.6
Iron & Steel	1025.0	1591.0	1387.0	1104.0	1000.0	-4.3	-1.8
Non-ferrous metals	418.0	752.0	483.0	537.0	388.0	4.2	1.7
Capital Goods	1857.0	1777.0	2206.0	2300.0	1877.0	4.4	6.1
Other imports	1881.0	2297.0	1339.0	3279.0	2956.0	7.9	7.3
Total Merchandise Imports	10348.0	11297.0	10797.0	11964.0	11112.0	3.6	5.8

Source: The Seventh Five Year Plan 1980-81 to 1983-84 figures from Dte Gen. of Commercial Intelligence and Statistics and the Reserve Bank of India bulletins 1984-85 are World Bank Estimates.

Table 1.11: India's Merchandise Imports 1974-75 to 1984-85

(*US$ Million at Current Prices*)

	1974-75	*1979-80*	*1981-82*	*1983-84*	*1984-85*
Food Grains	958	131	389	593	143
Edible Oils	15	552	700	525	698
Fertilizers	1450	4046	5592	3490	3213
Iron & Steel	885	866	1015	476	1530
Non-ferrous metals	531	1076	1348	934	654
Gems	224	438	446	358	290
Bulk Goods (Sub-total)	66	470	445	1049	865
Capital Goods	4129	7579	9934	7425	7393
Other Imports	873	1711	2219	2748	2202
Total (Customs)	663	2031	2876	3919	3468
Statistical Discrepancy	5665	11321	15020	14092	13064
Total (BOP)	-453	536	313	268	334
	5212	11857	15333	14360	13398

Source : Ministry of Commerce, Dte. General of Commercial Intelligence and Statistics; Ministry of Petroleum : Fertilizer Association of India.

Till 1982, India's external debt at the level of $ 19.4 billion amounting to 11.4 per cent of GNP was not so alarming as compared with Egypt at 52.8 per cent of GNP, Pakistan 31.5 of GNP and Brazil 16.9 per cent of GNP. As a result of decline in official concessional assistance and increase in commercial loans and soft loan from IDA the debt-service ratio had been rising since 1981-82. Debt-service ratio as a percentage of current receipts had more than doubled, from 12.26 per cent in 1984-85 to over 26 per cent in 1988-89.

Between 1985 and 1990 a number of developments in world economy put serious limitations on the availability of foreign capital for the developing countries. The recessionary tendencies in OECD countries and the additional requirement of capital for the development of East European countries after the disintegration of the USSR etc. diminished the prospects of required flow of foreign capital for financing trade-deficit of developing countries. Deficit in external trade and payment suddenly jumped from the first year of the Seventh Plan and was acute during the last two years of the Pan. The current account deficit more than trebled over the plan period. Over the Plan period, as a whole, the deficit was as high as 2.3 per cent of the GDP as compared to 1.2 per cent of GDP during the Sixth Plan. (Please see Table 1.12)

The balance of payment of India had been under pressure all through the eighties. The Seventh Plan was characterized by severe imbalance. The current account deficit ranged between Rs. 10,000 and Rs. 11,000 crore per annum which was not sustainable. One point of concern that emerges from the pattern of Balance of Payments Deficit of 1980s is that the deficit increased in spite of sharp improvement in export performance. In terms of Rupees, exports grew at an average annual rate of 16 per cent during Seventh Plan. The export-growth was neutralized by increase in imports. Despite growth in merchandise exports, a major factor behind the pressure on balance of payment was steadily mounting burden of external debt servicing. The share of short term commercial borrowing at market-rate of interest

Table 1.12: Balance of Payment in Seventh Plan

(Rs. Crore)

	Deficit on Merchandise Trade Account	*Current Account Payments*	*Current Payments Deficit as PC of GDP Deficit*
1984-85	5,390	2,352	1.2
1985-86	9,586	5,927	2.3
1986-86	9,345	5,830	2.0
1987-88	9,296	6,293	1.9
1988-98 (Prov)	14,010	10,429	2.7
1989-90(Estmtd)	13,975	10,975	2.6

increased and commercial borrowing plus NRI deposits increased as a percentage of external liabilities. The third factor was increasing import-intensity of both the industrial development programme and of exports.

India entered the decade of the nineties with large internal and external financial imbalances. The Gulf Crisis resulted in a higher import bill and the loss of export -markets and remittances. During 1990-91, total foreign exchange reserves declined by US $ 1137 Million. This was despite borrowings from the IMF to the tune of US $ 1814 Million under various facilities. As a corrective measure, the Government adopted a BOP adjustment strategy which comprised of three main elements viz. exchange rate adjustment, fiscal corrections and structural reforms in the area of trade and industrial policy. A downturn adjustment of about 18 per cent in the external value of the Indian rupee was effected in two steps in July 3 1991 followed by the abolition of cash export subsidies designed to improve export incentives and to make them more uniform.

In the field of trade and industrial policy the new measures replaced import licensing for a wide-range of intermediate products with the tradable import entitlements carrying a uniform replenishment rate of 30 per cent of export value. The new instrument known as Eximscrips provided added incentives to exports which enabled the allocation of imports according to market forces.

A look at the evolution of key BOP indicators during Sixth (1980-85) and the Seventh Plan (1985-90), clearly shows that emerging BOP crisis had begun to appear during the Seventh Plan (Please see the Table below).

This was aggravated by global developments. Subsequently the causes for the sharp deterioration in balance of payments 1990-91 were a surge in imports owing to an increase in POL import bill and a contraction in net invisible receipts as a result of escalation in interest payments. Superimposed on this situation were short term factors such as fall out of the Gulf crisis and unfavorable market appraisal about India at that time. On the current account, there was a steep fall in invisible receipts in the form of private remittances, travel and tourism earnings. The temporary loss of confidence resulted in virtual cessation of commercial lending by private foreign banks to India and in a massive erosion in accruals under non-residence deposits. Foreign currency non-resident account deposits were particularly hit. The net inflows into these deposits turned negative beginning October 1990. The result of all these factors was that as a percentage of GDP, the current account deficit went up to 2.5 per cent of the GDP in 1990-91 from 2.2 per cent during 1985-90.

The RBI estimated current account deficit in 1990-91 was at U.S. $ 7295 Million as compared to US $ 5900 Million during 1989-90. The sharp increase in the current account deficit of US $ 1395 Million was made up of a larger trade-deficit coupled with smaller net invisible receipts. Trade-deficit during 1990-91 on payment basis stood at US $ 8440 Million higher by U.S. $ 985 Million over the preceding year's US $ 7455 Million.

As will be seen from Table 1.14, persistent and increasing trade deficit continuously strained India's balance of payment since 1986-87. The table shows a trade-deficit of about $ 5.4 billion per annum during the last five years. The capacity of exports to finance imports (export/import ratio) declined in 1990-91 to about 75 per cent from around 78 per cent in the previous year. This decline was the result of fall in the growth of exports and sizable growth in the imports. During the first half of 1991-92 the trade deficit was curtailed by nearly sixty per cent (in dollar terms) due to sharp reduction in imports.

The high rate of growth of imports during the previous three years continued in 1990-91 when imports increased by 13.2 per cent in dollar terms or 22 per cent in Rupee terms. The acceleration in 1990-91 was mainly attributable to higher oil imports. As a result of structural changes in trade-policy announced in 1991 there was

Table 1.13: Key Indicators of India's Balance of Payment

(As per cent of GDP)

Year / Period	*Exports*	*Imports*	*Net Invisibles*	*Trade Balance A/C*	*Current balance*
Average 1980-85	5.0	8.4	2.2	-3.4	-1.3
Average 1985-90	5.1	8.2	1.0	-3.2	-2.2
1989-90	6.3	9.0	0.6	-2.8	-2.2
1990-91 (QE)	6.3	9.1	0.4	-2.9	-2.5

QE: Quick Estimates. Source: Economic Survey of India 1991-92.

Table 1.14: Trends in Foreign Trade

Year	*Imports*	*Exports*	*Trade balance*	*Changes in imports*	*Changes in exports*	*Trade bal. as % of exports*
	Rupees hundred Crore			Percent		
1986-87	201.0	124.5	-76.4	2.2	14.3	61.4
1987-88	222.4	156.7	-65.7	10.7	25.9	41.9
1988-89	282.4	202.3	-80.0	26.9	29.1	39.6
1989-90	354.2	276.8	-77.3	25.4	36.8	27.9
1990-91	431.9	325.5	106.4	22.0	17.6	32.7
1991-92	210.7	187.1	-23.6	9.0	23.9	12.6
	Billion US Dollars			Per cent		
1986-87		15.7	9.7	-6.0	-2.1	9.4
1987-88		17.2	12.1	-5.1	9.1	24.0
1988-89		19.5	14.0	-5.5	13.6	15.6
1989-90		21.3	16.6	-4.6	9.1	19.0
1990-91		24.1	18.1	-5.9	13.2	9.1
1991-92*		9.1	8.1	-1.0	-17.5	-6.2

Data for 1989-90 & April-September, 1991-92 are provisional. *April-September, 1991-92. Source : Economic Survey of India 1991-92 some import compression and during April-September, 1991, imports declined by 17.5 per cent in dollar terms. This decline was contributed by a 22.7 per cent fall in non-POL imports.

During 1990-91 India's exports grew only at 9.1 per cent in dollar terms or 17.6 per cent in Rupee terms. This reflected a major slow-down in export growth and indicated a reversal of the increase witnessed in earlier years. (Please see table below). This decline in exports was caused by a number of factors: a slow-down in the expansion of world trade from 7.3 per cent in 1989 to 4.2 per cent in 1990 and further to 0.9 per cent in 1991 and recession in some major industrial nations; loss of export-market in the middle East due to Gulf Crisis; and import-compression introduced during 1990-91 affecting export-related imports.

To boost exports, the Government took various measures such as lifting those import-restrictions which affected exporters i.e. on export related imports. The Union budget for 1991-92 contained certain export promotion measures. Tax concession was extended to exports of software and processed minerals. To promote leather exports, custom duty was reduced on certain raw-materials. Export-credit policy was liberalised. To provide added incentive to banks for extending export-credit, banks were provided export--credit refinance to the extent of 60 per cent of the increase in outstanding export credit over the monthly average level of 1988-89 up to monthly average level of 1989-90.

The new trade policy gave a massive export-thrust. It was recognized by policy-makers that conventional economic-policies had constraining effects on the growth of exports. It was also realized that high tariff walls and strict import-licensing had produced a domestic cost structure which was out of line with the world prices. The high cost-structure had resulted in the industry becoming uncompetitive in the international market which made it extremely difficult to export without extensive subsidies.

To redress the situation and to step-up the rate of growth of exports the new trade policy made major changes in the policies affecting exports. During July-August, 1991 the Government announced far reaching changes in the trade-policy. These policy changes aimed at strengthening export incentives and eliminating substantial volume of import-licensing. Imports of new materials and components were linked with export performance. The new trade policy made major changes in the import-licensing system by replacing large part of administered licensing of imports by import-entitlements linked to export earnings.

The new trade-policy also introduced the continuation of a system of advance licenses, designed to provide exporters with duty-free access to the inputs they need to produce competitively for world markets. Following the statement of industrial policy, the import of capital goods was also simplified. The new trade-policy also included measures to strengthen the development of export-houses and trading houses as instruments for promoting exports.

The new trade-policy also reviewed the policy of canalisation. Over the years, a number of items of exports and imports have been canalised for export or import through specified public sector agencies. The new policy aimed at progressively reducing the extent of canalisation. The export processing zone scheme which was introduced to provide for duty-free enclaves, enabling production exclusively for exports, was also reviewed. Several incentives in the form of reduction in customs duty on capital-goods imports etc. were given.

The sluggish rate of export-growth brought to focus the unduly high tariff protection which constrained the movement towards international competitiveness of Indian products. The budget and trade-policy statement of 1991-92 began the process of tariff reforms with a reduction in peak tariff rates to a maximum of 150 per cent and a moderate across the board reduction in tariff on capital goods.

On 31st March, 1992 the Government announced a new five year export-import policy which gave further push to liberalisation policies. The new policy included free import of all items except a negative list, decanalising a large number of raw materials including non-ferrous metals and further liberalising of

Table 1.15: Exports to GCA and RPA Areas

Year	*GCA*	*RPA*	*TOTAL*	*GCA*	*CHANGES RPA*	*TOTAL*
		Rupees hundred Crore			per cent	
1988-89	170.7	31.6	202.3			29.1
1989-90	225.1	51.7	276.8	31.9	63.8	36.8
1990-91	268.8	56.7	325.5	19.4	9.7	17.6
1991-92	169.0	18.1	187.1	39.4	-39.0	23.9
		Billion US Dollars				per cent
1988-89	11.8	2.2	14.0			15.6
1989-90	13.5	3.1	16.6	14.7	42.7	19.0
1990-91	15.0	3.1	18.1	10.8	1.6	9.1
1991-92	7.3	0.8	8.1	5.4	-53.8	-6.2

import of capital goods against export obligations. Other features of the new policy were enlarging the scope of duty-free imports under advance licenses and more incentives for 100 per cent export oriented units.

While presenting the budget for 1992-93 in his budget-speech, the Indian Finance Minister brought to focus the imperatives of managing balance of payments. The policies in the field of trade announced aimed at further liberalisation of Indian economy. Pointing out to the limitations of the policy of import-compression as a corrective measure for BOP problem, the Finance Minister stated that while imports of non-essential items should be discouraged, the only lasting solution for our BOP problem lies not in compressing imports but in the rapid expansion of exports.

The need for growth of exports for India's economic growth basically arises from the fact that a growing economy needs a growing volume of imports of fuel, industrial inputs, capital goods and technology. The concept of self-reliance in today's world of increasing global interdependence means that India should be able to integrate its economy with the global economy and a self-reliant economy should have the capacity to meet all its requirements through exports.

The BOP crisis in late 80s and early 90s affected India's growth-prospects adversely and as a result, the annual economic growth in 1990-91 and 1991-92 averaged at 2.5 per cent. The trade and development experience clearly showed that inwards looking trade policy which was adopted since 1950s could not lead to desired level of economic growth. The Government adopted a number of reforms in its economic and trade policies so as to avert critical payment problems and to create a suitable environment for exports-augmentation. While the crisis was temporarily averted, it was vital that the pace of liberalisation was sustained in future. The recent development experience also shows that accelerated economic development calls for a viable export-sector which can serve as an engine of growth.

2

Key Drivers of Globalization and Emerging New Forces in the Global Economy

Globalization refers to a set of trends in the world economy, which contributes towards integration of national economies with the global economy. It refers to the growing interdependence of countries worldwide through the increase in volume and variety of cross-border transactions in goods and services, international capital flows, and through the rapid and widespread diffusion of all kinds of technology. There were several phases in the history of world economy when barriers to international trade and international investment fell which led to expanding international trade, investment and the growth of multinational corporations (MNC). It is also possible to identify these phases in recent history of the global economy when increase in cross–border economic activities viz. trade, investment, MNCs etc occurred. In the 20thCentury, prior to World War-I, globalization of economic activities occurred through increase in international trade, foreign direct investment and multinational corporations. This wave of globalization collapsed when World War-I broke out in 1914. Again, the post-World War II period, the 1950s and 1960s, witnessed rapid growth of international trade, investment and the growth of MNCs.

The current wave of globalization through which we are passing is different from past waves in many ways, especially in speed and coverage. Several forces have emerged since 1980s which in combination with each other have accelerated the process of globalization. By analysing these forces and the resulting economic indicators such as the expansion of international trade, globalization of finance, the increase in Foreign Direct Investment (FDI) and growth of MNCs, one can assess the extent and speed of the current wave of globalization.

The study of these indicators becomes important because these are linkages through which national economies integrate with the global economy; and it is the degree of integration through trade, investment and the MNCs, which determines the extent of globalization in the world economy. International trade has become an important factor in international economic affairs. It has grown much more rapidly than the global economic output. Global exports of goods and services increased by 5.5 percent per year in real terms from 1978 to 2001; rising from just over 14 percent of output in the 1970s to almost 25 percent of output in 2001.

GLOBALISING FORCES

There have been several forces in the world economy which have led to expansion of world trade. A study of these forces will show how they have contributed towards increasing economic activities across the borders. These forces include sweeping waves of trade liberalization, fall in the transport and communication cost, and increase in intra-firm trade. Following the protectionist inter-war period, liberalization began with the lowering of import tariffs on trade in manufactures between industrial economies. Within Western Europe, trade was especially liberal following the Treaty of Rome and the formation of the European Free Trade Area.

Since World War II, trade barriers have declined significantly due to successive rounds of trade negotiations. For example, over the past half-century, average tariff levels of the United States and other industrialized countries on imported products have dropped from about 40 percent to only 6 percent, and barriers to trade in services have also been lowered. In addition, since the late 1970s deregulation and privatization have further opened national economies to imports.

The 1990s also witnessed a general reduction in average tariffs and non-tariff barriers in developing countries. In the mid-1990s, East Asia had an average tariff rate of 22 percent. By 1993, some countries such as Indonesia and Malaysia had already lowered their average tariffs to about 10 percent, while many Latin American countries had narrowed the gap by lowering their tariffs from 15 to 4 percent. In East Asia, tariff reduction in China was significant. China's average tariff in 1992 was 47.2 percent. Through a series of five downward adjustments, by October 1997 it had been lowered to 17 percent. Since 1992, China has reduced the number of products that require import licenses from 1,247 to 374 and reduced the number of products subject to import quotas from 26 to 13. Except for 14 price-sensitive raw materials and products that remain under state control, trade for all products has been liberalized.

Not only in volume and value of international trade, but also in its pattern there were significant changes. These changes included increasing share of developing countries in international trade, shift in the composition of trade to services and rise of intra-firm trade. The contemporary phase of globalization began around 1980. During this period, a group of developing economies stopped being onlookers from the sidelines and began to participate in the global economy. They harnessed their abundant human resources, produced labor-intensive manufactured goods and services in which they had comparative advantage, and exported them. Several of them handled their exports of labor-intensive goods in a pragmatic manner and succeeded in acquiring important market niches in specific product lines. Beginning from 25 percent in 1980, the percentage of manufactured exports in total exports of developing economies soared to 80 percent in 1998. This was an impressive spectacle of economic transformation in a short period.

Annual outflows of FDI grew more than six fold between 1983 and 1990 and have continued to grow more than twice as fast as goods trade in the 1990s. An intra-firm trade among MNCs is estimated to account for one-third of world trade, and another one-third is MNC trade with non-affiliates. During the 1990s, international portfolio investment was equally fast as FDI.

There have been several developments in the international economic relations since 1970s, which have led to a favourable environment for the emergence of FDI as an important source of finance. The end of the Cold War was a major reason for increased openness among countries and their participation in the global economy. Since the early 1990s, many countries have made substantial and consistent efforts to create more favorable conditions for FDI, both in the form of bilateral treaties and regional initiatives. The number of bilateral investment treaties totaled 1,513 by the end of 1997. Many countries have also been amending or introducing regulatory changes in order to be more competitive in attracting FDI. As many as 90 percent of these changes are in the direction of streamlining approval procedures, adding new promotional measures and decreasing tariffs. One notable feature is the liberalization of series like telecommunications; broadcasting; energy; tourism; and major urban infrastructure services, such as water supply transportation and education.

These changes, coupled with more liberal entry and operation rules and guarantees against privatization, have improved the macroeconomic environment for FDI. In the 1990s, the opening of domestic markets to products of foreign affiliates and of service sector to foreign participation has also been a significant development in fostering increased globalization and FDI inflows into developing countries. Because of these measures of liberalization, FDI has been growing faster than the expansion in international trade.

As a proportion of world gross product, the combined stock of outward and inward investment rose from 7.8 percent in 1967 to 14.0 percent in 1988 and 23.6 percent in 1997. There was also increase in Foreign Portfolio Investment. As a proportion of world gross product, the flow of outward and inward foreign portfolio investment rose over 14 times between 1970 and 1996 from 0.33 percent in 1970 to 1.94% in 1985, and 4.70% in 1996.

The growing importance of private capital flows since late 1980s flows reflects the trend towards liberalization and globalization of investment and finance. It was at this time that a number of developing countries dismantled barriers to current and capital transactions. Liberalization of restrictions on interest and dividend repatriation played an important role in attracting private capital. Technological advancements improved trading opportunities, and added to this, developing countries took efforts to widen and deepen their markets by introducing new instruments, allowing foreign participation in equity and bond markets, diversifying the currency denomination of bond issues and providing opportunities to hedge risks. The liberalization of capital markets was undertaken with a view of enhancing the supply of low-cost funds.

A special feature that distinguishes the current phase of globalization from the earlier phases is that developing countries emerged as an important recipient of FDI. The inflows of FDI in developing countries nearly doubled between 1981 and 1995, and there has been a trend of increase in the 1990s in their share of total inflows.

According to World Bank estimates, the ratio of FDI to GDP in developing countries jumped from 0.8 percent in 1991 to 2.0 percent in 1997. Developing countries also increased their share of global FDI inflows from 21 percent in 1991 to an estimated 36 percent in 1997. FDI flow to emerging markets grew by an average 36 percent per year between 1990 and 1997. The 1990s marked a shift in the composition of capital flows to emerging markets, with a significant increase in net private capital inflows to emerging markets and a decline in the share of official flows.

Privatization of infrastructure industries is another important new development that has boosted globalization through FDI. Infrastructure investments involve high costs and long gestation period, and therefore, it was not widespread in the developing countries before 1990s. In the 1990s, the development of new technologies and their increasing application had led to rapid expansion of the demand for such industries and services. The vast amount of firm-specific and un-tradable elements of the technologies and management involved changed the attitudes of governments of developing countries, leading to increased liberalization in these sectors to allow active participation by MNCs. A 1996 survey indicated that in 1991-95, a total of 25 developing countries had introduced measures to liberalize FDI in infrastructure.

Some developing countries that liberalized the infrastructure sector include China, India, Indonesia, Pakistan, the Philippines and Vietnam. Between 1988 and 1995, of the total revenue derived from infrastructure privatization in the developing countries, 51.1 percent came from FDI (UNCTAD 1996). China had quickly expanded the scope for foreign participation in infrastructure and services. By the end of 1996, it had signed contracts for such projects involving contractual FDI amounting to US$190 billion, which was 36.3 percent of the contractual FDI amount for the year.

The share of developing countries in total FDI more than doubled between 1986 and 1990s. A notable feature of the FDI flows to developing countries has been that these have concentrated in a small number of developing countries. In 1993, 83 percent of FDI inflows went to ten countries; China, Singapore, Argentina, Mexico, Malaysia, Indonesia, Thailand, Hong Kong, Taiwan and Nigeria, in descending order of magnitude. Over the past decade, these ten countries have consistently attracted between two-thirds and four-fifths of developing country inward investment.

Since the 1980s, developing countries have played a role not only as recipient of FDI but also as a source of FDI outflows.

The emergence of developing countries as an important source of FDI outflows is one of the trends indicating the speed of globalization, which marks the current wave of globalization. Developing countries, during the last ten years, have become important in FDI outflows. Between 1983 and 1987, these outflows accounted for about 5 percent of the total world outflows. The corresponding average figure for 1993-95 is about 16 percent i.e. more than three times.

The other important feature of speeding globalization in its current phase is the phenomenal growth of MNCs. The increasing importance of MNCs has considerably altered the structure and functioning of the global economy. These firms have become major determinants of trade-flows and of the location of industries and other economic activities around the world. Most investments are capital–intensive and technology-intensive sectors. These firms have become central in the expansion of technology flows to both industrialized and industrializing economies. Controlling much of the world's investment capital, technology, and access to global markets, such firms have become major players in international economic affairs.

In 1997 there were 53,000 MNCs worldwide with 450,000 foreign subsidiaries selling $9.5 trillion of goods and services across the globe (UNCTAD 1998B). Transnational production considerably exceeds the level of global exports and has become the primary means for selling goods and services abroad. MNCs now account, according to some estimates, for at least 20 percent of world production and 70 percent of world trade. They span every sector of the global economy activity within and across the world's major economic regions. In the financial sector, multinational banks are by far the major actors in global financial markets, playing a critical role in the management and organization of money and credit in the global economy.

As of 1995, MNCs accounted for quarter to a third of world output, 70 percent of world trade and 80 percent of direct international investments. MNCs channelised $7 trillion in sales through their foreign affiliates, an amount greater than the world total exports in 1995. And at the end of 1996, the MNCs total stock of FDI stood at over $3 trillion. Such globalization of economic activities is a result; partly of government policies on fiscal, foreign exchange rates, investment and wage; and partly of market forces involving product life-cycles, shifting market parameters and corporate strategies for survival and expansion.

Modern technological advances in production system supported the spectacular growth of MNCs. World-wide technology has extended the scope to sub-divide the process of production and distribution into parts that can be relocated anywhere in the world according to changes in comparative advantage. Globalization of production process has led to outsourcing through sub-contracting, joint- venture and FDI.

The resulting productivity growth in the industrial and services sectors is altering the key source of wealth of nations, which is moving ever faster away from natural capital to human capital (that is, from raw material and physical capital per worker to human skills and knowledge). In particular, wealth creation in the 21st century will depend mainly on the ability to access and make productive use of expanding stocks of knowledge and information, and to build on them through creative research and development.

The emergence of transnational corporations which require intra-firm movement of personnel, the growing skill shortages in the developed world owing to declining fertility rates and ageing populations, and the internationalisation of higher education, make global movement of labour, particularly skilled labour, one of the most important forces of globalization in the 21st century. First, the technological change in the form of information and communication technology has increased the number of jobs that can be moved to offshore locations, meaning that the outsourcing phenomenon is no longer limited to the manufacturing sector but also includes the outsourcing of highly skilled jobs in the service sector. Second, the opening up of labour markets in China and India has brought a vast number of low-wage semi-skilled workers into the global production system.

In addition to the key drivers of globalization of international trade, globalization of finance and growth of the multinational corporation, there are new forces which have further deepened globalization during its current phase. These new forces include the rapid growth of the services sector and information technology.

Developing countries have become increasingly integrated into global goods and financial markets over the last decade. Their export volume increased to 9 percent per year during the 1990s, up from 2 percent as compared to the 1980s. Net long-term capital flows, even after declining in 1998, remained almost three times the 1980s level. Globalization provides developing countries with significant benefits and spurs economic progress. GDP growth in developing countries, excluding the transition economies, averaged 5 percent during the 1990s compared with 3 percent during the 1980s. Poverty -the number of people living on less than $1 a day-fell from 29 percent in 1990 to an estimated 24 percent in 1996.

ASIAN FINANCIAL CRISIS

Globalization has thrown several challenges for developing countries in the process of their integration with the global economy. The development experience of 1990s has highlighted important concerns which need to be addressed.

Even in 1990, the four countries hit hardest by the Asian Crisis i.e. Indonesia, the Republic of Korea, Malaysia and Thailand– were relatively well integrated with global financial markets. Reflecting their integration and strong performance, they had ratios of private long-term non-guaranteed debt and private short-term debt to GDP higher even than large Latin American countries. Other large Asian countries – China, the Philippines and Vietnam – had much less private debt.

After 1990, the region entered a new phase of financial integration with the global economy. The four crisis-hit countries took on even more private debt, and at a faster pace than other developing countries, especially after 1993. Policy changes indirectly favored foreign borrowing. The ratio of private non-guaranteed and short-term debt to GDP rose by almost 3 percentage points a year. Short-term debt grew especially fast, with Thailand, and thereafter, Korea seeing the largest relative increase.

In addition, the four countries received enormous portfolio and FDI. Annual portfolio inflows averaged more than 1 percent of GDP, 50 percent more than in large Latin American countries. Significant FDI (above the average for large developing countries) went to Malaysia, Indonesia, and Thailand. The inflows were responding to these countries' continued good performance and increasingly open capital accounts. Thus, they benefited from and accounted for about one-quarter of the explosion in global private financial flows in the 1990s.

In the early 1990s, the inflows financed a sharp rise in domestic investment and international reserves. Higher net inflows to Korea, Malaysia and Thailand financed most of their sharp rise in investment increase (3 percent of GDP) and were largely financed by domestic savings, which was mainly due to two factors. First, short-term borrowing to finance long-term projects became increasingly important, especially in these three countries. This created a sizable maturity mismatch in the sheets of domestic financial institutions. Second, domestic banks lent to domestic firms in local currency, while borrowing short term in foreign currencies without hedging. This created a significant currency mismatch. Thus, the easy availability of credit fueled investment in increasingly risky assets. In some countries, the credit boom was translated into bubbles in real estate and poverty. In other countries, financial resources were direct toward over investment in narrowly specialized industries such as electronics or large, prestigious projects with unclear benefits. These poor and risky investments, in turn worsened the quality of the portfolios of domestic financial institutions, thereby creating the risk of panics and subsequent crisis.

In many cases, the domestic companies borrowed from foreign markets on a short-term basis to finance long-term debt. This constituted around 46 percent of the external debt of Thailand in mid-1997, and in South Korea it was as high as 67 percent. Several reasons have been attributed to the large increase in short-term capital inflows in Korea (Park 1998). First, the large increase in trade required a proportionate increase in trade-related credits but the growth in short-term capital inflows outpaced expansion in trade. Second, in 1994, the ceiling on foreign currency loans by commercial bank was lifted, but the ceiling on commercial banks' medium and long-term borrowings from international financial market was not eased. Finally, and this might be true of other countries also, the cost of short-term borrowing was lower than the cost of issuing medium-and long-term securities. The proportion of short-term debt to total debt in Malaysia and the Philippines was 39 percent and 24 percent respectively. The composition of capital flows which was initially dominated by FDIs, moved towards increasing dependence on short-term banking and portfolio flows which can enhance vulnerability to attacks. A high level of short-term debt makes a country vulnerable because of the continuous need of rollovers, which become extremely difficult at times of crisis.

In 1994-96, the four countries allowed themselves to become even more vulnerable, and there were signs that investors were becoming concerned about the sustainability of the boom. They increasingly used inflows to finance investment, which remained roughly constant as a share of GDP (except in Malaysia), while the current account widened by 1 percent or more of GDP. Moreover, short-term debt and unaccounted for capital outflows increased sharply. Finally, growth in international reserves slowed relative to rapidly growing short-term debt and domestic deposits, which meant a smaller cushion against shifts by short-term lenders and domestic depositors through the open capital account. This vulnerability was in addition to the potential of reversals in portfolio flows and any problems in rolling over long-term debt that would come with any loss of confidence. (Debt service obligations on long-term debt averaged 8.2 percent of GDP in Indonesia and 7.7 percent in Malaysia).

Avoiding the loss of confidence that would reverse capital flows and cause a crisis depended on using the inflows productively (so that the resulting assets could service the resulting debt) and maintaining sound macroeconomic policies (with consistency between monetary and exchange rate policies even if external or internal conditions changed). But during the 1990s and especially after 1993, the crisis countries increasingly did not meet these conditions – raising the risk of a sudden shift in funds.

After receiving large capital flows for four years or more, the four most affected crisis countries – Indonesia, Korea, Malaysia, and Thailand – suffered heavy losses following the sudden shift in investor sentiment. The penalties for policy mis-steps were excessive, fed as much by investor reactions to each other's behavior as by the underlying fundamentals. The region emerged from the crisis with ready to flee with alacrity investment attitude born of the recent experience.

The challenge of managing globalization is to capture its benefits without suffering the high costs of sudden capital reversals or trade shocks. This requires East Asia to put in place macroeconomic and structural policies for capital flows that encourage stability. It also means that transition economies – China and Vietnam – formulate options that minimize risks to exposure to the same forces that had wreaked havoc on the crisis countries. China is partway down the part of reform, and its trade and selective financial openness have already spawned an inevitable trend towards financial integration. Developing a coherent program to manage this process–and avoid disruption–involves difficult issues of pace and sequencing.

The crisis in East Asia in 1997 illustrates how financial integration without adequate institutional checks and balances can cause instability and affect the momentum of development adversely. The crisis adversely affected the growth prospects of Thailand, Malaysia, Indonesia and the Rep of Korea etc. In the process of financial integration, the economic strategy adopted developed several imbalances in important sectors. The firms depended on bank credit for their investment projects, which allowed them to rely heavily on bank credit. In the Rep of Korea and Thailand, for instance, the average debt-to-equity ratios in 1996 were above 200 percent. The other factor which led to the financial crisis was uncontrolled capital inflows. For many years, most Asian economies kept their financial systems relatively closed. Foreign borrowing controls ensured that the region's financial sectors remained immune from external shocks despite their domestic fragility. The controls checked the domestic flow of short-term and unhedged foreign debt. International capital markets were gradually opened and domestic markets were deregulated. This led to further increase in short-term capital flows.

The 1990s also saw a dramatic increase in foreign borrowing. Foreign debt financing became increasingly important. The pegged exchange rate eliminated exchange risks in borrowing in dollars. International investors were encouraged to lend because of higher interest rates in the countries affected by the crisis. Between 1991 and 1996, overall borrowing doubled in Malaysia and Thailand and grew by one third in the Rep of Korea.

In the first half of 1997, despite the worsening financial environment, capital inflows did not slow down but increasingly took the form of short-term inter-bank loans that could be readily withdrawn and could count on formal guarantees in the inter-bank markets. However, once the crisis began, international banks suddenly stopped lending and began to call in their loans. A huge amount of private foreign capital fled the region in the second half of 1997. Indonesia, the Rep of Korea, Malaysia, Philippines and Thailand received a net capital inflow of about $76 billion in 1996 but suffered a net capital outflow of around $36 billion in 1997.

Many of the affected countries ran a high current account deficit running well over 5 percent of GDP. In particular, current account deficits became large in Thailand and Malaysia in 1995. Even in Indonesia and South Korea, there was a worsening of the current account deficit in 1995 to 3.3 percent and 2 percent respectively from very modest levels in the preceding years. Under these circumstances, maintenance of high export growth rate became vital as the high level of current deficit made these economies vulnerable to external shocks. East Asian economies were preferred destination for private capital flows in the 1990s because of continuous high level of growth and high level of reserves. Once credibility came under a cloud, the outflow of capital gathered momentum. So long as a capital inflow filled up the current account deficit, the economies did well and performed well. However, once the sentiment changed and capital inflows were replaced by capital outflows, it had severe consequences.

The crisis also adversely affected the spectacular progress made by these countries in reducing poverty. The increase in the rate of unemployment in the affected countries was one of the social consequences of Asian financial crisis of 1997, which had directly impacted the poverty-profile of these countries. There was collapse in the demand for labour caused by retrenchment and bankruptcies. In the Republic of Korea, the unemployment rate increased from 2.3 percent in October 1997 to 8.2 percent in November 1998. The rate of unemployment also doubled in Thailand, Malaysia from 1997 to 1998. In Indonesia, the rate of unemployment varied between 15 to 20 percent by the end of the 1998.

The increase in insecurity is especially pronounced among low-income and urban households. In the five crisis countries and in China, the number of people living below the international poverty line of $1 a day (in 1993 purchasing power parity terms) jumped up to about 13 million between 1996 and 1998, pushing East Asia's total number of poor people to 278 million, of which 213 million were Chinese. Because another 150 million people had emerged above the poverty line only in the decade prior to the crisis -- 60 million East Asians and 90 million Chinese – the region also contained a huge group of near poor. The recession made their lot more precarious as demand for labor slackened and unemployment rose, especially in urban areas. In the crisis countries, many of these workers were young and had never experienced a serious recession. In China (and Vietnam) unemployment affected older workers – a painful by-product of state enterprise reform and government downsizing. In both groups of countries, the newly unemployed faced rising insecurity over jobs and incomes.

UNDP in its Human Development Report (1999) had identified two important lessons from the crisis. The first is that financial volatility is a permanent feature of today's globally integrated financial markets. The crisis was not an isolated accident—it is a symptom of general weakness in global capital markets. The second lesson is that extreme caution is required in opening up to foreign short-term (often speculative) capital, especially when financial market institutions are not well developed.

The East Asian financial crisis has several important policy lessons for developing countries in their integration with the global economy. It is clear that the process of global integration needs to be moderated and regulated in order to avoid financial instability and its adverse affects on growth prospects. The experience of countries affected by the crisis also shows that financial policies must avoid overvalued exchange rates and unsustainable current account deficits. More flexible exchange rates, greater reliance on fiscal policy and better and tighter domestic financial regulation are often needed to reduce excessive capital inflows and domestic lending booms. Financial sector liberalization must proceed carefully and in step with the capacity of countries to enforce tighter regulation and supervision. Efforts to improve prudential safeguards and banking operations need to be accelerated in most developing countries. The opening of the capital account flows needs to be carefully orchestrated to match the capacity of countries to manage risk.

CAPITAL FLOWS AND EQUITY

Although globalization of finance can stimulate growth under some conditions, it also has a profound impact on the distribution of the fruits of that growth. In some cases the link between growth and indicators of equity is positive; in others the relation is more ambiguous. Overall, the picture that emerges is one of great and perhaps increasing heterogeneity; with some regions, countries, sectors, and social groups taking advantage of the opportunities provided by globalization, while others fall ever further behind.

As we have already seen, there was great diversity in the distribution of capital flows across regions over the last two decades. Annexure **'A' (a&b)** summarizes the pattern, showing clear winners and losers in the period 1970-2003. East Asia and the Pacific were the main winners up to and including 1997, more than doubling their share of total capital flows to developing countries; the Middle East, South Asia, and Sub-Saharan Africa were equally clear losers, especially in the 1990s. Latin America and Europe and Central Asia saw their share decline between 1980 and 1990, but they more or less regained it by 1997. During the crisis years of 1998 and 1999, the main change was the temporary decline in capital flows to Asia.

Within the category of FDI, capital was even more concentrated than total flows, especially in the 1990s. Thus, while East Asia and Latin America together accounted for 50-70 percent of total flows, their share of FDI was nearly 80 percent. On the other side, South Asia and sub-Saharan Africa together received only about 5 percent of FDI flows compared with 10-20 percent of the total. In so far as we have argued that FDI is the most important type of capital for investment (and therefore, growth), these differences have a significant impact. Beyond the regional differences, there is additional evidence of concentration at the country level. According to UNCTAD (1999A: 115-120), in the period 1990-1997, the top ten emerging market economies accounted for over three-quarters of all FDI to developing countries. China, Brazil, and Mexico alone received almost one-half of such investment. Calculating FDI in per capita terms also shows great inequality; sub-Saharan Africa received less than $5 a year, the Association of South-East Asian Nations (ASEAN) $31, and Latin America $62. Among the highest individual recipients on this measure were Malaysia ($223 per capita), Chile ($170), Mexico ($ 79), Brazil ($35), and China ($21). The two sub-Saharan African countries with the largest amount of FDI were Ghana ($6 per capita) and Uganda ($3).

Poorer countries, then, must rely mainly on official flows, both loans and grants. Although these sources of finance have the advantage of low interest rates and long maturities (or no repayment at all in the case of grants), the volume of official development assistance (ODA) has lagged behind that of private flows. Bilateral aid, in particular, fell during the 1990s from 0.33 percent of the GDP of industrial countries in 1990 to 0.22 percent in 1998, before rising slightly to 0.24 percent in 1999 (OECD, Development Co-operation, various issues). Although multilateral funds increased somewhat in nominal terms during the decade, a significant share of these funds was concentrated in a few large countries that were hit by the financial crisis.

One issue of concern then is the failure of concessional funds (which go mainly to the poorest countries) to keep up with the private funds that are directed primarily toward middle-income countries. A related problem has to do with the high level of debt that characterizes the poorest countries; as a percentage of GDP, the levels are much higher than for wealthier developing countries. The particular mechanism designed to deal with this problem –the Highly Indebted Poor Countries Initiative (HIPC) –has made some progress. Nonetheless, the terms are onerous and the speed slow. Perhaps the most important element is the new link between the HIPC debt negotiations and the World Bank / IMF Poverty Reduction Strategy Papers. The latter are poverty-reduction programmes that are designed jointly by governments and various elements of civil society in the respective countries; although potentially very positive, they have not been in operation long enough for their effectiveness to have been evaluated. Globalization and liberalization seem to have increased the inequality of external savings across regions and individual countries; in addition, they have contributed to raising inequality within countries. Finally, identifying indicators of domestic inequality is not a simple task.

EMPLOYMENT IMPACT OF OUTSOURCING

Outsourcing (the contracting out of business functions previously performed in-house) has heightened concerns among workers about job security. More particularly, the increasing trend of offshoring (the contracting out to foreign as opposed to domestic affiliates) has promoted many to suggest that the phenomenon is leading to a reallocation of jobs from developed to developing economies.

It is certainly true that many multinational firms have shifted production facilities to developing economies to take advantage of lower labour costs, yet it would be an overstatement to assert that a large share of developed economy jobs have gone overseas. Recent statistics based on job losses due to outsourcing in some of the developed economies illustrate the point.

- In the United States, by far the largest outsourcer of the industrialized economies, estimates of job losses due to outsourcing represent only a small fraction of jobs lost in a given period. For example, in the first three months of 2004 less than 2 percent of mass layoffs in the United States were due to outsourcing (this includes domestic outsourcing).

- In Europe, the outsourcing phenomenon is not yet as widespread as in the United States. Germany is by far the largest outsourcer in Europe, perhaps due to its proximity to Eastern Europe. Outsourcing in Germany resulted in a loss of roughly 8,000 jobs per year from 1990-2001, mainly to Eastern Europe. This figure represents only 0.2 percent of Germany's labour force, which comprises 40 million people. It is also a small fraction of total jobs lost on a yearly basis.

For those in the business community with today's low figures on outsourcing, the future may bring a massive transformation in how goods and services are produced. The challenge for economies will be how to integrate themselves into the global production process in order to create decent employment opportunities for those seeking work. For developing economies, it undoubtedly will require increasing the absorptive capacity of their labour force, and for their institutions the ability to utilize technology transferred from the developed economies. For developed economies, it would require a stronger focus on innovation and expansion into new markets.

The benefits from outsourcing can be derived through a number of channels. Global linkages in the supply chain have created opportunities for increased income in the developing economies; however, it has to adapt to the rapid changes in technology, which are speeding productivity gains and the rate of job creation and destruction, and to provide social safety nets for workers who are displaced during the process.

As mentioned earlier, it is certainly true that globalization has been the cause of the loss of competitive advantage in certain labour-intensive industries in the industrialized economies leading to a loss of jobs, but there has been no net transfer of jobs to developing economies. Studies have shown that the decline in Industrial employment across economies is due more to gains in the efficiency of production than to the loss of jobs to developing economies, a trend that has been occurring worldwide. Innovations in the production process have increased efficiencies in traditional industrial sectors, not only in developed economies but also in developing economies, as increasingly more output can be produced with fewer workers. According to one study, "between 1995 and 2002 roughly 22 million jobs were lost globally, a decline of 11 percent. Yet, over the same period, global industrial production increased by more than 30 percent –a remarkable gain in productivity".

In addition to social protection for workers, international labour standards are necessary in order to ensure that low-cost labour is not synonymous with the exploitation of labour – and that decent work prevails. Some developing economies that have entered into the global supply chain have done so through the "low road" option to development. These economies are completely based on low-cost, low-skilled labour–a growth strategy that is not sustainable, because it often does not lead to productive work. For example, although the quantity of work has been increasing in the manufacturing sector in Mexico with the rise of the maquiladoras (Maquila factories), the quality of employment has not improved, leading to a "decent-work deficit".

3

Globalization as a Catalyst of Economic Growth: Emerging Concerns and Challenges in 21st Century

Global forces affect the path of economic development in many ways. It has been observed from the development experience of last three decades that countries which adapted their economic policies to the mechanisms and forces supporting globalization, succeeded in achieving a very high rate of economic growth; and subsequently, converged towards the income-level of developed economies. In other words, they succeeded in closing or narrowing the development gap. Globalization influences the momentum of economic development by creating new opportunities for developing countries to share the expanding trade, investment, technological and organizational innovations.

Foreign trade and FDI contribute to economic growth through various channels. Both exports and FDI contribute to the expansion of productive capacity because they bring foreign exchange, which the economy can then use to import foreign items necessary for the expansion of productive capacity such as high quality foreign capital goods, intermediate goods and technologies. FDI improves the productivity of the recipient economy because it brings technologies and managerial know-how, which are in short supply in developing economies. Foreign trade provides an economy with opportunities to improve the use of its productive resources or to improve its resource allocation. It also benefits by improving technical efficiency and by increasing productivity. Exports also put pressure on producers to achieve internationally competitive prices and quality. An expansion in imports improves the technical efficiency of domestic firms as imports create competitive pressures. In order to survive under competitive pressures, domestic firms have to improve their productivity by adopting strategies such as the introduction of new technologies and new products.

ASIAN CASE STUDIES

The role of globalization as a catalyst agent can be best demonstrated by the development experience of East and South East Asian economies. These economies out-performed the rest of the world for several decades while achieving spectacular and sustained economic growth. Foreign trade and FDI in these economies expanded rapidly in the 1980s and 1990s largely due to liberalization of trade and FDI policies. FDI inflows transferred funds for fixed investment, as also technology and managerial know-how which contributed to the expansion and improvement of productive capabilities. What has been remarkable in these economies is the interaction and simultaneous expansion of FDI inflows and exports, which reinforced the favourable impact of each. The regional production and trade networks established by multinationals through FDI contributed to economic growth by enabling multinationals and regional economies to improve their technical efficiency and achieve greater division of labor. An analysis of the growth experience of the Republic of Korea, Thailand, Malaysia and Indonesia from 1970s to 1990s, and more recently of China, captures the interaction between globalization and acceleration of economic growth in these countries. The table below depicts the same.

Table 3.1: Growth of real GDP per capita in East Asia, 1960-95

	Per-capita GDP, 1960 (in 1995$)	*Per-capita GDP, 1995 (1995$)*	*Rate of growth 1960-95 (%)*
Indonesia	621	2,602	4.1
Rep. Of Korea	883	8,505	6.5
Malaysia	1,381	6,613	4.5
The Philippines	1,112	1,756	1.3
Thailand	923	5,034	4.8
United States	**9,774**	**19,621**	**2.0**

Source: Barro and Lee 1994 and World Bank 1998.

Table 3.2: Growth of real GDP before the Crisis: East Asia Vs. the World (1980-96)

	Average annual rate of growth of real GDP (%)		
	1980-89	*1990-95*	*1996*
East Asia	5.6	6.9	7.1
Indonesia	5.3	8.0	8.0
Rep. Of Korea	7.8	7.8	7.1
Malaysia	5.8	8.8	8.6
The Philippines	1.9	2.3	5.7
Thailand	9.0	7.3	5.5
Industrialized countries	2.7	1.8	2.5
Developing countries	4.3	5.8	6.6
Latin America	1.0	2.9	3.5

Source: International Monetary Fund 1998.

Republic of Korea

The Republic of Korea has achieved a spectacular rate of economic growth since the 1970s. The real Gross National Product (GNP) grew at an average rate of 8.1 percent between 1970 and 1997. Between 1970 and 1996, per capita GNP increased from US$253 to over US$10,000. The share of agriculture in the Gross Domestic Product (GDP) decreased from 27 percent to less than 7 percent during that period. Exports recorded substantial increase from US$0.9 billion to US$128 billion, 70 percent of which comprised heavy machinery and chemical products. South Korea's successful economic development has been held up as a model for other developing countries to emulate. With a per capita income of US$100 it was one of the poorest countries in Asia in 1960, while in 1995 with a per capita income of US$10,076 it stood under the category of upper-middle income country. Its rapid economic growth has been accompanied by a big transformation in industrial structure. In 1960, only 1.8 percent of all workers were engaged in mining and manufacturing whereas 68.3 percent were in the agriculture, forestry and fishery sector. In 1995, employment in mining and manufacturing increased to 23.5 percent of total national employment; and in agriculture, forestry and fishery sector employment decreased to 12.5 percent.

One of the salient features of the economic development process has been the rapid expansion of the foreign sector propelled by the export-led growth strategy, which enabled it to participate in the expanding international trade resulting from globalization. The share of GDP in international trade increased sharply. The share of exports increased from 14 percent in 1970 to 40 percent of GDP in 1987, and the share of imports increased from 24 percent of GDP in 1970 to 41 percent of GDP in 1982. The increasing share of trade in GDP underlined the deepening of S Korea's integration with the global economy.

It responded to globalization by bringing suitable adjustments in its policies since mid-1960s. The outward oriented policy, which started in mid-1960s and continued through 1980s, further intensified with the adoption of a number of liberalization measures in 1980s and 1990s. In 1988, on the completion of the five-year import liberalization programme, the import liberalization ratio rose from 80 percent in 1983 to over 95 percent by 1988. Together with reduced quantitative import restrictions, the average nominal tariff rate was gradually lowered from 24 percent in 1983 to 13 percent in 1989. By 1993, the Govt brought down tariffs on industrial products down to 7 percent through annual cuts.

Since the mid-sixties, S Korea witnessed a robust expansion of trade, shown by the table below. Total trade in 1965 was equal to $ 630 million only, accounting for 21 percent of GDP. But the figure increased to $12.35 billion in 1975, $61.42 billion in 1985, and $260.18 billion in 1995. It rose more than twenty times within two decades. Since 1975, trade has consistently accounted for more than 50 percent of GDP, reaching 58 percent in 1997.

It responded to the adjustment of policies in trade and economic sphere right from mid-1960s and thus joined the category of early globalizers. In 1964, the government adopted a uniform exchange rate system and devalued the won by nearly 100 percent, in order to promote exports. In addition, short-term export credit was made available at a preferential rate, and tax rebates were allowed on raw materials imported for the production of exports. A number of free trade zones were also established and customs procedures were simplified. These measures enabled exporters to do business, in effect, under a free trade regime. Exports at current prices rose at an annual rate of 40 percent between 1962 and 1971. Propelled by the rapid growth in exports, GNP grew at an annual rate of more than 9 percent.

The simple average tariff was 23.7 percent in 1982, with two-thirds tariff lines subject to rates of 20 percent or higher. By 1994, the simple average was 7.9 and 93 percent of tariff lines were at rates less than 20 percent. Agriculture products tended to be subject to the highest rates (an average 31 percent in 1982 and 17percent in 1994), while raw materials attracted the lowest

Table 3.3: Trends of Export, Import and ratio of GDP (1960 – 1997)

Year	*Exports*	*Imports*	*Trade*	*GDP*	*Trade (%)*
1960	0.03	0.34	0.37	2.0	18.50
1965	0.17	0.46	0.63	3.0	21.00
1970	0.81	1.98	2.82	8.1	34.81
1975	5.08	7.27	12.35	21.3	57.98
1985	30.28	31.14	61.42	94.3	65.13
1990	65.02	69.84	134.86	253.6	53.18
1994	96.01	102.35	198.36	380.7	52.10
1995	125.06	135.12	260.18	456.5	56.99
1996	129.72	150.34	280.06	484.4	57.82
1997	129.72	15034	281.05	484.4	57.82

Source: 1. Exports & Imports 1960-1996, Bank of Korea, Ministry of Finance and Economy, Korea. **2.** GDP Bank of Korea

rates (12 and 2.8 percent, respectively). On this basis, it has liberalized trade significantly, however these figures are based on the low in-quota tariff rates, and South Korea applies many tariff quotas, especially for agricultural goods. If this is taken into account, the simple average applied tariff was 14.4 percent in 1996 and 13.8 percent in 2000. In both years, average tariffs on agricultural goods exceeded 50 percent, although the average on industrial goods fell from 7.7 to 7.5 percent. The import weighted average tariff was 10.9 percent in 1996 and 10.6 percent in 2000. In general, Korea has low tariffs, although agriculture sector is highly protected

More than four decades of exports drive have profoundly integrated the South Korean economy into a web of global economic interdependence. Total trade volume in 1965 was only a meager amount of $630 million, accounting for 21 percent of GDP, but the figure increased to $12.35 billion in 1975, $61.42 billion in 1985, and $260.18 billion in 1995. The trade volume rose more than twenty times within two decades. Since 1975, the trade volume has consistently accounted for more than 50 percent of gross domestic product, reaching 63.5 percent in 1997. In comparison with other countries, South Korea has become a truly trading state.

South Korea's export earnings posted strong performance through the whole year in 2004. On of the main factors in the export boom was the demand from China, which is now its most important export market. In addition to heavy reliance on a few major markets, its exports are relatively narrowly based on a limited range of products such as wireless communication equipment, automobiles and steel. This suggests that the country's export performance is quite vulnerable to negative shocks triggered by various external factors. Nonetheless, the merchandise exports registered rapid growth of 312 percent in 2004, up from 19.3 percent in 2003 and 8.0 percent in 2002. The major export items were passenger cars, metal goods, machinery and equipment, including electronics, telecommunications equipment and semiconductors.

Table 3.4: Capital inflows and outflows

(Unit US$ million)

	FDI from Korea	*FDI into Korea*	*FIDI into Korea*	*Total (FDI+FIDI)*	*FIDI Total Investment (%)*
1985	591	234	1,787	1,971	68.1
1990	1,052	789	218	1,007	21.6
1994	2,461	809	8,147	8,956	91.0
1995	3,552	1,776	13.875	15,651	88.7
1996	4,670	2,325	21,183	23,508	90.1
1997	4,287	2,341	12,546	14,887	84.3
1997-8	507	253	743	996	74.6

(Contd.)

(Contd.Table 3.4)

	FDI from Korea	*FDI into Korea*	*FIDI into Korea*	*Total (FDI+FIDI)*	*FIDI Total Investment (%)*
1997-9	180	40	1,760	1,800	97.8
1997-10	332	150	8852	1,035	85.5
1997-11	140	18	-1,481	-1,463	101.2
1998-1	124	43	308	351	87.7
1998-2	307	177	1,873	2,050	91.4
1998.3	360	146	690	836	82.5
1998-4	239	177	3,650	3,827	95.4

Source: Ministry of Finance and Economy, Korea. (Including investment into stocks and bonds).

Capital and financial flows have also been remarkable with Inbound and outbound foreign investments steadily rising. Total inbound foreign investment was $1.97 billion in 1985, but rose more than ten times by 1996 to reach $23.5 billion. Outbound foreign investment also rose from $591 million in 1985 to $4.6 billion in 1986. But external borrowing rather than foreign investment has played a more important role in foreign savings. Reflecting this trend, South Korea's external borrowing rose sharply from $467.6 billion in 1985 to $1,544 billion in 1997. Table 3.4 gives out the total capital flows in and out of S Korea.

Thailand

The Thai economy has grown rapidly during the past three decades. Real GDP grew at about 8 percent in the 1960s, and 7 percent in the 1970s. During the first half of the 1980s, the growth rate fell slightly to about 6 percent, but rose dramatically to 9 percent in the second-half. Growth rates of GDP in the beginning of the 1990s were well above 8 percent; however, they dropped to about 6 percent in 1996 and recorded a decline of 1.75 percent for the first time in 1997. After the onset of the 1997 economic crisis, the economy has tended to recover, although at a slower growth rate.

Over the years, the structure of the Thai economy has been changing from a labour-intensive agriculture base to a capital-intensive manufacturing base. The share of agriculture in GDP dropped sharply from nearly 40 percent in the 1960s to about 11 percent by the mid-1990s. These reductions were accompanied by a rapid expansion in the manufacturing sector whose share in GDP grew from 12.5 percent in 1960 to 60 percent by the mid-1990s, although it declined marginally after the crisis. Within manufacturing, the shares of food, beverages, tobacco and snuff fell, while the share of petroleum refining, electrical machinery, and wearing apparel, leather and textiles rose sharply.

These structural changes brought about by an outward-oriented policy have changed the structure of employment in the Thai economy. Over the years, manufacturing labour force expanded at a much faster rate than agricultural labour. The share of agricultural labour in total labour force declined from about 82 percent in 1960 to about 42 percent by the late 1990s. During the same period, the share of manufacturing labour continued to rise.

There has been a major change in the structure of Thai exports. A shift in trade and investment policy together with a favourable trading environment in the 1990s led to an expansion in labour-intensive exports. By the early 2000, the share of manufactured exports in total exports reached 75 percent. The export sectors that grew at the highest rates were computer parts and components, telecommunications equipment, electrical and electronic products, auto parts and certain miscellaneous consumer goods. Thailand's major traditional exports such as textiles, clothing and footwear grew at much lower rates and their shares in total exports declined steadily throughout the decade. The growth in production of these items, which were mainly exported to the US and the EU, generated substantial employment particularly for female workers.

Significant structural change was also evident in exports. Agriculture fell from around 85 percent of total exports in 1960 to 18 percent in 1990, whereas manufacturing rose from 2.4 percent to 73.8 percent during the same thirty-year period. The growth in manufactured exports after 1980 was especially striking; a 24 percent annual compound rate from 1980 to 1990 and 22 percent from 1990 to 1995 meant that Thailand had the highest rate of growth of both manufactured and total exports of all the Asian "high performing economies". Within this growth in manufacturing exports was a further shift; from 1985 to 1993, labour-intensive goods (e.g. garments, gems, shoes) dominated manufactured exports. As the growth of these products slowed in the early 1990s, medium-high technology products (computer parts, electronics, and electrical appliances) grew rapidly, so that by 1995 the export value of these products was 40 percent greater than labour-intensive goods.

Thailand's economy has been transformed from import substituting to export-led economy since 1972 when the Industrial Promotion Act came into force. Between 1986 and 1990, it stood as one of the fastest growing economies in the world with an average real GDP growth rate of 11.5 percent. An average real GDP growth rate during 1990-94, however, moderated to around 8 percent due to the tightening of fiscal and monetary policies as part of the government's objective to prevent overheating of the economy. The prudent financial management also stabilized inflation rate within the maximum band of 5 percent per annum during the early 1990s.

It witnessed an increasing flow of FDI during the 1980s. Net flows of FDI during the period 1981-85, 1986-90, 1991-95 and 1996-2000 averaged around 6,600, 30,900, 46,400 and 127,000 million respectively. FDI was relatively unaffected by the financial crisis, partly reflecting the political stability and investment reforms undertaken by the government, especially the partial opening in 1998 of several sectors such as banking, energy, and telecommunications. Most of the FDI was concentrated mainly in the industry sector, particularly electrical machinery and appliances, and transport equipment. The major investors were the United States, Japan, and the EU. However, ASEAN investors have played an increasingly dominant role recently.

In 2003, Thailand bound 72 percent of its tariff lines. A simple average bound tariff was 28.4 percent where a simple average applied, while most favoured nation (MFN) tariff rate was 14.7 percent, down from 17 percent in 1999 and 23 percent in 1995. Products with the highest simple averages were vegetable products, prepared good, transport equipment, footwear, headgear, arm and ammunition. As part of incentives granted by the Board of Investment (BOI), it continues to grant border tax exemptions to encourage investment in remote areas and production for export.

The foreign investment regime has remained liberal with the BOI promotion schemes that allow 100 percent foreign ownership in a number of activities. The other important investment legislation is the 1999 Foreign Business Act B.E.2542 (FBA) which replaced the old 1972 Alien Business Law. This Act allows foreign investors to have ownership of up to 75 percent or 100 percent in wide range of business activities subject to certain restrictions and requirements. In addition to the FBA there is the 1966 Treaty of Amity and Economic Relations with the United States. The treaty provides national treatment to U.S. investors, except for communications, transport, banking, exploitation of land or other natural resources, and domestic trade in agriculture products.

Foreign trade played a major role in giving a sustained high rate of economic growth between 1961 and 1996. During sixth and seventh plan, export grew at the rate of 25.7 percent and 44.2 percent respectively. The emergence of Thailand as an important player in the global trade can be assessed from the fact that the composition of exports registered a major shift from primary products to manufacturing products such as computers, electrical applications, electronics etc. An export-oriented growth resulted in economic prosperity during 1980s and 1990s. The expanding exports in manufacturing sector, especially exports of labour intensive products resulted in rapid expansion of employment opportunities.

Malaysia

The Malaysian economy entered a period of unprecedented growth in 1986. The economy expanded at an annual average rate of over 8 percent during the subsequent years up to the onset of the financial crisis in 1997. Per capita GNP increased from US$1,850 in 1988 to US$4,400 in 1997. Economic growth brought in radical changes in the contribution to GDP. Between 1987 and 1997, the manufacturing sector grew at an average annual rate of 14 percent and its share in GDP increased from about 20 to over 34 percent during this period, contributing to over 50 percent of the increment in GDP. The share of the agriculture in GDP declined from over 20 percent in the mid-1980s to less than 9 percent by the turn of the century, when the economy started to face severe labour shortages.

As in the other high performing East Asian countries, the Malaysian economic transformation was the result of export orientation. Merchandise exports as a percentage of GDP increased from about 50 percent in the mid-1980s to over 90 percent by the mid-1990s. The ratio of exports to total production in manufacturing increased from around 10 percent in the early 1970s to over 70 percent by the mid-1990s.

The sectoral composition of manufacturing output has been greatly influenced by growth of exports. In the early 1970s, the share of manufactures in total merchandise exports was about 10 percent. Since then, manufactured goods have emerged as the most dynamic elements in the export structure. By the mid-1990s, manufacturing accounted for 80 percent share in total exports, and Malaysia had become the sixth largest exporter of manufactured goods in the developing world, after the four dynamos of East Asia and China.

FDI played an important role in export-led industrialization in Malaysia. The entry of FDI into export-oriented production, particularly electronics assembly, began with the establishment of Free Zones in the early 1970s. This process intensified from the late 1980s reflecting the combined impact of both supply and demand factors for global production.

Foreign firms accounted for over 45 percent of total manufactured exports by the mid-1990s. There was a close association between foreign investment in product sectors and their relative contribution to total manufactured exports. The electronic industry (which is almost completely foreign owned) alone contributed to over 65 percent to total non-oil exports in 1995. Malaysia's efforts in attracting FDI in the electronics industry from the early 1970s were so successful that from the late 1980s it has been the largest developing–economy exporter (and one of the world's major exporters) of electronic components.

From the late 1980s, rapid growth was accompanied by persistent decline in the unemployment rate. By the mid-1990s, the Malaysian economy was at virtual full-employment with an unemployment rate of only 2.8 percent. Most of the new employment opportunities came from the rapidly expanding manufacturing sectors. The share of manufacturing in total labour employment increased from 14 percent in the mid 1970s to 35 percent in 1997. The direct contribution of manufacturing to the total increment in employment between 1987 and 1997 was as high as 63 percent.

Indonesia

Since mid-1980s, Indonesia had adopted several policy initiatives to liberalize its trade and investment regime which led to a progressive integration with the global economy. Between 1986 and 1995, tariff rates were reduced and quantitative restriction on import of many goods were removed. Average tariff rates fell from 27 percent in 1986 to 20 percent in 1991.

Towards the later part of 1980s, the Indonesian economy underwent major transformation in the structure of domestic and external sector. Agriculture's share of GDP declined from 53 percent in mid-1980s to less than 17 percent by mid-1990s. The share of manufacture in GDP grew from 8 percent in mid-1980s to 25 percent in 1996.

Structural transformation was also reflected in Indonesia's changing pattern of exports. Prior to the trade-reforms, oil and agriculture commodities dominated exports. Exports of manufactures were negligible till mid-eighties and rarely surpassed 5 percent of total exports during this period. The devaluation of the rupiah in 1983 and 1986, and the related trade and investment reforms, stimulated rapid expansion in non-oil manufacturing exports in the late 1980s. Manufacturing exports as a share of total exports grew from less than 3 percent in 1975 to around 8 percent in 1986 and to just over 51 percent in 1995.

The increasing diversification of exports was an important second feature particularly during the 1990s. In 1986, 76 percent of manufacturing exports came from three products: plywood (43 percent), garments (20 percent) and woven fabrics (11 percent). By 1995, the share of these three products had fallen substantially to 45 percent and by 2000 they accounted for less than 30 percent of all manufacturing exports. Exports had diversified into a much wider range of products. Rapid exports growth occurred in paper products, electronics, footwear, yarn, furniture, jewelry, toys and sporting goods in the 1990s.

On the investment front, substantial progress had also been made in dismantling many restrictions on investment during 1990s. The number of industries closed or restricted in the negative investment list fell from seventy-five in 1989 to thirty-four in 1995. In addition, equity restrictions and divestment rules on foreign investment were gradually eased between 1986 and 1994.

In addition: one-stop service was extended to regional investment boards; investment licensing procedures were simplified; a more liberal duty drawback scheme for foreign investors was introduced; joint ventures were allowed to export other firms' products in addition to their own; and the required export-production ratio in exported- oriented firms was reduced from 85% to 65%. In 1988, the entry of more foreign joint venture banks with a maximum foreign ownership of 85% was allowed, and foreign investors were allowed to distribute their goods domestically through joint venture. In 1993, FDI regulations were further relaxed. Regulations on licensing procedures were relaxed and the time needed for obtaining investment licences was halved.

China

The spectacular and rapid Chinese economic growth in the 1990s has clearly demonstrated the interaction between the forces of globalization and economic development. Among the late globalizers, it has outperformed developing countries in the South East and South Asia. Through far reaching changes in its economic, trade and investment policies, it has been able to benefit from the expanding international trade, increasing flow of FDI and transfer of technology through multinational corporations. In the external sector, the 1990s witnessed radical improvements in all the three important economic linkages through which globalization impacted economic development positively.

Foreign trade played an increasingly important role in the economic growth in 1990s. In 1980, the ratio of foreign trade to gross domestic product (GDP) was only 12.6 percent. In 1990, this figure reached 30.4 percent, and it advanced to 39.5 percent by 1995. Total trade, exports and imports, rose from US$115.44 billion in 1990 to US$280.85 billion in 1995. The trade surplus increased each year since 1990 and by the end of 1996 hard currency reserve exceeded US$100 billion. According to the National Statistics Bureau, China was the 10th largest trading country in the world as of 1995. The structure of foreign trade has also changed dramatically. For example out of US$62.09 billion in exports in 1990, primary goods accounted for 25.6 percent and manufactured goods 74.4 percent. This ratio changed to 14.4 percent and 85.6 percent, respectively, by 1995.

China started reforms in foreign trade from 1987, which included decentralization of export management, elimination of controls on imports/exports on commodities and implementation of a contract responsibility system on foreign trade offices. The government also modified controls on the use of foreign exchange. Instead of turning their foreign exchange over to government agencies and using trade quotas, exporting enterprises could use a large part of their foreign exchange earnings. A foreign exchange revenue settlement system was also started. This basically completed the reform of the foreign trade system.

One of the constraints that limited the growth of its participation in the expanding international trade during the era of globalization was the pegged exchange rate system. This resulted in over-valuation of the currency. This non-competitive exchange rate system had unfavourable effects on import and export. The exchange rate of Chinese currency did not fluctuate in accordance with changes in the value of foreign currencies, and it also did not fluctuate in accordance with changes in the value of foreign exchange. The persistent over-valuation seriously affected development of foreign trade. In 1994, China undertook major reforms of the foreign exchange system, which included unifying the official swap market exchange rate, permitting the currency to be converted freely for current account, adopting a managing floating exchange rate system. This permitted banks to operate foreign exchange business within limitation prescribed by the governance.

Significant liberalization in tariffs also contributed towards the development of imports. The average import-tariff rate decreased from 32 percent in 1992 to 19.4 percent in 1996. The proportion of import and export goods controlled by licences fell from 43.5 percent in 1992 to 25.3 percent in 1995.

The progress in Chinese integration with the global economy was also reflected from its increasing share in the flow of FDI. It increased its share in world FDI inflows from 2 percent in 1986 to 7 percent in 1998. Indeed, it was the largest recipient of FDI among developing economies and the third largest recipient in the world, behind the Unites States and the United Kingdom in 1998. By the end of 1997, the volume of foreign capital flowing in was growing at 30.5 percent annually. Accumulated foreign capital, including FDI, foreign loans, foreign securities and so on exceeded U.S. $360 billion. At present, about 240,000 are operating in China. It has been first among the developing countries in absorbing FDI for four years from 1993, and second to the United States in the world. In 1997, foreign capital inflow reached US$64.4 billion, increasing 13 percent over the previous year.

In order to attract foreign investors, the central and local governments implemented many preferential policies, of which taxation concessions and exemptions were dominant. For example, in the SEZs and EEAs: the income tax rate for FFEs is 15 percent; the tax rate is only 10 percent; and profit remittances, capital goods imports, and product exports are all tax-free. New enterprises are granted a tax holiday for two years and the income tax is levied at half the normal rate in the following three years. To attract foreign capital, China also enacted several laws since 1989; these laws included the taxation law, the labor law, the law of exchange management, the law of enterprise registration, the law of foreign economic contracts, and so on.

The increasing globalization of the Chinese economy is also manifested from its participation in the outflow of FDI. By the end of 1995, it had set up more than 5,500 enterprises in 130 countries/ regions, with total investment of US$40 billion. From 1980 to 1984, its foreign investment was only about US$50 million annually. From 1985 to 1990, such investment rose to US$2.5 billion annually. From 1991 to 1995, it increased again, to US$3.5 billion annually. Primary recipients include North America, Japan and South East Asia. Its overseas businesses are active in such fields as steel chemicals, electronics, textiles, machinery construction materials petrochemicals, and pharmaceuticals.

It responded to the forces of globalization by adopting technological innovations in the communications sector, which facilitated its global links. From 1990 to 1995, the revenue of the posts and telecommunications business grew from Rmb 8.17 billion to Rmb 98.89 billion, an increase of 11 times. Switchboard capacity in rural and urban areas rose 5.6 times and 3.3 times, respectively, in 1995 compared with 1990. Over the same period, the number of telephones nationwide increased more than 3 times. Mobile telephones, which were rare in the early 1990s, have become popular and reached 3.6 billion sets in 1995. The length of optical fibre cable has reached 113,000 kilometers. Consequently, telephone calls to abroad expanded 75 times from 1990 to 1995. The tele-density reached 5.8 percent in 1995 from about 2 percent in 1990. It also adopted new methods of communication such as public data network, electronic data interchange networks, e-mail and the Internet. It also developed the internet as an international network connecting more than 150 countries, 20,000 sub-networks and 30 million users.

CHALLENGES TO THE LEAST DEVELOPED

Developing countries have become increasingly integrated into global goods and financial markets over the last two decade. Their export volumes increased by 9 percent per year during the1990s, up from 2 percent per year during the1980s. In the 1990s, net long-term capital flows, even after declining in 1998, remained almost three times the 1980s level. Globalization provided developing countries with significant benefits and spurs economic progress. GDP growth in developing countries averaged 5 percent during the 1990s, compared with 3 percent during the 1980s. Poverty – the number of people living on less than $1 a day -fell from 29 percent in 1990s to an estimated 24 percent in 1996, along with boosting economic growth and increasing prospects for more trade and investments.

Globalization has thrown several challenges for the developing countries in the process of their integration with the global economy. The development experience of 1990s has highlighted three important concerns for the developing countries, which need to be addressed. First, integration with the global economy has made these countries vulnerable to financial instability. Second, globalization has very limited impact on the economic growth of LDCs. These countries have not participated in the dynamics of economic development and have suffered from stagnation. The third major concern for development arises from the fact that globalization has been selective and has not covered aspects of strategic importance for the developing economies.

The global economy has witnessed an emergence of a development gap in the developing world, which has persisted for the last three decades. Forty nine countries, as LDCs, have not been able to benefit from the momentum of development which has been generated by the forces of globalization during this time. This issue presents a major challenge for globalization i.e. to combine development with a human face in the global economy. In a situation where approximately six hundred million people suffer from stagnation and the vicious circle of poverty, a human face of globalization raises big doubts. The growing marginalization of LDCs during the era of globalization calls for an in-depth study of the various aspects constraints faced by these countries in their path to economic development.

The LDCs have been trapped in low-level income equilibrium, and as a result of weak linkages with the global economy through trade, finance and technology, they have suffered marginalization. There are several factors which keep the LDCs in the trap of low rate of economic growth and stagnation. These include lack of domestic resources for investment, high degree of dependence on the export earnings from primary commodities, huge external resources gap and increasing external indebtedness etc. The domestic resources are not sufficient to meet minimum requirements of investment for growth. In these economies, where a large part of the population survives at near subsistence level of consumption, private consumption takes a major share of GNP. In 1980s, per capita GDP growth for LDCs as a group was –0.1 percent and their GDP growth was 2.5 percent. The tables at Annexures **'B'** and **'C'** show the extent of marginalization of LDCs and rise in poverty.

Even though the 1990s witnessed a minor improvement in their growth performance, the real GDP of the LDCs as a group grew by 3.2 percent per annum during 1990–1998 as against 3.4 percent for the low and middle income countries. Taking into account a high rate of population growth, real GDP per capita of the LDCs grew at only 0.9 percent per annum during 1990-1998. A significant part of the aggregate growth was attributable to Bangladesh; and if we exclude it, GDP growth of LDCs was only 2.4 percent during this period.

During the period 2000-2002 the LDCs grew slightly faster than during the later 1990s. The average growth rate was 4.9 percent per annum during 2000-2002, which was 0.5 of a percentage point more than in 1998-2000. Bangladesh, whose economy constitutes a quarter of the total GDP of all the LDCs, pulled up the overall growth rate. In the rest of the LDCs, the rate of growth of real GDP per capita increased from 1.4 percent annum in 1998-2000 to 2.5 percent per annum in 2000-2002.

As stated above, the factors contributing to stagnation in LDCs economies include: Weak Impact of Trade on Economic Growth; Persistent External Resources Gap; and Rising External Indebtedness. These are now examined in some detail.

WEAK IMPACT OF TRADE ON ECONOMIC GROWTH

International trade is of major importance in these economies. During 1997-98, exports and imports of goods and services constituted an average 43 percent of their GDP. Even a high percentage of trade in GDP has not acted as an engine of economic growth. Although trade is of central importance, the smallness of the economies in global terms means that their participation in global trade flows is limited. In 2000, their total merchandise exports amounted to around $31.5 billion, which was equivalent to 0.5 percent of world merchandise exports and only 8 percent of the low-income countries. Total merchandise exports of the LDCs were accounted for by three countries – Angola, Yemen (both oil exporters) and Bangladesh. About 74 percent of total LDC merchandise exports came from just 10 countries – Angola, Bangladesh, Cambodia, Guinea, Myanmar, Nepal, Senegal, Sudan, Yemen and Zambia. The table at Annexure **'D'** highlights the direction of trade and the share of LDCs.

Their share in world trade has been declining, which reflects the fact that exports and imports are growing less quickly than overall world figures. This has resulted in their marginalization in the world economy. The share of LDCs in world exports of goods and services declined by 47 percent between 1980 and 1999, and stood at only 0.42 percent of total world trade in 1999. The share in world imports of goods and services declined by 40 percent over the same period and stood at 0.7 percent of world imports in 1999.

The marginalization process is strongest for non-fuel primary commodity exports and to a lesser extent in services, and in each case there was a bottoming out in the 1990s. But the share of LDCs in world oil exports rose in the 1980s and since 1988 the share of the world manufactures exports has also risen significantly. These increased from 0.1 percent of the world total in that year to 0.2 percent in 1999. Although still small, this represents a doubling of market share.

For the LDCs classified as exporters of manufactured goods or services there was no process of marginalization. Service exporters increased their share of world exports of goods and services in the early 1980s and although there have been significant ups and downs since then, they have maintained their increase in market share. Manufactured goods exporters were being marginalized in global trade flows in the mid-1980s, but since 1990 they have significantly increased their global market share. In contrast, it is the non-oil commodity exporters that have experienced a strong process of marginalization. This slowed down in the 1990s but their market share is still declining. In fact, in 1999, the share of non-oil commodity exporting LDCs in global trade had declined by more than 60 percent below its level in 1980. During the same period, LDCs exporting manufactures and services had increased their share of global trade by about 40 percent above their level in 1980s. In the beginning of the new millennium, merchandise exports of LDCs as a group increased from $26.1 billion in 1998 to a record level of $37.8 billion in 2002.

Weak export performance of non-oil commodity exporting LDCs is the result of falling commodity prices and lack of competitiveness. Falling world commodity prices had a major adverse effect on the export performance of commodity-exporting LDCs. Between 1980 and 2003, the price of food, including beverages, declined by 73.3 percent to 26.7 percent of its 1980 value. The price of agricultural raw materials declined by 60.7 percent to 39.3 percent of its 1980 value; and the price of minerals, ores and metals declined by 59.5 percent to 40.5 percent of its

1980 value. Declining commodity prices have affected some of the most important commodity exports of LDCs. In the first half of 2003, the price of coffee was just 17 percent of its 1980 value, cotton was 33 percent and copper was 42 percent.

The falls in commodity prices resulted in a significant loss of resources. The UNCTAD LDC Report-2004 has quantified the direct impact of the commodity prices changes on LDC exports by estimating what these would have been in 2001 if the world prices for selected commodities, for which price data were available, had remained the same as in 1980. They could have earned an additional $1.2 billion through the export of these commodities if their prices had not declined. This is an increase of 12.6 percent over the 2001 value of these commodities. Coffee exporting LDCs could have earned an additional $312 million, and cotton exporting LDCs an additional $386 million. Exports of minerals ores and metals would have been $715 million higher, which is about 25.1 percent higher than their 2001 level.

In the late 1990s, unprocessed primary commodities constituted 62 percent of the total merchandise exports of the LDCs as a group. Processed primary commodities made up a further 8 percent of merchandise exports, and manufactured exports were equivalent to 30 percent of merchandise exports. According to UNCTAD data, service exports were also important for LDCs, constituting 19 percent of total exports of goods and services in the late 1990s for the 35 LDCs for which data is available.

Falling prices of primary goods is one of important factors contributing to weak influence of exports on economic growth. It is worth recalling in this context that the World Bank (2000) has estimated that the cumulative losses to non-oil exporting countries in sub-Saharan Africa (excluding South Africa) from adverse terms-of-trade movements over the period 1970-1997 amounted to 119 percent of the combined GDP of these countries in 1997 and 51 percent of the cumulative net resource flows to them. Terms-of-trade losses associated with fall in commodity prices were equivalent to half the value of total capital inflows into those countries over that period.

A feature of the composition of LDCs imports is that machinery and equipment imports are much lower than in other developing countries. Such imports constituted just 1.2 percent of GDP in 1996 –1998, compared with 2.6 percent in other low-income countries and 3.8 percent in other developing countries. Machinery and equipment imports have been falling for LDCs as a whole since the early 1980s, a pattern, which contrasts markedly with that in other developing countries (although for the latter there has been a sharp downturn since the Asian financial crisis). The low level of machinery and equipment imports is significant as such imports can act as a centre of technology transfer for low-income countries and their level is also correlated with economic growth.

There are other contributory factors for their inability to augment their exports. These include slow export growth of commodities, loss of market share and concentration of exports in few products. According to LDC report-2004, their share in world exports of all foods, agricultural raw materials and minerals, ores and metals had remained the same in 2001 as in 1980. The report suggests that without loss of market share and the decline in world prices, as compared to 1980 level, LDC's exports of non-oil primary commodities would have totaled $16.7 billion rather that $9.3 billion. This difference is equivalent to about 3.8 percent of the GDP of the LDCs in 2001. The other factor is that export-structure tends to be concentrated on a narrow range of products. For the group as a whole, export concentration has remained about the same over the last 20 years. The three leading products accounted for an average of 78 percent of total exports in 1981-83, and 76 percent in 1997-1999.

In addition to constraining the economic growth of LDCs, weak trade performance had also resulted in a very high incidence of poverty for non-oil commodity exporting countries. To improve their export performance several policy initiatives have been taken in 1990s and in the new millennium, with preferential market access for LDC products being a key measure.

Following the Ministerial Conference of the WTO in Singapore in 1996, and particularly in the context of the Third United Nations Conference on the Least Developed Countries, many developed countries and developing countries have expanded or introduced market access preferences for marginalized developing countries, especially LDCs. In 2001, the WTO took note of a total of 28 market access initiatives in favour of LDCs, 19 of which are granted by developing countries, including transition economies, and 9 were granted by developed countries, including the Quad countries – Canada the European Union, Japan and the United States (WTO, 2001).

PERSISTENT EXTERNAL RESOURCES GAP

The other major constraint on the economic growth of LDCs has been the huge external resources gap. External resources have not been adequate to pull them out of their low level equilibrium trap, and they have always been more dependent than other developing countries on official financing. This was apparent during the period from 1975 to 1982, when private capital constituted only 13 percent of long-term capital inflows into LDCs in comparison with 55 percent in other developing countries. But this difference has been accentuated, particularly in the 1990s. The share of official finance in total capital inflows increased to about 89 percent of long-term flows in the period 1983-1989 and had remained at that level in the 1990s. At the same time, the share of official finance in total capital inflows into other developing countries had become progressively smaller. With the surge in private capital flows in the 1990s, private capital inflows have come to account for over 80 percent of the aggregate net capital inflows into developing countries in the 1990s.

In the late 1990s, the size of the external resource gap, measured as the net trade balance in goods and services, was equivalent to about 90 percent of investment in the poorest LDCs on average, and about 50 percent in the poor LDCs. This contrasts with just over a 10 percent average for the other developing countries. Similarly, the external resource gap was equivalent to over 100 percent of government consumption expenditure in the case of the poorest LDCs in contrast to an average of about 17 percent for the other developing countries. These ratios, which have remained at very high levels since the early 1980s, indicate that external resources have not been adequate to pull them out of their low level equilibrium trap. Another important feature of the LDCs is that the external resource-domestic resource gap is mostly composed of foreign aid and grants. Most of them do not have access to private capital markets, and the extent of FDI in these economies during the past two decades has been very limited.

With regard to specific components of capital inflows, the share received by LDCs is highest for grants. The share of FDI received fell from 3.6 percent in the period 1975-1982 to 1.4 percent in the 1990s. Moreover, they are largely rationed out of portfolio equity flows and commercial loans without a government guarantee. While official financing is crucial for economic growth of, aid flows as measured by the share of net Official Development Assistance (ODA) disbursements in donors' GNP, was almost half of the level in the 1990s. At the start of the decade, the total ODA of Development Assistance Committee (DAC) countries to LDCs stood at 0.09 percent of their combined GNP, whilst in 1998 it was down to 0.05 percent.

One of the dividends that the developing countries in general reaped from the process of globalization was the increase in the flow of private investment. In the 1980s and 1990s, LDCs could not share this dividend. As international trade becomes more and more knowledge-intensive, access to technologies becomes increasingly important to future competitiveness. The difficulties faced by LDCs in attracting foreign investment threaten to exclude them from the major sources of technology innovation. Net ODA flows from 1990 to 2002 are depicted in the table below.

Table 3.5: Net ODA Inflows into LDCs from All Donors, 1990-1994, 1995-1999, 2000, 2001 and 2002

	1990-1994	*1995-1999*	*2000*	*2001*	*2002*
	Annual average				
NET ODA (Current $, millions)					
LDCs	16,578.9	13,878.6	12,449.6	13,633.0	17,282.2
Of which					
Afghanistan	259.6	184.8	140.9	408.2	1,285.0
Others LDCs	16,319.3	13,693.8	12,308.7	13,224.8	15,997.2
Net ODA per capita (current$)					
LDCs	30.5	22.7	18.9	20.2	25.1
Of which					
Afghanistan	13.7	7.8	5.3	15.0	46.0
Other LDCs	31.1	23.3	19.5	20.4	24.2

(Contd.)

(Contd. Table 3.5)

	1990-1994	*1995-1999*	*2000*	*2001*	*2002*
	Annual average				
NET ODA (Current $, millions)					
LDCs	16,578.9	13,878.6	12,449.6	13,633.0	17,282.2
Of which					
Afghanistan	259.6	184.8	140.9	408.2	1,285.0
Others LDCs	16,319.3	13,693.8	12,308.7	13,224.8	15,997.2
Net ODA per capita (current$)					
LDCs	30.5	22.7	18.9	20.2	25.1
Of which					
Afghanistan	13.7	7.8	5.3	15.0	46.0
Other LDCs	31.1	23.3	19.5	20.4	24.2

Source: UNCTAD secretariat estimates, based on OECD/DAC, International Development Statistics, online data.

In recognition of the urgent need to increase development finance to LDCs, the donor countries reaffirmed their commitments at the Third United Nations Conference held in Brussels. They committed to reach the target of 0.15 to 0.20 percent of the GNP as ODA for the LDCs.

The International Conference on Financing for Development was held in Monterrey, Mexico, from 18 to 22 March 2002. In the Monterrey Consensus adopted at the conference, Heads of State and Governments pledged to undertake actions to improve financing for development. The conference marked the first quadripartite exchange of views between governments, civil society, the business community and institutional stakeholders on global economic issues.

As a share of the combined GNI of the 22 DAC donors, the overall level of ODA decreased from 0.36 percent in 1987 to 0.22 percent in 2001. Although ODA has recently begun to increase, rising to 0.25 percent in 2004 from its lowest point in the late 1990s, it is still far below the internationally agreed target of 0.7 per cent called for by the General Assembly 35 years ago. Only Norway, Denmark, Sweden, Luxembourg and the Netherlands have met and surpassed the United Nations ODA target of 0.7 percent. This indicates a large gap between these five countries and the other 17 DAC donor countries (with the exception of Portugal, which is close to meeting the target).

The declining aid flows to the LDCs gives particular cause for concern because of the multiple investment requirements for sustained economic growth and poverty reduction. There is limited scope for meeting those needs through domestic resource mobilization and the inability to attract large inflows of FDI and other private capital is a serious constraint. There are indeed positive signs that private capital inflows into the LDCs are actually increasing. However, aggregate trends obscure the fact that they are dominated by what is happening in four LDCs – Angola, Equatorial Guinea, Myanmar and Yemen – where oil and gas development is taking place, which absorbed 80 percent of private capital inflows during the period 1990-1994.

According to the latest World Bank estimates, aggregate net resource flows to LDCs reached a record level of $16.7 billion in 2002. This was up from $12.4 billion in 2000, which also was a record low since 1990. Net ODA flows into LDCs grew in 2002 for the third consecutive year. In 1999, aid inflows were $19.1 per capita (in current terms), which was the lowest level of the 1990s. In 2002, this had risen to $25.1 per capita.

The Programme of Action for the LDCs for the Decade 2001-2010 includes commitments by donor countries to increase aid to them and also to improve its quality; amongst other things, by untying most aid other than food aid and technical cooperation. The commitments are formulated with some flexibility. But there are long-standing targets, which are now also being monitored as part of the MDGs, namely that 0.20 or 0.15 percent of each donor's GNI should go to LDCs.

There are six DAC member countries, namely Denmark, Ireland, Luxembourg, Netherlands, Norway and Sweden, which surpassed the target of making net ODA disbursements more than 0.20 percent of their respective GNI in 2002. Between 2001 and 2002, Ireland increased its ODA to GNI ratio from 0.16 to 0.21 percent. Except for these six countries, all other DAC countries were below the 0.15 percent target.

RISING EXTERNAL INDEBTEDNESS

Another constraint on the economic performance of the LDCs in the 1990s was the persistent external debt burden. For the group as a whole, according to World Bank statistics, the nominal value of the total external debt stock rose from $121.2 billion in 1990 to $150.4 billion in 1998, and the total debt service paid amounted to $4.4 billion in 1998 as compared with $4 billion at the start of the decade. Total debt stocks corresponded to an estimated 101 percent of their combined GNP, up from 92 percent in 1990; half of this debt stock was concentrated in just six countries –Angola, Bangladesh, Democratic Republic of the Congo, Ethiopia, Mozambique and Sudan. According to the criteria adopted by the international community to judge the sustainability of debt under HIPC initiative, in 1998 the external debt was unsustainable in 27 of the 42 LDCs. Two-thirds of the LDCs entered the millennium with levels of external indebtedness which are unsustainable.

External indebtedness began to be a problem in the late 1970s; and following the second oil price shock, rising interest rates and economic recession in industrial countries in the early 1980s, the problem escalated. In 1976, only 2 out of 28 LDCs for which data are available had external debt-to-GDP ratios of over 50 percent and external debt-to-export ratios higher than 200 percent, but by 1982 over half of them were in this situation; and by 1987 two thirds of the LDCs for which data were available had levels of indebtedness beyond these thresholds. In that year, 19 LDCs had been to the Paris Club to reschedule their debts. Most of those experiencing debt problems were African LDCs, a fact which is related to patterns of external financing.

Those that have a serious debt problem have also become increasingly reliant on "exceptional financing" in the form of a reduction in actual debt service payments in any given year below those which are contractually due. Although measurement is difficult, it is clear that many LDCs are not highly dependent on these "virtual financial flows", which come either through formally negotiated debt relief which reduces the stream of debt service payments or through the disorderly accumulation of arrears. Indeed, if these "virtual financial flows" were not supplementing the actual flows, aggregate net transfers to LDCs as a whole would have been just 31 percent of their actual level during 19879-1993 and only 25 percent of their actual in 1994-1998. It is also estimated that exceptional financing has been critically important for a wide range of countries. Indeed, during 1989-1993, it constituted more than 2 percent of GNP in more than two-thirds (25) out of the 38 LDCs for which data are available, and during 1994-1998, it constituted over 2 percent in more than half (23 out of 41). For many severely indebted LDCs, "virtual financial flows" have become the main source of external finance after ODA. Although it is not helpful to treat such exceptional financing as a form of development finance, in practice, debt relief has started to function as such, which is making it natural for debt relief and ODA to be treated as analogous forms of assistance, and for ODA to be diverted into debt relief.

The persistent external debt burden greatly aggravates the task of escaping from the low-income trap which is at the heart of the development finance problem in the LDCs. A high level of external debt constrains domestic investment in various ways. Debt service payments absorb foreign exchange and thus reduce capacity to import capital goods. As much of the external debt is owned by government, debt service payments also reduce government expenditure on essential public service payments. The debt overhang creates uncertainty for domestic and foreign investors. It also adversely affects country credit ratings and perceptions of country risk.

By the time of the new millennium there was some reduction in the debt stock of the 46 LDCs. The debt stock declined from $154.4 billion to $137.3 billion between end of 1998 and the end of 2001. This decline was mainly the result of debt forgiveness and changes in cross-country valuation. However, in 2002, despite large amounts of debt forgiveness and a negative change in interest arrears, the total debt stock of the group of LDCs rose to $145 billion. This was mainly due to cross-country valuation effects and an increase in debt stock from multilateral concessional loans. As a consequence, the large debt stock to GDP ratio of LDCs, which had declined from 128.7 percent in 1999 to 117 percent in 2001, increased to 119.8 percent in 2002.

In 2002, the total debt service payments of the group of 46 LDCs, for which data are available, reached a record level of almost $5.1 billion, which is an additional $ 0.6 billion compared with 2001. This represented 3 percent of their combined gross national income.

The potential large financing needs associated with the MDGs pose a challenge to low-income countries in maintaining sustainable debt positions. The enhanced HIPC initiative has lowered debt burdens for participating countries: 27 countries have reached their decision points and are receiving debt relief, and 15 of these have reached their completion points—when creditors provide the full amount of debt relief committed at the decision points. Nevertheless, continued measures are needed by HIPCs and their creditors to ensure that financing the MDGs will not lead to excessive buildup of new debt.

A NET APPRAISAL OF LDC PERFORMANCE

The removal of constraints on economic growth of LDCs presents a major challenge for the international community in the 21st century. For globalization to be an effective instrument for global economic development, the emerging development gap cannot be allowed to widen further.

In the beginning of the new millennium the economic performance of the LDCs as a group had improved. In terms of real GDP growth rates, the late 1990s were better than the early 1990s. Similarly, the period 2000-2002, the latest for which international data are available, was better than 1998-2000. Indeed, GDP growth decelerated sharply in 2001 in many other developing countries. The annual real average annual GDP growth rate exceeded that of other developing countries in the 2000-2002 periods.

The encouraging growth performance of the group was underpinned by a significant increase in aggregate net resource flows to the LDCs. These capital inflows increased by 35.3 percent from 2000 to 2002. The increase was driven by increased FDI inflows in 2001 and by increased ODA inflows in the form of grants in 2002. Net ODA inflows have increased by 38.8 percent in nominal terms and 36.3 percent in real terms since 2000.

For the LDC group as a whole, continued progress has also been made in terms of increasing exports. But this has been much slower than during the period from 1998 to 2000, when merchandise exports surged by 36.7 percent, mainly owing to increased exports of oil and manufactures.

Within the overall growth performance, the tendency for increasing divergence amongst the LDCs continues, a trend that emerged since the early 1990s. Whilst the real GDP per capita growth rate exceeded 3 percent per annum in 14 LDCs during 2000-2002, it stagnated or declined in 24 countries, more than half of those for which data are available. Only seven achieved the 7 percent growth target of the Programme of Action for the LDCs for the Decade 2001-2010. Merchandise exports declined in nominal terms in 23 countries. Net ODA inflows increased by over 15 percent between 1999 and 2002 in 18 countries, but declined in 13. The four oil exporters, plus Chad, which is establishing an infrastructure for oil exportation, absorbed 68 percent of net FDI inflows into LDCs in 2001 and 63 percent in 2002.

One of the most encouraging aspects of the recent economic performance has been the improved performance in African LDCs, including some of those that have been dependent on non-oil commodity exports. But the fact that the African LDCs' growth rates exceeded those of Asian LDCs for the first time is a reflection of the slowdown in economic growth in the latter countries as much as of an improvement in the African countries.

The sustainability of recent growth improvements remains an important issue for all. Many of the countries which showed an improved economic growth performance in the period 2000-2002 are also those where the instability of GDP growth was highest in the 1990s. The high level of dependence on external aid inflows, as well as on primary commodity exports with volatile world prices, continues to give cause for concern. Moreover, it is notable that debt stocks in LDCs rose in 2002 for the first time since 1998.

Two recent trends deserve careful monitoring in terms of their potential effect on sustainability: the increase in the level of profit remittances on FDI; and the increase in multilateral debt. In 2000-2002, the sum of interest payment on long-term debt plus remittances on FDI were equivalent to 50 percent of grants (excluding technical cooperation) disbursed to the LDCs and 23 percent of grants disbursed to non-oil exporting LDCs. The increasing level of profit remittances is not necessarily a problem in itself, but it will become one if FDI inflows do not significantly contribute to the development of domestic productive capacities.

While analyzing marginalization of LDCs in world trade, it is necessary to take account of their export performance. Trends and instability in world commodity prices remain important determinants of trade and economic performance, and in particular in primary commodity-dependent LDCs. UNCTAD data on world primary commodity prices show price firming for cocoa and fish mean between 2000 and 2002. But world prices declined sharply over the same period for aluminum, coffee, copper, cotton, sugar and tea, and to a lesser extent for tobacco. World oil prices continue to be relatively high but volatile.

The growth rate of merchandise exports as a group slowed down in 2000-2002 after a major surge during 1998-2000. The divergence amongst LDCs in terms of their export performance continued. Those that exported manufactures experienced the steadiest growth. The merchandise exports of those that exported agricultural commodities also recovered after a decline in 1998-2000. But this increase was founded on the improved performance of a few countries, and the increase for agricultural exporters as a whole in 2000-2002 was not sufficient to offset the decline in 1998-2000. World price instability remained a significant influence on the export performance of all primary-commodity-exporting LDCs.

According the UNCTAD statistics, merchandise exports of the LDCs as a group increased from $26.1 billion in 1998 to a record level of $37.8 billion in 2002. In nominal terms this represents a 44.5 percent increase. In comparison, merchandise exports increased by 45.3 percent in other developing countries (without China) between 1998 and 2002.

In interpreting these figures it is important to recognize that a large proportion of the total exports come from a few countries and that performance is very mixed amongst the LDCs. The differences in performance are closely related to what products are exported. For the period from 1998 to 2002, exports decreased by 6 percent in nominal terms in those exporting agricultural products and by 16.6 percent in mineral exporters. The merchandise exports of those exporting manufactures and/or services increased by 43 percent and those of oil exporters by 134.4 percent.

The other area of concern has been concentration in the flow of FDI to the developing world. The spread of the FDI is an important channel through which the benefits of globalization can trickle to the developing countries where the majority of the poor live. It has been observed, however, that only few developing countries have been major recipients of FDI. A number of developing countries who need increasing flow of foreign investment have been almost bypassed. The continuation of this trend has adversely affected the trade prospects of those countries that have not been able to attract the much needed FDI. It has been estimated that richer developing countries (with a real per capita GDP of between $4,000 and $ 10,000) in 1990 received close to 60 percent of FDI investment in the Third World. The 51 poorest countries (with a per capita GDP of less than $1,500) received less than 5 percent. As the forces of globalization have intensified in the world economy, FDI has assumed the role of an important channel for the transfer of new technologies to the developing countries. In 1990s, FDI accounted for only 1.4 percent of the capital inflows for the LDCs. The study of trend and pattern of the flow of external resources to LDCs also shows that official financing is of much greater importance for these countries. During 1983 to 1989, the share of official finance was about 89 percent in the total external finance for these countries.

It is matter of great concern that the flow of ODA has also declined during recent years. It has been estimated that aid flows to LDCs, as measured by the share of the ODA disbursement in donor's GNP, had almost halved in the 1990s. Apart from insufficient inflows of capital, the majority of these countries continued to be burdened with serious problems of debt. In 1999, outstanding external debt of the LDCs as a share of the aggregate GDP amounted to 89 percent. A number of countries continue to be unable to meet their obligations and thereby accumulate further arrears on scheduled payments. The nineties have also witnessed a disturbing trend towards increasing external debt. The nominal value of total external debt has increased from dollar 121.2 billion in 1999, to dollar 150.4 billion in 1998.

But if these countries are taken out of the sample, it is apparent that long-term private capital inflows into the LDCs have increased from $323.1 million per annum during the period 1990-1994 to $ 941.9 million during the period 1995-1998, according to World Bank data. Average inflows in the late 1990s were higher than in the early 1990s for 29 out of 45 LDCs for which data is available.

However, although these trends are positive, large increases in private long-term inflows to LDCs are concentrated in just a few countries. In fact, about three-fifths of the increase in private capital inflows between the early and late 1990s noted in the last paragraph has been concentrated in four countries – Cambodia, Laos People's Democratic Republic, Uganda and United Republic of Tanzania. Uganda in particular illustrates the beneficial consequences of an upward growth spiral for private capital inflows, and Cambodia and the Laos People's Democratic Republic benefited until 1997 from the regional dynamics of East Asian growth and industrialization. For most LDCs, private capital are also generally such a small proportion of total capital inflows that even where these have been increasing they have been unable to offset the decline in official finance. There are in fact only three countries where the increase in the net private capital inflows was sufficient to offset declining net official finance. Also, it is apparent that the countries are failing to attract certain types of private capital.

In the early 1980s, long term international bank finance to LDCs collapsed and it has failed to recover. These countries have also been bypassed by portfolio equity flows and bond issues. FDI also remains highly focused on natural resource exploitation.

The overall effect of the inability of most LDCs to attract sufficient private capital inflows to offset declining aid is naturally decreasing the supply of external finance to them. Long-term capital inflows as a whole have declined by about 25 percent in nominal terms since 1990; and if the import price index of LDCs is used to deflate current values (i.e. to express them in terms of their purchasing power over foreign goods), long term net capital inflows are down by 39 percent since 1990.

The pattern contrasts markedly with what is happening in other developing countries. Whilst long term net capital inflows into the LDCs have declined, capital inflows into other developing countries have increased dramatically in the 1990s as private capital flows have come to dominate total flows. As a consequence, the LDC share in aggregate net resource flows into all developing countries has fallen dramatically. After peaking in 1987 at 18 percent, the share has fallen to less than 4 percent of total long-term net capital inflows into all developing countries. Moreover LDCs are largely rationed out of portfolio equity flows, bonds and commercial loans without a government guarantee.

It will be important to monitor the progress of untying at the recipient country level as well as at the OECD /DAC level. Given that about 50 percent of bilateral aid (excluding technical cooperation and food aid) was tied before the recommendation to untie aid to LDCs, the decision could have significant effects in improving the efficiency of aid. In order to maximize the economic benefits, not only will all donors have to proceed swiftly with untying and as comprehensively as possible, but also the LDCs will have to make major efforts to improve their government procurement systems. It is only in this way that the full economic benefits of the untying decision in terms of lower import costs will be realized. This issue will be taken up further in later parts of this Report.

4

Responding to Globalization: South Asia in the Global Economy and Prospects for its Rapid Integration

MACROECONOMIC PERFORMANCE

The South Asian economies entered the new millennium with a sound macroeconomic performance in 1990s. Earlier, during the decades preceding the 1990s, their rate of economic growth had greatly diverged from the spectacular economic growth achieved by miracle economies in East Asia. While the South Asian economies on an average achieved GDP growths at the rate of 3 to 4 percent, the East Asian economies and later the South East Asian economies registered an average 8-9 percent rate of economic growth during 1970s and 1980s. It was in 1990s that South Asia embarked on a series of economic reforms in domestic and external sector and that led it to a higher growth path. The growth rates of GDP during the period made the region comparable to the high performing developing economies.

A survey of changes in the rates of economic growth of South Asian economies during 2000 to 2004 shows wide variations across countries in the region. In Bangladesh, growth accelerated to 5.9

percent in 2000-01 from 4.9 percent registered in 1999. The growth momentum was sustained in 2001-02 and the economy grew at a rate of 5.3 percent. The higher rate of economic growth achieved by Bangladesh at the turn of the century was mainly the result of successive good crop harvest. In 2002-03 the rate of economic growth declined to 4.4 percent. This marginal decline was the result of falling exports and poor performance of agriculture. In 2003-04 the rate of economic growth was estimated at 5.5 percent provisionally.

During the initial years of the new millennium, Bhutan registered an increase in the rate of economic growth. GDP grew at 5.6 percent in 2001-02 as compared with 4.4 percent in 2001. While there was a marginal decline in 2002-03, the growth rate during 2003-04was estimated at 7.2 percent. Maldives registered a deceleration in its growth during the starting year of the 21st century. While in 1998-1999 GDP growth was at 9.8 percent, in the year 2000-01 it was under 5 percent. The deterioration in the rate of economic growth was mainly due to fall in tourism revenue. In 2002-03, Maldives registered an economic growth at the rate of 6 percent. In Nepal, GDP rose by 6 percent in 2000-01 in comparison to 4.5 percent in 1999-2000. The higher rate of economic growth was achieved primarily because of agricultural recovery. However, the rate of economic growth at this level was not sustained in 2001 and the economy registered only 4.9 percent during this year, and less than 1 percent in 2002. The decline in the rate of economic growth was mainly the result of loss of revenue from tourism.

In India, the economy grew at 4.4 percent in 2000-01 and at 5.06 percent in 2001-02. The growth rate was much below the 6.5 percent average of mid 1990s. The global economy slowdown and poor agriculture performance were some of the factors, which weakened the rate of economic growth in the beginning of the new millennium. In 2002-03 the Indian economy grew at the rate of 4.3 percent and 8.5 percent in 2003-04.

Pakistan registered 3.9 percent economic growth in 2000-01 as compared to 4.2 percent in 1999-2000. In 2001-02 and 2002-03 the GDP grew at the rate of 2.2 percent and 3.4 percent, respectively. Higher rates of growth in agriculture, manufacture and services supported the rate of economic growth which was estimated at 5.5 percent in 2003-04. As the new century began, Sri Lanka achieved a substantial gain of 6 percent in GDP in 2000-01. But there was sharp deterioration in the rate of economic growth in 2001-02 when the economic growth was –1.5 percent. This reverse trend was attributable to several external and domestic factors, which included sharp decline in export demand, and hence earnings. The trend was compounded by a weak agricultural production. In 2002-03, the economy registered higher rate of economic growth at 4 percent. In 2003-04, the estimated rate of economic growth was at 5.8 per cent.

FISCAL SITUATION

As South Asia entered the new millennium, fiscal imbalance continued to remain a major concern for the region. High fiscal deficits and large debt burdens characterized the government budgets. The persistence of relatively large fiscal deficits ranging between 9-10 percent in Sri Lanka to 5-6 percent in India and Pakistan, constrained the process of economic development in the region. In 2000, Bangladesh incurred high fiscal deficits at the rate of 6.2 percent of GDP. The large fiscal shortfall was also accompanied by increase in government borrowing from the banking system. Bangladesh was able to reduce fiscal deficit from 6.2 percent of GDP to 4.6 percent in 2002. Fiscal deficit was also a matter of concern for Bhutan. It registered a very high rate of fiscal deficit at 11.8 percent in 2001. The year 2002 registered some decline in fiscal deficit, which was at 4.5 percent of GDP.

Increasing deficit in the beginning of the new millennium marked the fiscal situation in India. In 2002, the fiscal deficit increased to 10.1 percent from 9.9 percent in 2001. Fiscal situation in Maldives also worsened in 2002 as compared with fiscal deficit in 2000, which was at 7.2 percent of GDP. Nepal registered a modest fiscal deficit at the rate of 3.3 percent of GDP in 2000. Similarly, Maldives registered a fiscal deficit of 4.4 percent in year 2000. The fiscal deficit expanded to 5.1 percent of GDP in 2001 from 4.4 percent in the previous year because of increased capital investments on large projects, including a housing project, an expressway project, and a renovation project for a former capital city.

Despite Sri Lanka's healthy economic growth, significant fiscal slippage was recorded in 2000 that continued through 2001. The overall fiscal deficit, excluding grants, rose to 10.8 percent of GDP in 2001. Several factors led to the increase of fiscal deficit and domestic borrowing, especially in the latter half of 2000. This rising included international oil price, increase in defense expenditures, unusually low rainfall that reduced hydropower generation and increased dependence on relatively costly thermal power generation, and delays in the privatization process because of depressed international market conditions.

INFLATION

Unlike the fiscal situation, which remained a major concern in South Asia in the 1990s and in the beginning of the 21st century, the countries on the whole succeeded in keeping the inflation at very moderate rates. In Pakistan, India, Nepal and Maldives, inflation did not pose any serious problem. Stable food prices and sound monetary management contributed towards controlled inflation in the region except in Sri Lanka. Inflation remained around 4 to 5 percent in India and Pakistan in 2001.

In Bangladesh, the inflation rate declined significantly during 2000-2001, the contributing factors being comfortable food supply, liberal import of consumer goods and good harvests. The inflation was only 1.5 percent in fiscal year 2001. In Bhutan also rate of inflation was 3.6 percent in 2000-01. The beginning of the new millennium was marked by low inflation in the Indian economy. In 2001-02, the rate of inflation was 4 percent and 3.9 percent respectively. In 2001, Maldives registered very low inflation rate at 0.7 percent, which was sustained in 2002 also. A similar trend prevailed in Nepal where inflation was only 2.4 percent higher in 2001. Pakistan also registered a very low rate of inflation varying between 4.4 and 3.5 percent during the initial years of the new millennium. In Sri Lanka, however, the high rate of inflation at 13 percent in 2001 was a matter of concern, the main reasons being increase in the prices of agriculture products including food as well as higher import costs of consumer items.

SECTORAL DEVELOPMENT

During the process of economic development, the South Asian economies have undergone massive structural transformation. From being primarily agrarian economies, they moved to industrial and service economies. The share of agriculture in GDP as compared to industry and services declined in all economies of South Asia. In the relatively less industrialized countries of the region such as Bangladesh, Bhutan, Maldives and Nepal, there has been a very sharp decline in the share of agriculture. The other common trend in sectoral development has been the increase in the share of services in the economies since 1990s in varying degrees.

Economic growth had been accompanied by a steady structural transformation of the Indian economy where the dependence on agriculture has gradually gone down from 39 percent in 1991 to 25 percent in 2002, with a corresponding increase initially in the share of industry and later in the share of services. In 2002 industry contributed 27.9 percent of GDP and services 49.2 percent. In 2005-06, the share of services and industry was estimated to be 80% of GDP.

While relatively the agricultural sector had declined in its share of GDP in South Asia, it continued to remain important for its contribution to the absorption of manpower in these economies. In India, agriculture accounts for employment of over 60 percent of manpower. In Sri Lanka, it employs 36 percent of the labour force. Similarly, in Bangladesh, Bhutan and Nepal agriculture employs a majority of the labour force.

One striking feature of the development pattern of these countries over the past decade has been an increasing convergence in the structure of the economies. At the beginning of the decade, the LDCs of the region were highly dependent on agriculture and had lower share of industry and services. By the turn of the century, the sectoral composition of the national incomes across the countries was more even as the LDCs of the regions speeded up the process of structural transformation towards industrialization and modernization of their economies.

EXTERNAL SECTOR

The initial years of the new millennium witnessed divergent trends in the external sector of the South Asian economies. For some countries in the region, the external sector emerged as a very sound and strong sector, which had a very positive impact on the parameters of economic growth. Some countries in the region continued to experience serious constraints such as availability of foreign exchange for financing development etc.

In Bangladesh, during initial years of the millennium, invisibles played a very important role in limiting the impact of trade deficit on balance of payment. With strong growth of worker's remittances, the current account deficit in 2000 declined to 1 percent of GDP from 1.4 percent in 1999. Despite an improvement in the current account, the overall balance of payments position remained fragile, and foreign exchange reserves were a mere $1.6 billion (2.3 months equivalent of imports) at the end of June 2000. During FY2002, the lower trade deficit was accompanied by a 32.9 percent increase in overseas worker's remittances due, in a large measure, to government efforts to encourage the flow of remittances through official channels. As a result of these developments, the current account balance (excluding official grants) moved to a surplus of $171 million (0.4% of GDP) in 2002 from a deficit of $1,090 million (2.3% of GDP) in FY2001.

The rate of export growth fluctuated sharply in India and it declined from almost 17 per cent in 2000-01 to 0.1 percent in 2002.

Export performance was adversely affected almost across the board. In particular, garments and textiles have traditionally been a major foreign exchange earner for many countries in the region. Their exports faltered as a result of the external economic slowdown and demand contraction in the developed region. In addition, the bursting of the information technology bubble led to a steep fall in external demand for IT products, including software. In 2002-03, exports grew at the rate of 11.4, which was a marked improvement over the contraction witnessed in the corresponding period of 2001. The current account realized a small surplus of 0.3 of GDP for the first time in 23 years in FY2001, and it continued to improve during the first half of FY2002 with a surplus of $1.7 billion, mainly due to a surplus on the invisible account.

The year 2002 witnessed a marked improvement in the external debt position of India which, according to a World Bank classification, had been transformed from a "moderately indebted country" to a "low indebted country" as of 1999. According to ESCAP Report 2003, the debt-to-GDP ratio declined continuously from 38 percent in 1999 to just over 20 percent in 2002. It was estimated that India's external debt, both short-term and long-term amounted to around $102.3 billion at the end of March 2003.

The beginning of the new millennium also witnessed rising foreign exchange reserves, which reflected soundness of its external sector. Foreign exchange reserves increased steadily from about $40 billion at the end of 2000 to around $70 billion as of 31January 2003. Towards the end of 2003 this increased to approximately 100 billion US dollars. The FDI flow increased from $1.5 billion in 2001 to $2.4 billion in 2002.

In the year 2000, Maldives' exports increased by 13.2 percent and there was a slight increase in imports. The trade deficit fell from 45.1 percent of GDP in 1999 to 39.1 percent in 2002. The increase in tourist arrivals positively impacted the current account balance. The current account deficit decreased from 11.1 percent of GDP in 1999 to 4.6 percent in 2000. The overall balance also improved due to a stronger inflow of foreign grants and loans. The total external debt position improved slightly from 36.6 percent of GDP in 1999 to 36.2 percent in 2000. External debt comprised almost entirely medium-and long-term debt. The debt-service ratio of 3.7 percent in 1999 deteriorated slightly to 3.8 percent in 2000.

Nepal's current account balance, which registered a surplus in 1999 of 0.1 percent of GDP, switched to a deficit in 2000 of 1.5 percent of GDP, largely due to strong growth in imports. Non-aid imports increased in 2000. Loan disbursements from aid agencies decreased slightly from the 1999 level, but foreign exchange reserves continued to rise. By the end of the year, such reserves amounted to $981 million (sufficient to cover more than six months of imports). External debt as a proportion of GDP declined slightly in 2000 to 48.0 percent. However, because of the concessionary nature of this lending, the debt-service ratio for external debt declined and remained a manageable 5.3 percent of export in 2000. The trade account deficit increased from 16.7% of GDP in 2000 to 22.6%. However, the improvement of services and transfers helped narrow the current account deficit from 30.6% of GDP in 2000 to 27.5% in 2001. Capital inflow in the form of grants and loans, primarily to fund the power sector, continued to exceed the current account deficit by some margin despite the lack of FDI. Grants, having surged in 2000, returned to the 1999 level in 2001, while the volume of loans increased. The net effect was to keep foreign exchange reserves at a level equivalent to 16 months of merchandise imports. In 2001, India accounted for 94% and 74% of Nepal's total exports and imports respectively, and 70% of total grants and loans. Total external debt increased by 37% largely in response to loans from India for the new hydropower projects.

The Initial years of the new millennium witnessed an improvement in Pakistan's external sector over the decade of nineties when it suffered from a serious foreign exchange situation, continued trade deficit and from increasing external debt. The narrowing of current account deficit from 3.9 percent of GDP in 1999 to 1.6 percent in 2000 reflected this improvement. The trade deficit shrank to 2.3 percent of GDP because exports grew strongly while imports were contained. Exports, while recovering, grew by 8.4 percent in dollar terms. Cotton manufactures exports, which account for about 60 percent of the total value of exports, expanded by over 12 percent. The near doubling of the import bill for petroleum products was offset by reductions in virtually every other category of imports, in part because of lower non-oil commodity prices.

Pakistan managed to sustain its export momentum, although the rates of growth in exports earnings declined somewhat, from about 10 percent in 2000 to under 8 percent in 2001. Traditional items such as rice, raw cotton, leather and non-traditional products (chemicals and pharmaceuticals etc.) continued to dominate Pakistan's export receipts. For example, cotton products contributed over $2.1 billion and rice over $0.5 billion to the total export value of $9.2 billion in 2001. External debt services on medium and long-term debt rose as a percentage of exports of goods, non-factor services and private transfers to 30.4 percent in 2000 from 29.4 percent in 1999. Gross official reserves fell by nearly half from $1.7 billion in 1999 to $0.9 billion in 2000, or about four weeks of imports of goods and services as large capital outflows swamped an improvement in current account deficit.

Pakistan faced a serious external debt situation in 2001, with the debt-to-GDP ratio standing at over 44 percent. However, it was successful in debt-rescheduling negotiations with creditors both in and outside the Paris Club. Consequently, the debt-service ratio was brought down from 20 percent of export earnings in 1999 to 17.5 percent in 2001.

According to Pakistan's Economic Survey during July-April 2002-03, exports grew by 20.8 percent as against a decline of 1.8 percent during 2001-02. Imports also grew by 22.5 percent during the period as against a decline of 6.9 percent during 2001-2002. It had a trade deficit of $1.5 billion during 2002-2003, but there was a sharp increase in worker's remittances, which played a critical role in the country's balance of payments. These remittances stood at approximately $3.5 billion. The year 2002-03 ended with a surplus of current account balance worth $2562 million. Heavy inflow of remittances with a sharp increase in exports resulted in a surplus current account. The foreign exchange reserves stood at $10.5 billion sufficient to finance eleven months of imports. Along with improvement in the trade performance, it also improved its external debt situation during this time. As compared with the decade of 1990s when external debt had reached alarming proportions, the total external debt decreased from $36 billion in 2000 to $26 billion in 2002. The debt-services payments were projected at 2.1 percent of GDP.

In 2000-01, Sri Lanka's exports increased by 19.8 percent as against 3.9 percent contraction in 1999. Merchandise import surged by 22.4 percent in 2000 after 1.5 percent growth in 1999. Imports of consumer goods except rice increased. Intermediate goods imports representing a little more than 50 percent of total merchandise imports rose faster than imports of consumer goods and investment goods. Imports of petroleum went up by 76 percent. As a result, the trade deficit widened to 8.7 percent of GDP, while the current account deficit deteriorated to 6.0 percent. The capital account also worsened, because foreign direct and portfolio investment fell and long-term capital flows declined. Reduced inflows of foreign funds required the central bank to draw down on its reserves, with the result that by the end of 2000 official reserves were only sufficient to finance 1.5 months of imports of goods and services. In subsequent years also viz. in 2001 and 2002, it experienced falling export earnings.

The textiles and garment sector, which accounted for a little over half of the total receipts on merchandise exports, remained depressed. It experienced a large contraction in 2001 and production further declined by 8 percent in 2002. Tea exports, which accounted for about 15 percent of the total export earnings, also fell, although at a slower pace, in 2002.

The survey and analysis of macro-economic performance of the South Asian economies during initial years of the new millennium brings out several challenges faced by the region in achieving sustained high rates of economic growth; necessary for wiping out poverty and deprivation from the region. The challenges included constraints on external and domestic resources which are reflected by a low savings-investment ratio, a persistent deficit in current account balance and a fragile foreign exchange situation faced by some countries of the region. The survey also highlights the emergence of a sound and strong external sector of some countries in the region which enabled them to take advantage of the forces of globalization.

TRADE LIBERALIZATION

From the case studies in chapter-III, we noted how globalization influences the momentum of economic development by creating new opportunities for developing countries to share the expanding trade, investment, technical and organizational innovations. The development experience of East and South East Asian economies demonstrated the interaction between globalization and acceleration in the rate of economic growth. The positive impact of globalization on the accelerated rate of economic growth of these economies was fostered to a great extent by change in the policies of these economies from inward looking policies to outward oriented ones. The fast growing economies in East and South East Asia liberalized their trade regimes by significantly reducing tariff and non-tariff barriers, and exports became increasingly important in these economies. Most of the East Asian economies had a ratio of exports to GDP exceeding 30 percent. This was significantly higher than the average ratio of approximately 23 percent for the developing economies in 1997.

Trade and economic growth are closely inter-related. Export expansion provides a developing economy with an opportunity to improve the use of its productive resources. It also benefits these economies by increasing productivity. Exports also put pressure on producers to achieve internationally competitive prices and quality. An expansion in imports improves the technical efficiency of domestic firms as they create competitive pressures. In order to survive under these pressures, domestic firms have to improve their productivity by adopting strategies such as the introduction of new technologies and new products.

Opening up of the economy in South Asia commenced in 1980s and continued through 1990s. The region embarked on an outward oriented trade policy, which is an important pre-requisite for participation in a global economy. Average tariff rates, which were among the highest in the world at the start of the 1990s, fell rapidly in all countries of the region by the end of the decade. Since the early 1990s, it moved gradually away from a strategy of industrialization through import-substitution and public sector production to a more open market-orientated trade and investment regime.

Bangladesh carried out wide-ranging trade policy reforms during the past two decades covering both tariff and non-tariff barriers. Trade liberalization included the following:-

- Reduction in the number of commodity categories in the control list. Measured at four digit level, this was reduced from 200 in 1990-1991 to 150 in 1991-92 and finally to 50 by of the end of 1990s.

- Reduction in the average nominal protection rate from 94 percent in 1988-89 to 50 percent in 1992-93 and 16 percent in 1998-99.

- Elimination of QRs. In 1992-93, nearly 11.5 percent of 10,000 tariff lines were subject to QRs, compared to only 3.4 percent in 1998-99.

- Maximum tariff (custom duty) was reduced from 350 percent in 1991-92 to 40 percent in 1998-99.

Bangladesh's trade regime has become quite liberal in terms of removal in the level of interventions and transactions. In the post-reform period the economy performed fairly well as measured by the importance of trade in the economy and the macro-economic performance. The share of merchandise plus non-factor services trade in the economy, having remained around 19 percent of GDP during the 1990s rose rapidly to 30 percent in 1997-98. Exports being only 4-6 percent of GDP in the 1980s rose to 12.2 percent in GDP in 1997-98, while imports rose from 12 percent to 17.8 percent during the same period, increasing foreign trade impacted economic growth. Per capita GDP accelerated to 3.2 percent during 1991-98 as compared with 1.7 percent during 1984-1990.

Prior to 1994, India's import duties were among the highest in the world. The Government lowered its average applied tariff rate from 125 percent in 1990 to 71 percent in 1993, to 41 percent in 1995, and to 35 percent in 1997. The corresponding levels of average import-weighted tariffs were 87 percent in 1990s, 47 percent in 1993, 25 percent in 1996 and 30 percent in 1998. The average imported weighted tariff on consumer goods was also reduced from 153 percent in 1990s to 39 percent in 1998. On the other hand, the maximum tariff rate declined from 355 percent in 1990s to 45 percent in 1997 and to 40 percent in 1999. It was reduced to 35 percent in 2000 but has been subjected to a 10 percent surcharge, thus making it 38.5 percent.

As a result of trade-liberalization measures, the economy became much more open with share of imports of goods and services going up from 9.9 percent in 1990 to 16.6 percent in 2000 and of exports from 7.3 percent to 14 percent. Export and import have grown at 11.7 and 9.5 percent growth respectively during 1990s.

Trade liberalization also led to stronger economic growth, which accelerated from 5.9 percent per year during 1980-90 to 6.7 percent per year during 1992-96, and then slowed to 5.8 percent per year during 1997-99. Real per capita GDP grew from 3.8 percent per year during 1980-90 to 4.7 percent per year during 1992-96, slowing to 4.1 percent per year during 1997-99. Inflation declined from almost 14 percent in the early 1990s to 6 percent in 1996-97 and has remained at or below 6 percent since then. Foreign exchange reserves increased to $32 billion in 1999 from $1 billion in 1990. India's total external debt of $95.2 billion at the end of March 1999 represented approximately 25 percent of the GDP, down from 38 percent in fiscal year (FY) 1991-92.

Nepal opened up its economy in the early 1990s with the adoption of reforms. The reform measures have since covered almost all sectors of the economy including trade and investment, fiscal and monetary policies, financial and capital markets, and other economic and social sectors. The support licensing system and quantitative restrictions were eliminated and tariff rates were reduced and rationalized to make the trade sector competitive. The trade weighted nominal rate of protection declined from about 80 percent in the early 1990s to about 31 percent in 1994. The number of slabs subject to protection fell from more than 1000 in the 1980s to 5 in 1996.

Since late 1980s, Pakistan took a major shift in trade and industrial policy from the inward-looking substitution policy to an outward looking export promotion policy. The following reforms were initiated to liberalize foreign trade regime since July 1988.

- In 1987-88 most of the non-tariff barriers on imports were replaced with tariffs; maximum tariff rate was reduced from 225 to 100 percent in 1990-91. Tariff slabs were reduced from 17 to 10 and various sales tax rates across commodities was replaced by a uniform sales tax rate of 12.5 per cent.

- The maximum tariff (except automobiles) was further brought down to 70 percent in 1994-95, 65 percent in 1995-96, 45 percent in 1997-98 and finally to 35 percent in 1998-99. All Para-tariffs have been merged into statutory tariff regime. All items are now allowed to be imported with the exception of a few on religious, health and security grounds.

- In May1999, the managed float exchange rates, operative since 1982, switched over to a market determined inter-bank floating rate with currency convertibility extended to trade account.

There has been a radical pruning of the "negative list" i.e. items subject to import bans/QR. As a consequence, there are now only 57 items whose import is not allowed. These restrictions are strictly on grounds of public health, environmental concerns and national security considerations. Similarly, there are 190 items on the "restricted list".

Sri Lanka's shift to outward oriented trade policy started in late 1970s. International trade was liberalized, tariffs were reduced and simplified and quantitative restrictions were almost abolished. From a situation where all imports were subject to license, less than 3 percent of all imports remained under license in 1977, with a rate of 500 percent on luxury items and zero percent on essential consumer goods. In 1991, the number of bands was cut to four. A three-band tariff structure with 10 percent, 20 percent and 35 percent was introduced in 1995. The proportionate value of all imports subject to import duty fell from 71.8 percent in 1978 to 36.5 percent in 1995. Sri Lanka is South Asia's most open economy with total trade accounting for more than 70 percent of GDP.

Spurred on by the economic liberalization of 1977, industrial exports became more significant beginning in the early 1990s. The share of plantation agricultural commodities in total exports declined from 74 percent in 1977 to 15 percent in 2000. Industrial exports continued to be the major contributor to expanding exports, the share of which increased from 14 percent in 1977 to 78 percent in 2000.

Economic performance is the result of the influence of a host of factors – quantitative and qualitative. It is rather difficult to disentangle precisely the contribution of trade liberalization to economic performance. However, the influence of trade on economic growth can be indicated by associating trade liberalization to the change in some macroeconomic indicators like GDP growth rate, the rate of inflation, export performance, current account balance, etc. Thus, trade liberalization appears to have contributed, together with other market-oriented reforms and sound macroeconomic management, to an improvement in macroeconomic performance.

Compared to 1970s and 1980s, South Asia's export performance has improved rapidly. The share of export in regional GDP increased in 1990s. Exports grew extremely fast at 10 percent per annum during the 1990s; almost double the rate of a decade earlier and among the highest in the developing world.

Trade liberalization also impacted the export structure of the countries. Fast integrating countries, such as those in East Asia, have progressively increased the share of manufactured goods in merchandise exports. Over the past two decades, South Asian merchandise exports have also followed this trend, gradually shifting away from primary commodities, such as, unprocessed cotton, jute and tea, towards more manufactured goods. The share of manufactured goods in the region's total merchandise exports grew from 53.8 percent in 1980 to nearly 77.6 percent in 1997, comparable to the world (79.6 percent). The ratio in 1998 ranged from 91 percent in Bangladesh to 73 percent in Sri Lanka.

Liberalization also positively impacted the trade balance in the 1990s. South Asia's trade deficit actually improved from an average of 4.6 percent of GDP during the 1980s to 3.5 percent during the 1980s, the result of strong and sustained export growth that outpaced import growth by one percent per year on average. The current account moved broadly in line with the trend in the trade balance, remaining in deficit over the past two decades, but also improving during the 1990s in most of the countries. There were large variations in current account deficits, ranging from quite low in India (1.2 percent of GDP) during the 1990s, to quite high in Bhutan (13.3 percent). The external payments situation in several countries remains vulnerable to cyclical downturns, as they have poorly diversified export bases.

The trade liberalization process during the past decade and a half contributed to the region's progressive integration with the world economy, as is clear from the rising trade-to-GDP ratios. The table below shows that the trade-orientation ratio for most of the countries has increased. Despite varying base values, the trade-GDP ratios have increased substantially between the mid-1980s and late 1990s for Bangladesh (from 16 percent to 28 percent), India (from 12 percent to 21 percent), Nepal (23 percent to 43 percent), Sri Lanka (54 percent to 72 percent). Pakistan is the only exception to this pattern where the trade-to-GDP ratio has actually declined from 38.5 percent in the early 1990s to 33.7 percent in the late 1990s.

Table 4.1: Proportion of Trade in GDP of South Asian Economies

(In percent)

	1985-87	*1990-92*	*1996-99*
Bangladesh	15.81	17.2	27.92
India	11.80	16.13	20.92
Nepal	23.34	29.82	42.90
Pakistan	32.75	38.53	33.73
Sri Lanka	54.22	58.94	71.74

Source: South Asian Development Coop Report 2001-2002

Trade-to-GDP ratio for the region as a whole rose from 19 percent during the 1980s to 26 percent during the 1990s. The rate of integration has been rapid, with trade to GDP ratios increasing from an average of 0.1 percent per year during the 1980s to 3.6 percent per year during 1990s; only slightly slower than East Asia (5 percent), but faster than Latin America (2.2 percent). Trade liberalization also contributed to increasing the share of exports from the region from 0.698 percent in 1980 to 1.08 percent in 2002.

LIBERALIZATION OF FDI REGIME IN SOUTH ASIA

One of the salient of globalization has been a tremendous increase in the global flow of FDI as compared with other forms of external resources. Compared to the average annual growth of trade in goods and services of about 6-7 percent over the 1990s, FDI inflows have grown at an average annual rate of 20 percent over 1991-95 and at 32 percent during 1996-99.

FDI contributes to economic growth through various channels. It contributes to the expansion of productive capacity because it brings foreign exchange, which the economy can use to import foreign items necessary for the expansion of productive capacity such as high quality foreign capital goods, intermediate goods and technologies. It improves the productivity of the recipient economy because it brings technologies and managerial know-how. Compared to other modes of external resources, FDI has certain advantages for economic development. These advantages include: A less volatile source of finance; the servicing burden of inflows arises only when the investor enterprise makes profit, and so these inflows are non-debt creating; Inflows also bring assured market access along with financial resources and entrepreneurial resources.

FDI inflows received by developing countries had expanded from under US$ 42 billion in 1991 to $240 billion 2000 and are maintaining this trend. The growth of FDI inflows in developing countries seems to have been slower than that of global inflows, especially in the late 1990s. The share of developing countries rose sharply during the early 1990s from 26 percent in 1991 to over 40 percent in 1994. The sharp rise in the share of developing countries in the early 1990s was largely owing to the emergence of China as the most important host of FDI in the developing world. South Asia had a negligible share in 1980s primarily because of high degree of restrictiveness in investment regime. Since mid-1980s, the economic policies of South Asian countries witnessed a visible shift towards liberalization of investment regime.

Most South Asian Countries have drastically changed the entire spectrum of industrial policies and their attitudes towards foreign investment. Several factors have led to this shift. These included: An increasing resource-gap and a resultant foreign debt burden of a huge magnitude; and the influence of high growth performance of the countries in the East and South East Asia in the 1980s based on their outward looking policies.

FDI flow started picking up in the mid 1980s. As compared to the inflow in 1986, the increase was almost 17 fold from $255 million to $4379 million in 1996. As a result, its share of global FDI flows gradually reached over one percent from a mere 0.33 percent. Similarly, its share in the total FDI inflows to developing countries and Asian countries also recorded a remarkable increase from 1.8 to almost 3 percent and from 3.6 to over 4 percent respectively in the twelve year period of 1986-98. Annexure **'E'** shows the increase in FDI flow to South Asia. The increasing trend of FDI since 1990s was visible in several countries of region.

The 1990s witnessed several liberalization measures in the investment regime of Bangladesh. In 1991, a comprehensive reform in economic policy was introduced which included tax reform, liberalization of tariff and liberalization of the industrial sector. The industrial policy of 1991 emphasized the role of private sector to accelerate the rate of industrialization and to simplify procedures of private investments. The major liberalization provisions of this new direction in policy include.

- No limit on foreign equity participation (i.e. up to 100 percent)
- No obligation for joint venture or wholly-owned foreign companies to sell shares through public issues irrespective of the amount of paid-up capital.
- Allowing foreign investors to obtain working capital loans equivalent to their foreign equity amount.
- Allowing foreign investors to buy shares through stock exchange

- Provision for rules to protect intellectual property rights such as patents, design and trademarks and copyrights.
- Tax exemption on royalties, technical know-how and assistance, interest on foreign loans, and capital gains from transfers of shares.

The policy initiative and other macroeconomic reforms have led to greater foreign capital inflows. The number of private foreign investment projects approved by BOI and the amount of foreign capital inflow increased dramatically, especially during 1993-94 to 1995-96. Investment inflows in EPZs also increased significantly during this period. The average investment inflows in EPZs during the 1991-92 to 1995-96 period exceeded US$30 million per annum compared to US$5.98 million per annum during the 1983-84 to 1990-91 period. It has one of the most liberal FDI regimes in South Asia, with no limits on foreign equity participation. It registered an increase in FDI from an annual average of 8 million dollars in 1991-99 to 79 million dollars in 2001.

Bhutan has also adopted liberalization in its FDI policy. The current FDI policy allows international investors to hold up to 70 percent equity in joint projects and sets a minimum project size of $1 million in the manufacturing, financial services and tourism. As a result of these capital inflows, international reserves went up from $316 million in fiscal 2002 to $374 million, equivalent to 23 months of import, in the following year.

Foreign investment played a very limited role in the Indian economy prior to 1991. It was permitted in industries where foreign technology was necessary for economic growth. Foreign equity participation was regulated, usually limited to 40 percent of total equity capital. A new industrial policy announced in July 1991 liberalized FDI in the Indian economy; automatic approval was permitted for investments of up to 51 percent equity in 34 industries. In February 2000, the Government took a major decision to place all items under the automatic route for FDI except for a small negative list. This was an important step in dispensing with the previous case-by-case approval procedure and in imparting greater transparency to the foreign investment process. Furthermore, subject to sectoral policies and caps, the automatic route was made available to all foreign and non-resident Indian investors who could secure 100 percent foreign investment. Policies relating to investments by foreign institutional investors (FIIs) and to global depository receipts (GDRs) have undergone various changes since 1991. Indian companies were permitted to raise capital through Euro-market issues of GDRs and foreign currency convertible bonds, and to have access to international capital markets in 1992.

FDI inflows since the liberalization of policy in 1991 registered a significant increase, growing from a magnitude of around US$ 1085 million in the early 1990s to a peak of $3.6 billion in 1997. India has also been able to increase her share in FDI inflows to developing countries that peaked in 1997.

Despite the continuing weakness in the global economy, FDI flows into India grew by 2.4 percent to $3449 million in 2002 reflecting the ongoing improvement in infrastructure, and further liberalization of foreign investment policies. The bulk of FDI went into ICT activities, engineering industries, services, electronics and electrical equipment, chemicals and allied products, food and dairy products.

Policy towards foreign investment in Nepal was relaxed significantly during the 1980s. The Industrial Policy and Industrial Enterprise Act of 1987 marked a departure from previous thinking with a focus on outward looking private-sector oriented strategy. Private foreign investment was welcomed in every sector of medium and large-scale industry with the exception of defense activities. Joint ventures were the preferred form of investment and limitations were set on the level of foreign equity holdings. In the case of medium-sized industries, foreign equity of up to 50 percent was allowed. In large industries, with at least 90 percent export sale, there could be 100 percent foreign ownership. In other large industries 80 percent was normally the maximum.

Under the 1987 Act, a new set of incentive was introduced to attract foreign investors. Full remittance of dividends for investments in convertible currency was allowed. Repatriation of capital was also permitted with an annual limitation of 20 percent of the initial investment. A five year tax holiday from taxation on profits was available for investment in most activities and exporters were allowed to import their input requirements duty-free either through a duty drawback or a bounded warehouse facility. These measures resulted in an increase of FDI from an annual average of 8 million dollars in 1991-1996 to 12 million dollars in 2001.

The 1990s also witnessed liberalization of FDI regime in Pakistan. In early 1990s, the Government took a number of policy and regulatory measures to improve the business environment and attract FDI, which are detailed below:

- The requirement for government approval of foreign investment was removed with the exception of new industries.

- Foreign equity participation of up to 100 percent was allowed and foreign investors were allowed to purchase equity in existing industrial companies on repatriable basis.

- Foreign investors were allowed to negotiate terms and conditions of payment of royalty and technical fee suited to them as well as acceptable to the multinational for transferring technology.

- The government also liberalized the foreign exchange regime. Foreigners were allowed to bring in, possess and take out foreign currency and to open accounts and hold certificates on foreign currency. Remittances of principal and dividends from FDI and from portfolio investment made by foreign investors were also allowed without prior permission or clearance from the State Bank of Pakistan.

- The government has also given an extensive set of investment incentives including credit facilities, fiscal incentives and visa policy.

In 1997, the government also opened the agriculture services/infrastructure and social sectors for foreign investment on repatriable basis. While there was no immediate impact of liberalization on the flow of FDI to Pakistan, the new millennium witnessed a visible trend towards increasing FDI from an annual average of dollar 501 million 1991-1996 to dollar 823 million in 2002.

The promotion of FDI inflows, particularly export-oriented ones, assumed centre stage in Sri Lanka's reforms process since 1977. This included the establishment of various institutional structures, like Greater Colombo Economic Commission (GCEC) and Foreign Investment Advisory Committee, for establishing export processing zones and for speedy clearance of foreign investment. The first investment promotion zone, at Kutunayake near the Colombo International Airport (henceforth KEPZ) was opened in June 1978. The remarkable success of KEPZ paved the way for setting up a second KEPZ in Biyagama (BEPZ) in 1982 and a third in Koggalal (KGEPZ) in June 1991. The investment promotion policy package offered by the GCEC to EPZ investors included: allowing complete foreign ownership of investment projects; a tax holiday for up to 10 years with complete tax exemption for remuneration of foreign personnel employed, royalties, and dividends of shareholders during that period; duty exemption for the importation of inputs and assistance with customs clearance; industrial services at subsidized rate; and unlimited access to foreign currency credit at interest prevailing in world financial markets.

While the GCEC programme was to act as the major instrument of promoting export oriented FDI, many other elements of the 1977 policy package were aimed at improving the general investment climate in the country for export oriented production by both local and foreign firms. These elements included the removal of most of the quantitative restrictions on import, considerable relaxation of controls on capital and profit repatriation etc. In addition, a wide range of export promotion schemes, including an all-encompassing duty rebate scheme with a flexible operational procedure, were introduced under a newly established Export Development Board (EDB). With regard to these concessions and incentives, the non-EPZ joint-venture firms were treated at par with locally-owned firms.

The beginning of 1990s witnessed moves towards further market-oriented policy reforms. A new Investment Policy Statement announced in 1990 introduced several important changes in the foreign investment policy framework in line with the increased outward orientation of the economy. These included, abolition of various restrictions on the ownership structures of joint-venture projects outside EPZs, providing free-trade-zone status to export-oriented foreign ventures in all parts of the country (in addition to the area demarcated by the original GCEC Act), and the establishment of a new Board of Investment (BOI) in order of facilitate and speed up investment approval within a unified policy framework applicable to both import-substituting and export oriented investors. The various liberalization measures outlined above resulted in an increase of FDI from dollar 125 million during 1991-96 to dollar 823 million in 2002.

Most countries in the region have reformed their investment regimes to encourage these inflows by reducing foreign ownership restrictions, domestic-equity and licensing requirements, and by introducing fiscal and financial incentives. In response to these measures and owing to improving macroeconomic fundamentals more generally, the flow of foreign direct investment to South Asian countries has increased over the past decade. Most of these flows have originated from either the developed countries or from the newly industrialized countries of East and Southeast Asia. The United States and Europe have been the main providers of FDI to India and Pakistan during the 1990, while Japan, Hong Kong, Korea and Malaysia have been important for Bangladesh and Sri Lanka.

However, cross-regional comparisons point to South Asia's stagnating share of total FDI to that of other developing countries.

During the 1990s, its share remained less than 2 percent of the developing countries total, the lowest among developing regions. In contrast, Central and Eastern Europe, Latin America, the Middle and North Africa, and Sub-Saharan Africa all managed to increase their share over the same period. With the reforms of FDI policy regimes undertaken during the 1990s, South Asian countries have now emerged as more important destinations of FDI inflows than they were before. In the region, India has increased her share of FDI inflows from 41 percent in early 1990s to nearly 74 percent in the late 1990s. Similarly, Bangladesh has also increased the absolute magnitude of FDI. The analysis of recent trends in the flow of FDI to the developing countries, however, shows that South Asia has been marginalized in global trends in the expansion of FDI. The four LDCs viz. Bangladesh, Nepal, Maldives and Bhutan will need increasing flow of FDI in order to reduce the gap in the external resources.

PROSPECTS: RAPID INTEGRATION WITH THE GLOBAL ECONOMY

Globalization has led to expanded trade opportunities, increased flow of global finance and enhanced technological capabilities. It is through progressive integration with global economy that South Asian economies can reap dividends from these opportunities. The growth experience these countries in 1990s has amply demonstrated that by responding to globalization and adopting appropriate economic reforms and lIberalization in the field of trade and investment, the region was able to achieve a strong external sector, macro-economic stability, and enter higher growth-trajectory as compared to 1970s and 1980s. Its integration with global economy has been much limited and its participation with the global flow of trade, investment and technology has been much less than it's potential.

For globalization to effectively impact the development process, it is necessary that the region shares expanded trade opportunities in sectors where it has comparative advantage. Market access in the global market is an important determinant for availing expanding trade opportunities in the global economy, however, this continues to be restricted in two sectors viz. agriculture and services. These two sectors have huge potential for expanding exports from the region because of the comparative advantages enjoyed.

Agriculture has emerged as the key sector for the creation of employment opportunities in South Asia where poverty and unemployment have continued to remain major concerns for policy makers. In Sri Lanka, the agriculture sector employs 36 percent of Sri Lanka's labour force and contributes around 20 percent of the GDP. In Pakistan also agriculture has maintained its dominant position in the economy providing work for 47 percent of the active population. In Bangladesh, agriculture accounts for 30 percent of GDP and employs 63 percent of the labour force. In India, over 63 percent of the labour is engaged in agricultural activities. While agriculture plays a crucial role in the economic development, it has failed to generate sufficient income for these economies, which can eliminate poverty from the region. One of the constraints on the capacity of agriculture to generate sufficient income has been falling prices and reduced export earning for agricultural commodities. A factor in the decline of contribution of agriculture to the economic growth is the persistence of a severely distorted international market. These distortions result from high tariffs, domestic support and export subsidies in the developed countries. According to some recent studies, developing countries loose about US$ 24 billion annually in export earnings because of protectionism in development countries.

Developed countries provide significant domestic support to agricultural production along with substantial export subsidies. In 2001, subsidies to the agricultural sector in the OECD countries amounted to US$ 311 billion, adding up to as much as 31 percent of the agricultural output in these countries.

Simple average applied tariff rates on agricultural products compared to those on industrial goods have been higher by 641 percent in Japan, by 353 percent in the European Union and by

100 percent in the case of the US. A very high proportion of the agricultural products are subject to peak tariffs and specific duties in the developed countries. Nearly 98 percent of peak tariffs in the European Union and as many as 85 percent in Japan are related to agricultural products. The rate of import duty on rice and milk products illustrates this very clearly. Japan levies 550 percent import duty on rice. United States imposes $865 import duty on import of every tonne of milk. European Union imposes $1188 import duty on every tonne of milk and milk products, which amounts to 171 percent of import duty on these products. Canada levies import duty of the level of 300 percent.

The benefits to developing countries in terms of increasing their exports will occur only after complete elimination of export subsidies and substantial reduction in domestic support in the developed countries. It was expected that negotiations in Cancun (Sep 2003) to liberalize agriculture by eliminating the high levels of agricultural support and reducing tariff barriers to agriculture trade in developed countries would succeed. The negotiations did not succeed in achieving this objective and collapsed because the developed countries did not accept the demand from the developing countries to eliminate domestic support and export subsidies. Thus, the objective set in the Doha Ministerial Declaration, to achieve: "substantial improvements in market access; reductions of, with a view of phasing out, all forms of export subsidies; and substantial reductions in trade-distorting domestic support", remains un-fulfilled. It has been observed that the developed countries have been resisting elimination of agriculture subsidies and domestic support which they provide to their agricultural sector.

The progress since the Doha Ministerial conference has been far from satisfactory and suggests a going back on the spirit of the Declaration. The Fifth Ministerial Conference to WTO, held in Cancun in September 2003, was to advance the Doha Agenda; however, it could not adopt a ministerial text and collapsed because of a sharp polarization on the North-South lines. Developed countries had shown their resistance to phase out the billions of dollars of export subsidies and domestic assistance that they give to protect their farm sector, while seeking to extract new concessions from developing countries in the form of a negotiating mandate on Singapore Issues. The draft modalities for market access in agriculture as well non-agricultural goods that were proposed by developed countries at Cancun suggested that the principle of less-than-full-reciprocity as enshrined in the Doha Mandate had been undermined.

Even though the negotiations in Cancun collapsed, there is an important lesson for South Asian countries to make further progress in putting across their demands in future WTO negotiations. For the first time, a total of 20 developing countries made an impact on the developed countries during negotiations. While developed countries did not accept the demands for elimination of subsidies and other forms of protection, they were not able to ignore the concerns of developing countries when these were voiced not individually but by a group. The Cancun negotiations provide a very significant milestone for the South Asian countries to forge a joint stand vis-à-vis industrialized countries in WTO negotiations.

SERVICES

One of the salient features of the globalization has been the emergence of services as the most dynamic sector in the global economy. This has offered expanded trade opportunities for developing countries. According to an estimate by the World Bank Report titled "Global Economic Prospects for Developing Countries – 2001", liberalization of services could provide as much as $6 trillion in additional income to the developing world by 2015, four times the gains that would come from liberalization in trade in goods.

In South Asia, the sector has been growing at a higher rate than agriculture and industry. While there are inter-country variations, at present it accounts for over 50 percent of the GDP in

South Asia. The sector has undergone considerable growth in India. Over the past two decades, it has replaced agriculture as the dominant sector in India. Its share in GDP has risen from 40.9 percent in 1991 to 49.2 percent in 2002. The average annual growth rate of the sector increased from 7 percent in the 1980s to 8 percent in the 1990s making it one of the driving forces of the India economy. It accounts for nearly one quarter of trade in goods and services.

The service sector contributes most to the growth of GDP in Bangladesh. Its share rose from 49.4 percent of GDP in 1991 to 52.6 percent in 2002. Within the sector, professional and miscellaneous services made the largest contribution followed by transport-storage-communication services, housing services and so on. Services make up the largest part of the Pakistani economy. The share (including construction, electricity / gas distribution) in GDP rose from 48.6 percent in 1991 to 53.4 percent 2002. Between 1995 and 2000, the sector's share in total employment remained stable at around 42.7 percent. Wholesale and retail trade, and transport, storage and communications have been by far the leading service activities; other important service activities being public services, ownership of dwellings, distribution of electricity, gas and water, and construction.

The huge potential of global trade in services has found recognition in the General Agreement on Trade in Services (GATS) which currently lists out 12 sectors and 161 sub-sectors of services. Global trading is presently taking place in all these sectors and sub-sectors. Under Article XIX of GATS, member-nations "shall enter into successive rounds of negotiations beginning not later than five years from the date of entry into force of the WTO Agreement, and periodically thereafter, with a view to achieving a progressively higher level of liberalization. The Agreement recognizes four modes of delivery of services:

- Cross-border supply, e.g. supply of diskettes, blue prints etc.
- Consumption abroad, e.g., a tourist availing services abroad.

- Commercial presence, e.g., in the form of legal entity established abroad like a bank branch.

- Movement of natural persons e.g. physical movement of professionals, skilled and unskilled labour for temporary work not covering permanent migration.

As far as liberalization of services is concerned, it has only progressed in mode three in which developed countries have substantial comparative advantage. In the increasingly globalized and liberalized world, most developing countries are seeking investment and technology from the developed countries and in turn are opening their economies to the latter.

For developing countries in general and especially in South Asia, the major mode of interest is mode IV which relates to the movement of natural persons. Considering the abundance of skilled manpower and professionals that it possesses across a vast range of services, opening of access in mode IV of services is crucial for South Asia. The extent of liberalization by the developed countries in mode IV is very much limited. Complex administrative procedures and strict entry and stay conditions restrict market access for professionals from developing countries. There are immigration laws and labour market policies of individual countries which add to the list of entry barriers. Not separating temporary movement of labour from the permanent category in the immigration rules aggravates the situation for professionals seeking access. The restrictions imposed include strict eligibility conditions for application and processing of visas and work permits, control over length of stay and transferability of employment in the overseas markets etc. These naturally raise the direct and indirect cost of entry of professionals from the developing countries, thereby eroding the cost advantage of service suppliers of such countries. Besides, insistence of wage parity by the developed countries neutralizes the cost based advantages of the developing countries in exporting labour intensive services.

Increasing worker's remittances and its contribution towards strengthening the external sector points to the need for the region to take policy initiatives for harnessing its manpower resources. This is an area where it has distinct comparative advantage and it has the capacity to avail the opportunities which globalization has created in this sector. The sluggish flow of FDI and diminishing ODA also add to the importance of worker's remittances as much needed means to narrow the external resources gap.

The structural transformation in the economies of the developed countries such as USA and EU has resulted in a situation when they are finding it difficult to ensure competitiveness in their products because of lack of manpower and high cost of local work force. The emergence of outsourcing in the form of Business Processing Outsourcing (BPO) by developed countries clearly indicates that developing countries have the comparative advantage in providing services to the developed countries.

Outsourcing has created new opportunities for South Asia to realize its comparative advantages in skilled manpower. India has shared the new opportunities and has made significant progress in capturing the market for services through BPO. The recent opposition to the supply of services under BPO in the USA and in other developed countries on the ground of loss of jobs in those countries poses a threat for India and other countries that have the potential for utilizing the new opportunities in the global economy.

The process of economic growth has brought out a very significant sectoral transformation, which has enhanced the region's potential for playing a dominant role in the international trade in services. The emergence of service sector as one of the most dynamic sectors in the economy coincides with the global trends of increasing share of services in the global GDP and in international trade.

According to recent trends in global economy, the developed countries face a labour constraint which has led to a growing demand for skilled manpower from developing countries including South Asia. With its rich manpower resources, the region enjoys a comparative advantage in fulfilling the global requirement of workforce in the global economy. The global demographic transition has opened up vast opportunities for the export of manpower. The United States Bureau of Labour Statistics has reported that the American economy will be faced with a 10 million labour shortage by 2010. According to a projection made by the department, the US will be able to support 167 million jobs in 2010 but will have a skilled labour pool of not more than 157 million. This demand-supply gap has significantly increased the potential of the service sector to act as an important earner of foreign exchange, which is of crucial importance to the region.

India's emergence as the most dynamic supplier of software services reflects the potential of South Asia for playing a dominant role in the trade in services. India's share accounted for 17 percent in software exports compared to 3.2 percent in textiles. While there is a potential for expansion of export of skilled manpower in the changing production structure and the dynamics of comparative advantages in the world economy, the countries in the region are facing problems of restricted market access in developed countries for the supply of services under Mode IV.

Information technology has a big potential of acting as an effective linkage between globalization and economic development. The revolution in information technology (IT) offers new opportunities for realizing the benefits of globalization. Through the development of IT, South Asia can participate in the global information structure. The applications provide new tools for improving access to information and knowledge, and it has enormously lowered long distance communications costs and enabled the global economy to rapidly access knowledge, information and ideas from anywhere in the world. The 1990s have witnessed a digital revolution of the kind which is unprecedented.

The lack of information infrastructure in South Asian countries considerably limits the capacity in realizing the new opportunities that the revolution in IT has offered. The countries can not participate in the global Information and Communication Technology (ICT) revolution without being connected to the global information infrastructure. They should be able to obtain access to global information and share its information by being connected, because lack of connectivity can further marginalize them in global trade. The level of connectivity in South Asia is at present very low as depicted in the table below. According to World Development Report 2006, average availability of telephones, mobile telephones and internet users in 2004 in South Asia is far behind that of high -income countries.

Indian success in computer software development showcases the link between globalization and the IT industry. India has seen a dramatic rise in the computer software industry in the 1990s from total revenues of less than US$200 million in 1990 to over $8 billion at the end of the decade, with 75 percent of the revenue coming from exports. The sub-sector is of increasing importance in the India economy, in terms of both export revenue and employment generation. It is the main driver of the industry and accounts for the bulk of IT products, which generated over $10 billion in sales revenue, up from a mere $15 million 10 years earlier. In addition, the industry created 92,000 new jobs and provided 250,000 people with indirect employment during that period. The industry is highly export-oriented; its export-revenue was $7.6 billion in 2001. With a projected growth of 30 percent in 2002, export revenue could reach $10 billion. Overall, IT software and service exports accounted for over 16 percent of India's total export in 2001. It is expected that by 2008 the industry will account for 7.7 percent of India's GDP and 35 percent of its total exports. India's IT software and service industry represents a mere 2 percent of the global software market. The Government and the software industry, however, have set an ambitious goal for software exports of $50 billion by 2008, a share equivalent to 6 percent of the relevant global market.

As stated, software is one of the vital sub-sectors of ICT industry. The Indian success in export of software underlines the

Table 4.2: Connectivity per 1000 Persons Select Countries

Country	*Telephones*		*Cellular Subscribers*		*Internet Users*	
	1990	*2004*	*1990*	*2004*	*1990*	*2004*
High income OECD(avg)	462	551	12	770	3	563
S Korea	310	542	2	761	_	657
Malaysia	89	179	5	587	0	397
China	6	241	_	258	0	73
Philippines	10	42	0	404	0	54
Indonesia	6	46	_	138	0	67
Viet Nam	1	76	0	60	0	71
Sri Lanka	7	51	_	114	0	14
India	6	41	0	44	0	32
Pakistan	8	30	_	33	0	13
Bhutan	3	33	0	20	0	22
Bangladesh	2	6	0	31	0	2
Nepal	3	15	0	7	0	7

prospect for IT becoming a significant source of foreign exchange. South Asia enjoys a huge reservoir of manpower and its transformation into a skilled manpower resource can enhance the export-capability of Information Technology Enabled Services (ITES). The outsourcing of skilled and technical services by USA and by other developed countries has increased the potential of IT for economic development.

The Indian experience in ICT is also relevant for the region in bridging the digital divide between rich & poor. The poor lack access to information about income earning opportunities. This is reinforced by the lack of access to knowledge, education and skills to improve their livelihoods. These observations have been confirmed in several projects where ICT has been applied in breaking the poverty, low productivity cycle and bringing some hope to their age of darkness and ignorance. At the village of Manchal in Rangareddy district in Andhra Pradesh, the farming community has learned to use computers to manage their water resource, updating of village records, gain access to vegetable prices, etc. All this is managed by village women themselves in self-help groups. The National Institute of Agriculture Extension Management and the NIIT has helped train school drop outs to become computer operations.

REGIONAL COOPERATION

The spectacular economic growth in a number of East and South East Asian developing countries during 1980s and 1990s was marked by a strategy of export–led growth. In other words, trade had acted as an engine of growth in these countries. The various stages in their export-led economic growth have shown a close interaction between the expansions of export and accelerated economic growth in these countries. One of the features that marked the increasing share of their global trade was the gain in the export competitiveness of their products through building up strong regional economic and trade cooperation. ASEAN showcases the interaction between regional cooperation and gain in competitiveness and acceleration in economic growth.

Modern technology calls for organizing production and distribution on a global scale and also requires huge expenditure on research and development. To meet the challenge of competition, it is necessary that through regional cooperation the scale of production is increased. The main driving factor in the creation of EU, NAFTA, ASEAN and MERCOSUR was to acquire competitive edge in trade and production. The regional groupings have resulted in expanding trade and investment and that led them to a higher growth path. The success of economic and trade groupings provides a very important lesson for South Asian countries for adopting regional cooperation as a strategy of economic development of the region.

Regional groupings such as NAFTA, ASEAN, the EU and MERCOSUR are enjoying gains from trade in goods and services with intra-regional trade touching 63 percent in the case of the EU and 51 percent in NAFTA. An increase in regional trading has resulted in higher employment opportunities and bigger tourist traffic movement. There have been investment and joint ventures because a large barrier-free area helps in attracting more FDI. It enables foreign investors to reap the benefits of vertical integration of production across the region, leading to an expansion of intra-firm and intra-industry trade.

For South Asia, intensification of regional economic cooperation is of crucial importance to enhance external competitiveness and to attract foreign capital. SAARC provides an institutional framework for strengthening of trade and economic cooperation among the countries. There is immense potential in the region for strong economic cooperation.

The members of SAARC are at different levels of economic and industrial development and have different natural resource endowments. Hence, the complementarities between them are substantial. Although the intra-regional turnover is small, it is increasing faster than the overall trade of member countries. Full potential of intra-regional trade remains untapped because of tariff and non-tariff barriers, poor communication and transport links, lack of information about the supply capabilities etc. Similarly, intra-regional investment is negligible despite tremendous potential that exists for market seeking as well as efficiency seeking investment within the region. Regional economic integration may help in exploiting this hidden potential of intra-regional cooperation for mutual benefit.

The recent conclusion of an Agreement on the South Asian Free Trade Area (SAFTA) underlined the growing recognition on the advantage of regional economic cooperation among the countries. At the twelfth SAARC Summit, held at Islamabad from 4-6January 2004, member States (Bangladesh, Bhutan, India, Maldives, Nepal, Pakistan and Sri Lanka) signed the Agreement on the SAFTA to promote and enhance mutual trade and economic cooperation. The Agreement was to come into force on 1st January 2006 upon completion of formalities, including ratification by all member states. The main provisions of the Agreement are briefly explained below.

Under the trade liberalization programme, tariffs are to be brought down to 0.5 percent in two stages. Member-states agreed that India, Pakistan and Sri Lanka would reduce their tariffs from the existing levels to 20 percent within a two-year timeframe from the date on which the agreement comes into force. States are encouraged to adopt the reductions in equal annual installments. It was also agreed that the LDCs viz. Bangladesh, Bhutan Nepal and Maldives, would reduce their existing tariffs to 30 percent within two years of the coming into force of the Agreement. The subsequent tariff reductions by India and Pakistan from 20 percent or below to 0.5 percent are to be completed within a second five year time frame, beginning from the third year from the date on which the agreement takes effect. However, the period of subsequent tariff reductions by Sri Lanka will be six years. The subsequent tariff reductions by LDCs from 30 percent or below to 0.5 percent are to be done within a second eight-year timeframe beginning from the third year from the date of the coming into force of the Agreement. LDCs are encouraged to adopt the reductions in equal installments, but not less than 10 percent annually.

The tariff reduction schedules will not prevent member states from immediately reducing their tariffs to 0.5 percent or from following an accelerated schedule of tariff reduction. It was agreed that India, Pakistan and Sri Lanka would reduce their tariffs by 0.5 percent for the products of LDCs within a three–year timeframe beginning from the date of the coming into force of the agreement. The rules of origin will be negotiated by member States and incorporated as an integral part of the agreement. Under the rules of origin, a product is considered to be of a particular country only if it has a certain pre-specified level of value added content by the country.

It was also agreed that member States would eliminate all quantitative restrictions, except as otherwise permitted under GATT 1994, in respect of products included in the trade liberalization programme. Moreover, members agreed to consider the adoption of trade facilitation and other measures to support and complement SAFTA for their mutual benefit. The conclusion of SAFTA among the countries has greatly enhanced the prospects of the region to increasingly integrate with the world economy, and thereby, to play a more effective role in the global economy.

All the member countries have implemented SAFTA in full except Pakistan which is still trading with India on the basis of a positive list. When SAFTA came into effect in 2006, Pakistan allowed tariff reduction on import of 4,872 products from Sri Lanka, Bangladesh, Bhutan, Nepal and Maldives. However, in case of India it limited these concessions on the products in the positive list of 773 items. In November 2006, it expanded this list to 1,075 items. India on the other hand had offered MFN status to Pakistan and expects similar facility from Pakistan. Pakistan has refused to reciprocate. The main reason behind this is political. It wants the resolution of Kashmir issue first before moving whole hog on

SAFTA. This approach of Pakistan has kept the trade agreement in limbo. Though SAFTA has been implemented, South Asia has not been able to draw the full benefits of the agreement.

Despite Pakistan's reluctance to open up to India, bilateral trade is booming. It grew 129 per cent year-on-year in April-October 2006 to $977 million. India's exports increased 141 per cent to $789 million while imports from Pakistan were up 59 per cent to $187 million. It is estimated that trade between India and Pakistan could rise to over $ 9 billion over the next five years from the current $ 1 billion if barriers relating to policies, infrastructure, corruption and red tape are eliminated. Despite a common location and history, South Asia remains the least integrated region in the world. Countries here have significantly opened up trade with the rest of the world but remain closed to each other, with protective policies, poor infrastructure, corruption and red tape hampering the growth of trade. Countries of the region now need to work towards reducing the costs of doing business, improving institutions and addressing infrastructure constraints. The region is now faced with increasing challenges such as the high cost of doing business, weak institutions, weak knowledge economy and infrastructure from second-generation policy reforms.

India should take all initiative to bring the region closer by increasing connectivity, which will result in greater volume of trade. Besides, it will also bring other regions like South East Asia and Central Asia closer to South Asia. To expand the scope of SAFTA, India should stress on including trade in services under the ambit of agreement. These measures will have immense potential to multiply trade taking place in the region.

South Asia's increasing participation in expanding global finances is one of the key determinants in the rapid integration with the global economy. Growth prospects of the economies depend, inter-alia, on the availability of external resources. In 1970s and 1980s most of the developing countries including South Asian countries faced constraints on the growth process because of limited availability of external resources. One of the positive outcomes of globalization for developing countries has been the increased availability of external resources especially through FDI in the 1980s. FDI inflows received by developing countries have risen steadily from an annual average of US$30 billion in the second half of the 1980s and to a peak of $246 billion in 2000. It has been estimated that official resources flow to developing country have declined from $62.2 billion in 1991 to $36.5 billion in 2001. Private flows now account for over 80 percent of total long-term resources. FDI emerged as the most important channel of external resource transfers to developing countries, and these inflows contribute to development process by bringing technology, organizational skills and also by expanding market-access for developing countries, as has been explained earlier.

The recent in-flows and direction of FDI have not been entirely favourable to the developing countries including South Asian economies. Major changes have taken place in the international financial system in terms of changing magnitudes and destination of external resource flows to developing countries. While the private capital inflows such as FDI and portfolio investments have expanded in magnitude, they are determined by the levels of development and infrastructure in recipient countries. There is an important policy lesson for South Asia that liberalization has its limitation in attracting FDI to low income countries that need external resources. It is, therefore necessary that 0.4 percent of GDP as aid target by development countries should be implemented urgently.

The Asian financial crisis of 1997-98 provided an impetus to regional economic co-operation and policy coordination, as Asian economies were severely disrupted by certain aspects of globalization. Asian integration is, in a sense, a subconscious effect to avoid another Asian crisis; but crises are events, whereas integration is a process. For integration to succeed there must be a process to manage the process. Structure must follow strategy, and strategy cannot be put in place until there is a consensus on what the ultimate goal should look like.

Since then, while the affected countries have recovered, Asia has seen a major trade and investment expansion. The dramatic increase in intra-Asian trade and the growing interdependence has provided a new impulse to integration within Asia. Market-driven economic integration through trade and investment has been a major force in East Asia's growth over the past two decades. In fact, there is already de facto economic integration in East Asia, with intra-regional trade as a share of total trade having risen from 35% in 1980 to 54% in 2003.

ASEAN's intra-regional trade has gone up from 18% to 24% in the same period. India-Asean trade expanded more than five times from $3.5 billion in 1994 to $17.7 billion in 2004. India's trade with China has gone up from $260 million in 1990 to reach $20 billion this year. By 2010, it is expected to rise to $40 billion. Japan continues to play a leading and active role in Asia. It is also a leading investor in all ASEAN countries.

There is a spurt in bilateral FTAs or CECAs being entered into among Asian countries. India is engaged in regional or trans-regional agreements like SAFTA or BIMSTEC. Such agreements go far beyond their commercial or economic utility. They also act as useful building blocks for developing overall closer understanding and cooperation.

INDIA AS THE ENGINE OF SOUTH ASIAN ECONOMIC GROWTH

The current accelerated growth of the Indian economy will naturally have positive externalities for the neighboring countries. Proactive policies to increase economic integration with other South Asian counties could multiply these benefits many fold, and the impact on the economic development of the neighboring countries could be dramatic.

Investment climate surveys frequently reveal that poor roads, congested ports and unreliable power and water are important disincentives to investment. After successive rounds of multilateral trade negotiations, tariffs on most goods are now low enough that improvements in trade efficiency offer much greater potential for expanding trade than further tariff reform. Infrastructure contributes to economic development through a variety of ways, such as increasing market access and thereby broadening the inclusiveness of growth, facilitating production, trade and investment, as well as access to productive inputs. These directly increase incentives for greater trade and investment. Perhaps the greatest benefit of infrastructure's contribution to regional integration is the enhanced competition that lowers process and widens choices for consumers, while stimulating greater efficiency and innovation among producers.

As India shares borders with most South Asian countries and has good marketing capability and linkages in the major importing countries, it could become a hub for spurring the growth of intra-industry trade in the Sought Asia region. With its central location and size, India could serve as an assembly and exit point of high value South Asian goods, as well as service, for both domestic and international markets. Intra-industry trade could also be posted by greater cross-border foreign direct investment. In brief, India is not only crucial for the success of regional trade cooperation in Sought Asia; it could also transform the development and growth pattern of the entire region.

The developing countries in East and South East Asia were able to reap the dividends of the increased availability of global finance. South Asia's comparative performance has been poor. Liberalization alone is not a sufficient condition for attracting FDI. The attractiveness of destination for the inflow of external resources to a great extent depends on the state of infrastructure, the size of market and the scale of production etc. On a national level, it may not be possible for countries in the region to fulfill all the necessary conditions for attracting investment. The development of infrastructure calls for huge investment, and therefore, for a national economy it may not be possible to do so. The strengthening of regional economic co-operation in South Asia is, therefore, necessary for the development of adequate infrastructure. While there are several areas where development of infrastructure is required, the need for ensuring adequate supply of energy in the region is of paramount importance.

The energy sector presents an area of potentially mutual beneficial cooperation. The South Asian region comprises of countries with high energy production potential and fast energy demand, which in turn opens up avenues for cooperation. Moreover, the region is also endowed with the technical capabilities and skill needed in the field of energy production and distribution. Most of the South Asian countries have the advantage of being located on a single landmass, which is convenient for planning and developing integrated power infrastructure like power grids and gas pipelines. Such a network of electricity grid and pipelines will increase energy security in the region, reduce cost of fuel transportation and help in the more efficient harnessing of energy resources. Also, for small countries like Nepal and Bhutan, regional cooperation is indispensable, as their domestic demand is limited while the production potential is enormous.

The Heads of States met at the Thirteenth Summit Meeting of the South Asian Association for Regional Cooperation (SAARC) in Dhaka Bangladesh on 12 –13 November 2005. They noted that the Thirteenth Summit was taking place at an important moment in the evolution of South Asia when SAARC stood at the threshold of a new decade of its existence. They agreed that the Summit provided a unique opportunity to consolidate the gains made in regional cooperation during its first two decades and to chart a forward-looking strategy to promote effective cooperation at all levels to realize the objectives and principles set out in the Charter of the Association.

They noted that cooperation and partnership within the framework of SAARC is based on the sound foundation of shared values, beliefs and aspirations. The objectives and goals of SAARC, they affirmed, were of continuing relevance and importance to all member states. The dynamics of recent political and economic changes in South Asia and the world highlighted the importance and the compelling logic for a more vibrant and effective process of constructive regional cooperation. They emphasized their commitment to making such cooperation an enduring feature and thus contribute to the region's peace, progress and stability.

5

Human face of Globalization: Challenging poverty in the 21st Century

The impact of the process of globalization's current phase on economic development has been a subject of intensive debate. The key issue is whether economic development has been with a human face during the era of globalization. In chapter III, the interaction between economic growth and globalization has been analyzed. In the developing world, which embarked on the task of economic development during the last four decades, the persistence of poverty deprives large segments of people from enjoining a decent standard of life. This chapter examines to what extent, during the current phase of globalization, economic growth in the developing world has combined with elimination of poverty and deprivation.

TRENDS IN POVERTY: A MIXED STORY

At the global level considerable progress has been made in reducing poverty over the past three decades, largely as a result of acceleration in rate of economic growth and more focused anti-poverty programmes. The proportion of the world's population living in extreme or absolute poverty (surviving on US $1 a day) declined noticeably between 1981 and 2001, dropping from 40 to 21 percent. At the regional level, only East Asia and the Pacific,

Table 5.1: Decline in Income Poverty, 1981-2001

Region	*1981*	*1984*	*1987*	*1990*	*1993*	*1996*	*1999*	*2001*
East Asia & Pacific	56.7	38.8	28.0	29.5	24.9	15.9	15.3	14.3
Europe & Central Asia	0.8	0.6	0.4	0.5	3.7	4.4	6.3	3.5
Latin America & Caribbean	10.1	12.2	11.3	11.6	11.8	9.4	10.5	9.9
Middle East & North Africa	5.1	3.8	3.2	2.3	1.6	2.0	2.7	2.4
South Asia	51.5	46.8	45.0	41.3	40.1	36.7	32.8	31.9
Sub-Saharan Africa	41.6	46.3	46.9	44.5	44.1	46.1	45.7	46.4
World	**40.4**	**33.0**	**28.5**	**27.9**	**26.3**	**22.3**	**21.5**	**20.7**

Source: HDR 2003.

the Middle East, North Africa and South Asia registered sharp declines during the period. Table 5.1 shows poverty declining at regional level between 1981 and 2001.

In 2002, more than 1.1 billion people worldwide were struggling to survive on less than US $1 a day. Poverty is more prevalent and persistent in certain regions. In sub-Saharan Africa, for example, the number of poor people increased by almost 90 million in a little more than a decade (1990-2001). Even in regions that have achieved significant progress, such as South and East Asia, rates of poverty reduction have been uneven.

The Role Models

One of the most striking aspects of development in East & South East Asia over the period around 1970-1990 is that many countries achieved remarkably high rates of economic growth accompanied by steep reductions in poverty. For example, based on national poverty lines, poverty declined over this period: in China from 33 to 10 percent; in Indonesia from 60 to 15 percent; in Malaysia from 18 to 6 percent; in the Republic of Korea from 23 to 8 percent; and in Thailand from 26 to 18 percent. This constituted one of the largest decreases in mass poverty in social history. The table below shows the rapid rate of decline in the incidence of poverty in there countries.

A number of developing countries in East and South East Asia succeeded in achieving growth with equity by ensuring a significant reduction in poverty and thereby a high level of human and social development. Those that succeeded in the alleviation of poverty along with attainment of high rates of economic growth include the Republic of Korea, Malaysia, Indonesia, Thailand and China. In order to address the problem of poverty and deprivation suffered by poor people across the globe, it is important to note the policies which combined growth with reduction poverty in these countries. They succeeded in not only reducing the incidence of income-poverty but also improved indicators related to human and social development.

Table 5.2: Trends in Poverty in Asian Countries (based on national poverty lines 1970 –2000)

	Population below the national poverty line (percentage)				*Annual Change (Percentage)*	
	1970	*1980*	*1990*	*2000*	*1980s*	*1990s*
China	33.0	28.0	10.1	4.6	-6.4	-5.4
Republic of Korea	23.0	10.0	8.2	11.6	-1.4	6.9
South East Asia						
Indonesia	60.0	29.0	15.1	27.1	-4.8	8.8
Malaysia	18.0	9.0	6.1	8.1	-3.6	3.3
Philippines	61.6	59.7	45.2	40.0	-4.0	-1.3
Thailand	26.0	17.0	18.0	14.2	0.3	-2.1
Vietnam		75.0	58.0	37.0	-4.5	-7.2

Source: ESCAP Report; MDG in Asia and Pacific.

The development strategy of Malaysia which was adopted in the New Economic Policy (NEP) in the period 1970-90, played a major role in alleviating poverty. The rapid growth of export-oriented and labour-intensive manufacturing sector provided employment for poor people. In the process of economic growth, the rapidly growing rural labour was absorbed in the urban industrial and service sector, which provided a major avenue for the reduction of rural poverty.

The incidence of poverty declined from 18 percent in 1970 to 9.6 percent in 1990. Among others, a very significant factor contributing to the persistence of poverty was the lack of employment opportunities. The growing economy created jobs in many non-traditional sectors which increased the income of the poor. With availability of more jobs, the share of household income from wages and salaries began to increase. The shift among rural household to salaried jobs was an important contributing factor in the reduction of poverty.

Malaysia also achieved a very high rate of success in providing health care to its population. In 1975, 62 percent of the population had access to safe water. It rose to 78 percent in 1980. In case of sanitation also, it achieved considerable improvement in expanding access of population to clean habitation; in 1980, 75 percent of the population had access to sanitation. Similarly by 1993, approximately 88 percent of the population had access to health care services.

In health providing accent–services the achievement was remarkable. During the sixth Malaysian development plan, almost 88 percent of the urban poor and 77 percent of the rural poor could access either a government or a private clinic within 9 kilometers. It was the policy initiatives of the NEP since 1971 which contributed to achieving social development along with the process of economic growth. It laid emphasis on rural development programmes, education and employment.

In Indonesia also, economic growth was combined with rapid reduction in poverty. In 1970, according to some estimates almost

60 percent of the population, nearly 70 million people, was living in absolute poverty. During two decades (1970-93), the proportion of the poor fell from 60% to 15%. The absolute number of poor fell from 67 million to 24 million. There were three major factors which contributed to reduction in poverty in Indonesia: improvement in agriculture; shift to labour intensive manufacturing; and human development.

During the process of growth, the country also achieved commendable improvement in social indicators. From 1960 to 1990-2001, life-expectancy increased from 55 to 66 years. Infant mortality rate was reduced from 79 per thousand live births to 33 per thousand live births during this period. Adult illiteracy decreased from 61 percent in 1960 to 23 percent in 1990 and the percentage of primary enrollment during this period was raised from 71 to 118 percent.

It is also a notable fact in Indonesian development strategy that basic services were given priority in public policy. It allocated a major proportion of total public expenditure to basic education. In the health sector also high percent of total public expenditure was allotted to rural health sector, family planning, and disease control and child health. It is worth mentioning that it attained near universal education by 1980s. Gross primary enrollment rate rose from 75 percent to over 100 percent between 1970 and early 1980s. The Indonesian experience also showed that with an appropriate policy choice, economic growth can lead to minimizing human deprivations.

The Republic of Korea achieved a very high rate of reduction in the incidence of poverty in a short span of time. In 1970, the incidence of poverty was at a level of 23 percent. It was reduced to 11.6 percent in 1990. A high degree of economic growth sustained through several decades generated conditions which enabled Korea to significantly eliminate the scourge of poverty. Between 1972 and 1997 the GNP grew at an average rate of 8.1 percent, and per capita GNP increased from US dollar 253 in 1970 to US dollar 10,000 in 1996.

A high degree of economic growth sustained through several years in continuation also contributed towards social development. Life expectancy at birth increased from 67 years in 1980 to 74 in 2001. Infant mortality decreased from 61.8 deaths per one thousand life births in 1965 to 31.6 deaths in 1990. The population growth rate per annum also declined from 2.3 percent in 1965 to 1 percent per annum in 1980.

Apart from the expanding employment opportunities generated by rapid economic growth and industrialization, human resource development played a very important role in the success of poverty reduction. Formal education and skill–training are the most effective means of preventing the transmission of poverty from generation to generation. In a developing economy, it is necessary that opportunities should be generated for all individuals so that they can participate in the growth process. Human resource development has played a critical role in Korea's rapid economic growth and poverty alleviation. It accorded priority to education in its public expenditure policy. Through expanding education, the demand for skilled workers was met and economic growth did not suffer for lack of the same.

In the study of relationship between economic growth and reduction in poverty, the experience of some developing countries in other regions such as Latin America and Africa is also of crucial importance. In Latin America, Chile achieved considerable reduction in poverty in a relatively short span of time. Between 1985 and 1997, its GDP grew at an annual average of 7 percent, more than double the average rate of economic growth of 3.3 percent in the region. Along with accelerating economic growth, in the ten years or so, poverty fell drastically. The percentage of the population living with per capita income below the poverty line fell from 45 percent in 1987 to less than 25 percent in 1996. This success is comparable to the performance of East Asian countries. Chilean policies reflected a combination of priority on economic growth and social development. Public expenditure policy played a very important role in improving the quality of life by meeting the basic needs of the population. In 1990s, the social spending grew and was well targeted towards the poorest 40 percent of the population. It was concentrated on providing public goods and services such as health care and education. In providing the basic needs of the population, Chile ranked third among developing countries in the Human Poverty Index of the UNDP 1997. This index measures longevity, access to basic knowledge and minimum level of consumption. The ranking reflected its success in the fulfillment of basic needs of the population along with achieving very high rate of economic growth.

The above analysis brings to focus the relationship between high rate of economic growth and reduction in poverty. Globalization through linkages of expanding trade, investment and technology created opportunities for attaining high rates of economic growth in some developing countries. Combined with right choice of policies, these countries were able to remove the deprivations suffered by their people.

The potential of globalization to reduce poverty can also be assessed from the development experience of countries which have started integrating with the world economy since 1980s. In the current phase of globalization, since 1980s the two most populous countries of the world, China and India, started adapting their economies to the mechanisms of globalization and thereby progressing towards integrating with world economy. Through participation in the process of globalization they have achieved a much higher rate of economic growth then in earlier decades. While achieving this, they also succeeded in a significant rate of reduction in both income and human poverty. Their development experience underlines a close interaction between globalization, high rates of economic growth and reduction in poverty. China is one of the few countries in the developing world to make substantial progress in reducing its total number of poor in the past two decades. The number of poor started declining from 1978 onwards, at which time there were 250 million rural poor (33 percent of the rural population). This changed dramatically after the rural reforms, which started in the same year. By 1984 only 11 percent of the rural population was living below the poverty line, decreasing to 8 percent in 1994 and 3.7 percent in 2000, representing only 30 million people. Even by taking the more conservative World Bank figures (which are generally higher), there was a reduction of rural poverty from 31 percent in 1990 to 11.5 percent in 1988. A reduction in poverty on this scale and within such a short time is unprecedented in history. Contributing to this success were policy and institutional reforms, promotion of equal access to social services and production assets, and public investment in rural areas.

Agriculture reforms were introduced by Deng Xiaoping in 1978 in order to raise the living standards of the people and to eliminate poverty by 2000. These reforms consisted of dismantling the commune system, granting farmers decision-making power, introducing the contract responsibility system and raising producer prices. It created a mixed economy where central planning coexisted with markets. The introduction of the "household production responsibility system", for example, allowed farmers to retain a certain proportion of outputs after fulfilling a production quota. Grain output increased dramatically as did per capita income, which increased on an average at a rate of 15 percent a year between 1978 and 1984; but at a much slower pace of 3 percent between 1985 and 1999 (mainly because of stagnation in agricultural production after the reforms). Much of the success in raising per capita agricultural income – and thereby reducing poverty – was attributed to productivity improvements. With crop prices stagnating, rural income gains had to come from increased productivity in agriculture or from employment outside of agriculture.

Among the factors that contributed to sharp declines in income–poverty and improvement in social indicators in the developing countries in the East and South East Asia, education was an important factor. It was the investment in health and education that resulted in higher life expectancy and skill–formation. In both the sectors, these countries invested a much higher amount as compared with other developing countries. A comparative expenditure is given at Annexure **'F'**. Education is the most powerful tool for accelerating economic growth and reducing poverty, and the fast growing economies of East and South East Asia had invested in the range of 3.5 to 5 per cent of GNP in education.

LDCs: THE DOWNSIDE STORY

Development experience of fast growing economies in East, South-East and South Asia has established that in a globalizing economy, economic growth can be combined with marked reduction in poverty. Poverty has been nearly eliminated in some parts of the developing world as a result of economic growth combined with right choice of public policies. However, many parts of the developing world did not participate in the process of poverty–alleviation. While poverty still persists in various parts of the developing world, the poverty profile of the LDCs as a group consisting of 49 countries in Africa and Asia presents a serious challenge to the global economy. It appears that these countries have been by-passed by the positive forces of globalization. Poverty among these countries is unique in its dimension and characteristics. According to analysis by UNCTAD in its various LDC reports, the LDCs poverty has been characterised as persistent and generalized. It is generalised because it affects 50% of population and it has been persistent because it doesn't decline. The economies of a number of countries grouped under LDCs present a contrast with the countries that succeeded in wiping out poverty from their economies.

The UNCTAD through its annual reports on LDCs has brought to focus the grim situation of income and non-income poverty reflected from the deprivations and non-fulfillment of that basic need. According to its report on LDC, 2002; 50 percent of the population during the 1995-1999 lived in extreme poverty viz. less than $1 a day. The intensity of the poverty can be measured from the fact that the average per capita income in the LDCs is about 72 cents a day. The total number of people living on less then $1 day in all the 49 LDCs was 307 million people out of their total population of 630 million. It is also a matter of concern that incidence of poverty has been increasing. During 1965-1969 the population in extreme poverty was 48 percent, while in 1995-1999 it rose to 50 percent of the population. According to the report, the LDCs suffer from generalized poverty and have become the primary locus of extreme poverty in the global economy.

In human and social development, the LDCs have lagged behind other developing countries on several counts. Because of slow rate of social progress, their social indicators show considerable gaps between the international development goals and their achievements. Table 5.3 gives comparative rates of social progress of LDCs and developing countries.

In conditions of generalised poverty, sources of government revenue are limited and hence total public sector expenditures on social services are relatively low. According to LDC Report 2004, the Asian and African LDCs on an average spend $4.6 a year per head on public health expenditure in contrast to an average of $73 in other low-income and middle-income developing countries. The stark reality is even more glaring when compared with the per capita public health expenditure of $1,456, and per capita total health expenditure of $2,391, in the high-income OECD countries.

Rapid and sustained economic growth is an effective mechanism for reducing poverty in LDCs. The interaction between the rate economic growth and the extent of poverty reduction was projected by UNCTAD in its report LDC–2002. Table 5.4 shows the impact of economic growth on poverty reduction in these countries.

One of the forecasts in the table is based on the assumption that a GDP growth rate of 7 percent per annum will be achieved. This is the target growth rate in The Programme of Action for the LDCs for the decade 2001-2010 which was agreed at the Third United Nations Conference on the LDCs in Brussels in May 2001. The report suggests that poverty will increase in these countries

Table 5.3: Comparative Rates of Social Progress of LDCs and Developing Countries

Year	*Social Indicators*	*LDCs (percent or Live Births)*	*Developing Countries*
2001	Life expectancy at birth	50.4 Years	64.44 years
1998-00	Under nourishment	38 percent	18 percent
2001	Illiteracy	33.7 percent	15.2 percent
2001	Infant mortality Rate	100 per 1,000 LB	62 per 1000LB
2001	Under five mortality rate	16 out of 100 LB	9 of every LB
1995	Maternal mortality rate	1000 per 100,000 LB	463 per100,000
2000	Sustainable access to water source in rural areas	55 percent	69 percent

Source: Compiled from LDC Report 2004.

between 1990 and 2015 if the growth trends of the 1990s are maintained. If a 7% growth target is achieved, poverty will reduce to half by 2015.

Several policy initiatives have been taken at the global level in helping LDCs to break-out of the low level equilibrium of low income, low domestic savings and low investment. These initiatives have centered on increasing access to global finance, increasing market access for LDC products and reducing the burden of external debt.

Poverty of LDCs and work trade performance is clearly related. The LDC Report 2002 showed that during 1997-1999, 69 percent of the population of non-oil commodity-exporting LDCs was living on less than a dollar a day, and in mineral-exporting LDCs the proportion was over 80 percent. The share of the population living on less than $1/day was lower on the average in service-exporting LDCs (43 per cent), whilst in LDCs that had managed to diversify into exporting manufactured goods the incidence of extreme poverty was even lower (25 per cent). There has also been a general tendency for the incidence of extreme poverty to be more persistent in the commodity-dependent LDCs. In the mineral exporters, the incidence of $1/day poverty rose on average from 61 per cent to 82 percent on average between 1981-1983 and 1997-1999.

Following the Ministerial Conference of the WTO in Singapore in 1996, and particularly in the context of the Third United Nations Conference on LDCs, many developed countries and developing countries have expanded or introduced market access preferences for marginalized developing countries, especially LDCs. In 2001, the WTO took note of a total of 28 market access initiatives in favour of LDCs, 19 of which were granted by developed countries.

The EU originally granted two sets of market access preferences to LDCs. It provided relatively far-reaching market access preferences to the group of African, Caribbean and Pacific

Table 5.4: Projections of the Incidence of Extreme Poverty in LDCs in 2015; Three Alternative Scenarios

			I	*II*	*III*
	1990	*1999*	*2015*	*2015*	*2015*
Share of population living on less than $1 a day (%)	49.1	50.5	50.6	43.7	24.0
Number of people living on less than $1 a day (millions)	214.4	270.5	383.6	331.0	181.8
Number of countries on target to halve poverty between 1990 and 2015	-	-	7	6	28

Source: UNCTAD Secretariat estimates.

(ACP) countries which includes many LDCs, and provided less far reaching market access to other developing countries, including non-ACP LDCs. The market access for the former was regulated through the Rome Conventions and is now being regulated through another agreement, while the market access conditions for the latter have been provided in accordance with other GSP schemes. The existence of different market access schemes meant that the ACP LDCs benefited more from better market access conditions than non–ACP LDCs. In 2001, however, the EU introduced the Everything But Arms (EBA) initiative, which has consolidated and improved the market-access preferences for the group of LDCs as a whole. It grants duty-free market access to all types of exports from the LDCs, with the permanent exception of arms and ammunition.

The chapter-III analysis of constraints on economic growth of LDCs has shown that external resources gap limits growth prospects and perpetuates poverty. ODA accounts for nearly 55 percent of external financial flows to LDCs. After stagnations in 1990s, it has shown a recovery since 2001. Post Monterrey, commitments for increased ODA to LDCs has improved the prospects for higher level of development assistance. In 2003, ODA increased by $11 billion and between 2003-06 it was assessed to have grown by 30%.

Despite the progress in expanding ODA since Monterrey, donors' aid lags behind those of the early 1990s and before. At 0.25 percent in 2003, ODA as a share of donors' average gross national income (GNI) was three-quarters the level in the 1970s, 1980s and early 1990, and only about half the level in the 1960. Five countries viz. Denmark, Luxemburg the Netherlands, Norway, and Sweden have achieved ODA shares of 0.7 percent of GNI or more. Finland, France and the United Kingdom have announced timetables for achieving that level. Implementation of such pledges will be vital in raising aid flows to poor countries; the target of $ 5 billion in annual assistance by fiscal 2006 under the U.S. Millennium Challenge Account is now unlikely to be reached until fiscal 2007.

Even on announced pledges, DAC donor's aid effort is expected to reach only 0.3 percent of GNI by 2006 and 0.32 percent by 2010, lower than the level of the early 1990s.

MILLENNIUM DEVELOPMENT GOALS

The millennium declaration adopted in the United Nations Millennium Summit held in September 2000, affirmed the commitment made by the international community to the eradication of poverty in all its aspects viz. income and non-income poverty. The summit was attended by 189 heads of states who pledged to adopt new measures in the fight against poverty, hunger, illiteracy etc. The declaration adopted aid development goals and eighteen time–bound targets for the first time. The eradication of poverty both in terms of income–poverty and non-income poverty was one of the key development goals adopted at the summit. To achieve this goal, the fixed target was to halve the proportion of people whose income is less than one dollar a day between 1990 and 2015. One of the indicators to evaluate this was percentage of people below national poverty line. The deceleration provided a framework which can be utilized to measure progress made by countries in reducing poverty (details of MDG targets and indicators are at Annexure **'K'**).

Progress towards achieving goals related to income and non-income poverty has been uneven across regions and countries. Earlier in this chapter, we have seen that most of the developing countries in East and South East Asia have already achieved these goals. We have also seen that in South Asia some of the countries have made significant progress in meeting these goals.

In the case of LDCs, there appears to be a gap between the present state of human and social developments and the targets set in the millennium submit. The low level of human development as evident from the above indicators presents serious challenges. For assessing progress towards achieving MDGs, some broad targets are as follows:-

Halve, between 1990 and 2015, the proportion of people who suffer from hunger:

- Ensure that, by 2015, children everywhere, boys and girls alike, will be able to complete a full course of primary schooling.

- Eliminate gender disparity in primary and secondary education, preferably by 2005 and at all levels of education no later than 2015.

- Reduce by two thirds, between 1990 and 2015, the under-5 mortality rate.

- Halve, by 2015, the proportion of people without sustainable access to safe drinking water.

The UNCTAD LDC report 2004 has prepared a detailed chart showing the progress made by the countries in reaching MDGs. The report points to the limited national statistical capacity in the countries to provide data on the implementation of MDGs. In brief, the finding of the report causes concern for the policy makers both at national and international level. The findings are as follow:

- In the case of the target to halve hunger by 2015, only eleven countries out of 34 LDCs will be able to achieve this by 2015.

- In the case of primary education, out of 25 LDCs only seven countries had achieved targets by 2000.

- In gender equality in education, out of 29 LDCs only 9 countries have fulfilled the targets.

- In case of child mortality, out of 48 LDCs it is expected that 11 countries will be able to achieve the target by 2015.

- As regard access to safe water, only 7 countries out of 22 LDCs have the achieved the targets.

While in general the progress towards achievement of MDGs is very slow, there are some countries that have made progress.

- The proportion of the population that is undernourished has fallen sharply from very high levels during the 1990s in Chad,

Haiti, Malawi and Mozambique. In these four countries, the proportion undernourished during 1990-1992 was 58 percent, 64percent and 69 percent respectively. During 1998-2000, the proportion had fallen to 32 per cent, 50 percent, 33 percent and 55 percent respectively.

Net primary school enrolment rates increased substantially from 1990 to 2000 in Bangladesh (from 64 percent to 89 percent), Benin (from 19 percent to 70 percent), Eritrea (from 24 percent to 41 percent), Gambia (from 51 percent to 81 percent) Malawi (from 50 percent to 100 percent),Mali (from 21 percent to 43 percent), Rwanda (from 66 percent to 97), Senegal (from 48 percent to 60 percent) and Togo (from 75 percent to 92 per cent).

The ratio of girls to boys in primary and secondary school rose impressively from 1990 to 2000 in Bangladesh from (from 72 percent to 103 per cent), Gambia (from 64 percent to 85 percent), Mauritania (from 67 percent to 93 percent), Nepal (53 percent to 82 percent) and Sudan (from 75 percent to 102 per cent).

It is encouraging to note that there is a global consensus on the utilisation of aid for supporting social and human development in the low-income countries. During the initial years of the new millennium, the LDCs in sub-Saharan Africa received 24 billion $ as ODA which was 33 percent of total ODA as compared to 27 percent in 2000.

Estimates of MDG financing needs vary widely, but all point to the need for a major increase. The UN Millennium Project (2005) conducted detailed MDG-based needs assessments for five low income countries- Bangladesh, Cambodia, Ghana, Tanzania, and Uganda. In Ghana, for example, per capita expenditure needs are projected at $80 in 2006, rising to $124 by 2015. The bulk of such spending will have to come from external financing; $52 in 2006 and $70 in 2015(during this period domestic resource mobilization is expected to rise by about 4 percentage points of GDP). The assessments for the other low-income countries suggest similar external financing needs: $42-$50 per capita in 2006, rising to $77-%98 in 2015. The study projects the MDG financing gap in low-income countries to be $73 billion in 2006, rising to $135 billion in 2015. The gap in middle-income countries is projected to be $10 billion a year. Meeting the MDGs and other needs in low-income and middle-income countries implies additional ODA over 2003 levels of $66 billion in 2006 and $126 billion in 2015- a nearly threefold increase in net ODA by 2015. This implies that the share of ODA in donors GNI will be 0.44 percent in 2006, rising to 0.46 percent in 2010, and reaching 0.54 percent by 2015.

The Commission for Africa (2005) estimates that achieving MDGs in sub-Saharan Africa will require $75 billion a year in additional financing. Two-thirds of the increase ($50 billion) would have to come from external sources. The Commission recommends proceeding in two stages. In the first stage, an additional $25 billion a year would be required within three to five years (2006-2008/10) – doubling aid to Sub-Saharan Africa over 2004 levels. Implementation of the second stage would be based on an assessment of the improvements in governance and aid quality achieved in the first stage.

The adequacy of current aid and debt-relief efforts must be considered in the proper context. From an MDG perspective, what matters is how current aid commitments square with the financing requirements for reaching the targets. Estimating MDG financing gaps is an inexact science. Cost structures vary widely from country to country, and there is a dynamic interaction among the MDGs; progress on, for example, girls' education can reduce the costs of achieving progress on child mortality. The UN Millennium Project estimates that overall aid will need to roughly double by 2006 and then rise by another 50% by 2015 to meet the MDG targets. The proposals set out in the report by the UK-sponsored Commission for Africa are broadly consistent with this assessment. They recommend a doubling over the next three to five years of the $25 billion in aid currently provided to the region, with a further $25 billion increase to 2015. Current aid projections fall far short of these levels.

The G-8 communiqué makes some important commitments. The pledge to increase aid by $50 billion over 2004 levels, with half the increase going to sub-Saharan Africa, could close a substantial part of the MDG financing gap.

The GSP scheme of Japan was recently reviewed, and extended for a new decade (until March 2014). During the 2001/2002 fiscal year, the special treatment granted to LDCs was improved by the addition of a number of tariff lines. All exports from LDCs, under the Japanese scheme, are eligible for duty-free entry and exemption from ceiling restrictions for a list of relevant products. In early 2003, Japan further improved its GSP scheme for the benefit of LDCs. While many industrial goods have already benefited from far-reaching market access preferences under the previous scheme, the new scheme has improved market access preferences primarily for agricultural goods and food items, such as prawns and frozen fish.

MDG: THE ASIAN STORY

The East Asian countries in their fight against poverty have also shown that employment was central to reducing poverty. The economic growth created employment opportunities in the non-farm sector and that in turn absorbed low income poor people. It may be pointed out that in the late 1950s, less than 30% Malaysian work force was in wage-paying industrial and service jobs. By the end of 1980s, the share of the workforce in industries and services rose to approximately 60 percent. Similarly in South Korea, agricultural employment fell from 50 percent of the work-force in 1970 to 20 percent in 1980. In East Asia, growth in rural non-farm employment-opportunities has been a major feature of rural income growth. This had a cumulative effect on other variables of economic growth. Higher agricultural income increased the demand for goods and services and that helped in financing investment in off-farm industries.

In the case of China also, rural non-farm employment grew by 130 million jobs between 1980 and 1999. Agriculture productivity grew rapidly between 1979 and 1984 during the early stages of agricultural reforms. Productivity growth continued but at lower pace from 1984 onwards. This slow rate is mainly the result of opening up the rural industrial sector and the rapid growth of China's township–village enterprises, which drew higher quality labourers (over 28 per cent of the rural labour force in the 1990s in certain rural areas) away from traditional agriculture. In sum, growth in agricultural productivity was through: Improvements in Technology (machines and fertilizer); Research and Development; Increased Production (extension); Better Infrastructure (irrigation, road, etc.); Institutional Reforms; and Better Education

Other parallel measures were also taken to reduce poverty, such as instituting higher agriculture wages, increasing non-farm employment opportunities, rural reforms, public investments, and targeted poverty investment programmes. It should also be mentioned that progress in reducing poverty has generally occurred during improvements – such as greater production and revenues, increased home consumption and increased nutritional value of good. Encouraging technological innovations among these poor farmers will have direct benefits vis-à-vis reducing poverty. In much of Asia, to take another example, most of the poor are landless and live in rural areas. Here, the indirect effects of agricultural growth would be reduced foods prices and positive employment creation for alleviating poverty. A third example is Latin America, where poverty is mainly urban and large farmers own a majority of the land. Here, the best way to reduce poverty with productivity improvements is through reductions in the prices of the types of food that the poor most often consume. In all cases, it is important to focus on a stabilization of the prices of export goods.

Economic development in East Asia has been impressive over the past ten years, with an average annual GDP growth rate of 8.3 percent since 1993 and this is expected to continue in the near term. China, the largest economy in the region, mostly drives this progress. Because of the strong growth in the region and relatively low unemployment rates, East Asia is on track to achieve the MDG of halving the share of people living on less than US$1 per day by 2015. In fact, China has already achieved the goal. Additionally, because the workforce represents 95 percent of the labour force in the region, it has also halved the number of working poor since 1990. The absolute number of workers unable to lift themselves and their families above the US $ 1 a day poverty threshold fell from 242 million in 1990 to 139 million in 2003, a reduction of 43 percent. If growth continues on its current path it is expected that the region will more than halve the share of US$1 and 2 a day working poverty by 2015.

Overall poverty reduction statistics mask wide national and regional differences and the uneven pace of progress. The advances made in China and India has contributed substantially to the positive picture at the global level. Because these two countries account for 38 percent of the world's population, the rapid expansion of their respective economies has led to a significant reduction in the number of people living in absolute poverty worldwide; between 1990 and 2000 this figure declined from 1.2 billion to 1.1 billion (International Labour Organization, 2004). In China alone, the proportion of people living on less than US $2 a day fell from 88 to 47 per cent between 1981 and 2001 and the number of people living on less than US$1 per day was reduced from 634 million to 212 million. In India, the proportion living on less than US$ 2 per day declined from 90 to 80 percent, and the number living in extreme poverty decreased slightly from 382 million to 359 million.

THE FUTURE

Economic stagnation has been a widespread feature of the globalization era during the 1990s, exemplified by 25 countries in sub-Saharan Africa and 10 in Latin America. The past two decades have witnessed one of the most rapid revolutions in global poverty.

Its reduction has been driven largely by the extraordinary success of East Asia, particularly China. At the other end of the spectrum, sub-Saharan Africa has almost 100 million more people living on less than $1 a day in 2001 than in 1990. South Asia reduced its incidence of poverty, though not the absolute number of poor people. The chart at Annexure **'G'**, based on UNDP's 2006 Human Development Report, makes a comparison of progress in MDGs between countries of East Asia/Pacific, South Asia and the LDCs.

While global integration has been associated with accelerated growth for some countries, current growth patterns remain incompatible with achieving the MDGs. In 1990-2003 more than 1 billion people were living in countries growing at less than the prescribed rate to halve poverty over a 25-year period as envisaged under the MDGs – with about half of them in sub-Saharan Africa.

6

India: A Tryst with Globalizing with a Human Face

ECONOMIC PERFORMANCE

Rapid economic growth and strong external sector comprising of increasing trade, foreign direct investment, invisibles and sustained increase in the foreign exchange resources have enabled India to progressively integrate with the global economy. It has emerged as one of the fastest growing economies in the new millennium. Recent trends in economic growth have strengthened its potential to emerge as a key player in the world economy. It achieved 8.5 percent rate of economic growth in 2003–04, 6.9 percent in 2004–05 and 7.2 percent in 2005–06. In per capita income growth, the performance since 2003–04 has been very encouraging. In 2004–05, per capita income reached Rs. 12,416 as compared to Rs. 11,799 in 2003–04. In other economic parameters also the performance has been noteworthy. The significant improvement in the rates of savings and investment witnessed in 2002-03 continued through 2004-05. Savings rate, which are gross domestic savings as a proportion of GDP at current market price, increased from 23.4 percent in 2001-02 to 25.1 percent in 2002-03. The corresponding increase in investment rate (gross domestic capital formation as a proportion of GDP) was from 22.6 percent to 24.8 percent. There were further improvements in savings and investment rates in 2003-04 to 28.1 percent and 26.3 percent, respectively. The savings rate in 2003-04 is the highest recorded so far and the investment rate in 2003-04 is the highest since 1996-97. The rise in savings and investment rate continued in 2005-06. India has been able to come out from savings trap of 1990s. The rate of investment also improved in 2004-05 and in 2005-06.

The late 1990s and the initial years of the new millennium witnessed a progressive integration with the global economy. Trade policy reforms since 1991 have aimed at creating an environment for achieving rapid increase in exports, raising India's share in world exports and making exports an engine for achieving higher economic growth. The focus of these reforms has been on liberalization, openness and transparency.

Since the introduction of economic reforms in 1991-92, impressive trade policy reforms have been carried out. The peak level of tariff on industrial products had already been brought down from 300 percent prevailing in 1991-92 to 35 percent in 2001-02. During the Tenth Plan, the general peak rate has been further reduced in successive years. In the Union Budget for 2005-06 it has been brought down to 15 percent on all non-agricultural products, with a few exceptions. These changes have further reduced the tariff average from 22.4 percent in 2004-05 to 18.3 percent in 2005-06.

At the commencement of economic reforms, import controls were withdrawn on virtually all raw materials, intermediates and capital goods. With effect from 1st April 2001, virtually all the remaining quantitative restrictions had been eliminated except those maintained for protecting human, animal or plant life and for other reasons specifically provided for in the WTO Agreement. The process of liberalization continued during the Tenth Plan and 83 products were placed on open general license (OGL) in 2002-03, 69 in 2003-04 and 42 in 2004-05.

Exports in the recent past have continued to grow at a rate higher than that of world exports or exports from developing countries, except in 2003 when there were large US dollar price changes. Its share in world exports rose from 0.6 percent in 1999 to 0.8 percent in 2003. Currently, it is the 31st leading exporter and 24th leading importer in world merchandise trade. The value of Indian exports has shown a rising trend since 2002–03, and in 2005-06 Indian exports were worth $100 billion.

One of the main benefits of trade has been modernization and technological upgradation of industry. The consequent improvements in efficiency have enabled Indian industry to increase its share in world exports, which has substantially mitigated the adverse effects of the domestic cyclical slowdown. Another beneficial effect of trade liberalization has been to keep inflation under check. The possibility of import of goods from abroad after quantitative restrictions were lifted, introduced an additional competitive dimension in the markets and eased domestic supply constraints. In addition, access to cheaper import of raw materials and intermediaries has led to reductions in domestic production costs and prices, which has further strengthened efficiency in industry.

Merchandise exports are predominated by manufactured items, which accounted for more than three-fourths of its total exports during the 1990s. This is also the pattern of global trade. Within manufactured items, there has been a considerable change in the relative importance of different products; the products which increased their share were chemicals and allied products, engineering goods, readymade garments, textile yarn, fabrics, gems and jewellery. With increasing share of manufactures there has been a decline in the exports of primary products since the 1990s and India has been moving up the value chain. The unit labour cost of manufacturing exports is one of the lowest among the developing countries and this comparative advantage has been enhanced by the productivity growth since the 1980s, which has outpaced the real wages in this sector. With sizeable growth in exports of auto-parts and pharmaceutical products, it has been demonstrated that it has an emerging competitiveness in skill intensive manufactures.

Rising surpluses in the current account have been one of the distinguishing features of India's balance on payments in the current decade. While for the predominantly exports-oriented East and South-East Asian economies (e.g. Korea, Malaysia, Philippines, Singapore, Taiwan and Thailand), strong growth in merchandise exports has been the main driver behind their current account surplus; buoyant invisible inflows, particularly private transfers comprising remittances, along with software services exports, have been instrumental in creating and sustaining the Indian current account surplus.

One of the distinguishing features of its trade in the new millennium has been the rise in the share of trade in services in overall trade. Trade in services has been growing faster than merchandise trade. In 2004-05, growth in services trade was 78.6% as compared with 33.6 per cent in merchandise trade. The share of services in total trade increased from 23.5 percent in 2003-04 to 34.4 percent in first half of 2005-06. Rising share of services in the overall exports has brought out a significant transformation in the composition of India's export basket. The share of invisibles, comprising, services, income from financial assets, labour and property, and current transfers are rapidly catching up with merchandise exports as the principal foreign exchange earners for the country.

There are several factors which have led to the rising share of services in trade. On the macro-front, there has been an evident shift in which services have assumed an important position in the production structure and become a key driver of growth. This is evident as they now account for more than half of India's GDP. In addition, structural reforms and liberalization in the sector have released new growth impulses and enabled productivity and cost efficiency to provide a cutting edge in international competitiveness.

Remittance flows have been a source of strength for India's external profile. As an important constituent of net invisible earnings – besides software earnings and tourism – it has ensured an overall surplus on the current account since 2001-02. According to RBI estimates, net invisible earnings as a whole amounted to $25.4, which more than offset the trade deficit of $16.7 billion in 2003-04 resulting in current account surplus of 8.7 billion or 1.4 percent of GDP in 2003-04 - an all-time high. India has emerged as the highest remittance receiving country in the world in 2004, followed by China, Mexico, France and Philippines. Indian share in total global remittances of US$ 225 billion in 2004 was almost 10 percent according to Global Economic Prospects 2006.

The year 2004-05 marked a significant departure from surplus in balance of payment to deficit. The current account turned into a deficit in 2004-05, from a surplus of $14.1 billion in 2003-04. The deficit was at the level of $5.4 billion, while in 2005-06 the deficit had widened further. The emergence of the deficit can be attributed to a large merchandise trade deficit. Imports fuelled by high global crude oil prices and sustained demand for non-oil imports from a buoyant domestic industry, grew rapidly by 39.0 percent. The widening trade deficit could not be compensated by surpluses in invisibles (net).

The steady growth of non-factor services, receipts and the concomitant strengthening of the invisible balance can be, inter-alia, attributed to the rapid rise in software services exports. From a relatively low share of only 10.2 percent in 1994-96, exports of software services came to occupy 48.9 percent of India's total services exports in 2003-04. Thus highlighting the country's growing comparative advantage in production and export of such services. The growth in ITES and BPO has strengthened the service sector.

The flow of FDI in the global economy has been one of the prime drivers of globalization since 1980s. In recent years, there has been a phenomenal increase in the magnitude and in the rate of growth of FDI. In developing countries like India, FDI is seen as a means to supplement domestic investment for achieving a higher level of economic growth. FDI benefits the domestic industry as well as consumers by providing opportunities for technological upgradation and access to international quality goods and services. The growth in FDI has surpassed the rate of growth in GDP and also the growth of global trade. A distinguishing feature of FDI flow in 1980s and 1990s has been that developing countries have emerged as an important destination.

The Government of India has put in place a liberal, transparent and investor friendly FDI policy, wherein up to 100 percent is allowed under automatic route for most of sectors/ activities, where the investor does not require any prior approval. Only notification to the Reserve Bank of India within 30 days of inward remittance or issue of share to non-residents is required. Cases requiring prior government approval are considered by the Foreign Investment Promotion Board (FIPB) in a time-bound and transparent manner. A liberal investment regime has enabled India to attract increasing amount of FDI during recent years. It attracted an amount of US$7.5billion in 2004-05 and $4.3billion in 2003-04. This further underlines India's progressive integration with global economy.

Rising level of foreign exchange has further strengthened the external sector. The level of foreign exchange reserve had increased from less than $ 1 billion as of end-June 1991 to $140.4 billion on 11thMarch2005. This has been fuelled by FII inflows and remittances from workers, the latter being $23.2 billion in 2003-04. India's foreign exchange reserves are adequate for about 17 months of imports. The accretion to foreign exchange reserves creates an opportunity for providing a part of the huge financial requirement for development. At the end of March 2005, India's total foreign exchange reserves including foreign currency assets [FCA], gold, special drawing rights [SDR] and reserve tranche position [RTP] in the IMF) stood at US $141.5 billion, reflecting an increase of US $ 28.5 billion as compared with US $ 113.0 billion at end of March 2004.

India's external debt at US $123.3 billion during 2004-05 reflected marginal increase in the absolute amount of external debt. Even through there was an increase in the absolute amount of external debt, India's debt to GDP ratio suggested an improvement in the external debt-situation during 2004-05. The total external debt to GDP ratio was 17.3 percent in 2004-05. In the international comparison of top ten debtor countries-2003 declared by Global Dev. Fin. (2005), India has been categorized under less indebted countries. Please see Annexure **'H'** for selected indicators of the external sector.

Through its increasing trade and investment linkages with expanding international trade and finance, India is firmly on the path of integration with the global economy. The response to emerging new opportunities in the global economy in the new millennium has been encouraging and it has further strengthened the economy to play a major role in the global economy. There are a number of factors such as high rate of sustained economic growth, strong external sector and advanced technologies, which will enable India to seize on new opportunities, created by globalization, and emerge as a major player in the global economy.

The emergence of services sector as one of the engines of growth in the global economy has created new opportunities for India's integration with the global economy. Services today account for 20 percent of global trade and 68 percent of global GDP. They are a high employment-generating sector and employ as much as 40 percent and 70 percent of the work force in developing and developed countries respectively. In 2000-01, the share of services in the country's GDP was 52.4 percent, up from 51.5 percent recorded in 1998-99. More significantly, this sector accounted for around a quarter of the trade flows in the same period. The high growth rate of services exports explains the higher rate share of India in the global services trade: 1.4 percent compared to 0.9 percent in the case of global merchandise trade. The year 2004-05 was especially very encouraging in terms of services export growth. It saw exports doubling to US $ 51.3 billion from US $ 24.9 billion in 2003-04 an astounding growth of 105.7 percent.

The growth and dynamism of the sector in India is fuelled by its export potential, though domestic growth is also at a robust nine percent. The country's main source of comparative advantage in services is its labour endowment. Its global competitiveness in this regard is striking. In recent years, the country has accounted for 70 percent of all specialty occupation (H1-B) visas granted by the US in computer services. Overall, Indian professionals across services as diverse as accountancy, engineering, consulting, medical and management accounted for nearly half of all H1-B visas granted to foreigners in the US in the late 1990s.

India is ranked as the leading global outsourcing destination in services. In all, 60 percent of fortune 500 companies are outsourcing services to India, ranging from simple back-office services like processing and billing to intermediate services like technical help and systems design, to specialized services like research and development, and technical analysis. The cost and quality advantage in labour-baled services combined with India's high quality institutions has also enabled the country to diversify its services exports considerably into emerging areas like healthcare, research and development, and educational services.

Indian progress in the field of IT was spectacular and has accelerated the place of integration with the global economy. Total spending on products and services in the sector increased from US $ 5 billion in 1997-98 to nearly $ 20 billion in 2003-04 and software exports reached US $ 17.2 billion in 2004-05, as per a NASSCOM study. Employment in the sector grew by 30.1 percent per year between 1999-00 to 2003-04. By 2008, the industry is projected to grow from 4.1 percent of GDP in 2004-05 to 7.0 percent of GDP and account for 35 percent of total exports.

It accounted for 65 percent of the global market in offshore IT services and 46 percent of the global BPO market in 2004-05. With an annual growth of over 25 percent, these two can generate export revenues of US $ 60 billion by 2010. Studies suggest that growth will be driven by traditional outsourcing services lines –

such as hardware and software maintenance, network administration and help desk services.

The BPO industry has grown at phenomenal rates in the past few years. Exports grew from a mere $ 565 million in 1999-2000 to $ 2.6 billion in 2003-04. Despite emerging constraints, the industry is expected to grow rapidly, given cost pressures and demographic shortages in developed countries and India's comparative advantage based on its labour endowment and skill base. BPO exports are projected to rise to $20 billion by 2007 and employment in this sector projected to rise from its current level of around 300,000 to one million by 2012. Given this, the industry has far-reaching socio-economic and cultural implications, beyond the employment and foreign exchange earning effects. The sector in India has been growing at almost 60-70% per annum. According to NASSCOM, the projected revenue of the BPO industry in India is expected to grow to touch $ 12 billion in 2006-07. This is nearly four fold growth from the 2003-04 revenue estimates of around $ 3.6 billion.

Agriculture's share in national income has declined more rapidly than its share in employment. This has led to the widening of agricultural-nonagricultural sector income disparities. Currently, labour productivity in non-agriculture is several times higher than what it is in agriculture and wage rates in the rural non-farm sector are higher than in the farm sector. In the short and the medium term, the challenge is to increase both productivity per hectare and the productivity per worker of the people who remain in agriculture, while simultaneously taking steps to create as many non-farm jobs as possible with a view to accelerating the shift of workers from low productivity employment in the agricultural sector to more productive employment in the non-farm sector.

A weak agricultural sector, in any region, in terms of employment growth and productivity levels gets reflected in a similarly weak non-agricultural sector in that region. Both non-farm employment levels and the productivity of rural non-farm employment depend critically on the performance of the agricultural sector. The development of the rural non-farm sector has to go hand-in-hand with the development of agriculture itself.

Simultaneous development of both sectors does not come "on the cheap". It demands heavy and sustained investment on infrastructure, especially rural infrastructure development. Evidences from SAARC countries show that infrastructure development tends to reduce poverty by increasing labour productivity and reducing costs of production in both the farm and the non-farm sectors. It also helps in promoting rural-urban stimulates non-farm sector development and tends to push-up real wage rates. In regression analyses, the impact of better infrastructure is more significant than any other factor. The impact of a workforce shift in favour of non-farm employment has the second most significant favourable impact on poverty reduction. This underscores the importance of achieving higher levels of domestic resource mobilization in the interest of higher rates of investment in infrastructure.

The emerging areas in agriculture like horticulture, floriculture, organic farming, genetic engineering, food processing, branding and packaging, and futures trading have high potential of growth. Development of rural infrastructure, rural extension services and agro-based and food processing industries are essential for harnessing this potential. Indian agriculture suffers from low yields per hectare, volatility in production and wide disparities of productivity over regions and crops. Domestic production of pulses and oilseeds are still below the domestic requirements. A distinct bias in agricultural price support policies in favour of food grains in the past may have distorted cropping pattern and input usage, and may require corrections. Market for farm output continues to depend heavily on expensive government procurement and distribution systems. A shift from the current MSP and public procurement system and developing alternative product markets are essential for crop diversification and broad-based agricultural development.

INDIA'S EFFORTS AT HUMANISING ECONOMIC GROWTH

We have seen from the case studies in chapter IV that the process of economic growth of developing countries in East Asia and South East Asia was accompanied by enhanced level of human and social development. The lesson of development strategy adopted by these countries is that for globalization to positively impact economic development, it is necessary to create capabilities in the population in terms of fulfillment of basic needs such as sound health, good living conditions, high level of education, skill etc. The case-studies also underlined the fact that the benefits of economic growth are not automatically transmitted to society. It is the choice of appropriate policies that leads to an all–inclusive and broad-based economic development. The last decade of the 20th century has seen a visible shift in the focus of development planning from a mere expansion of production of goods and services and consequent growth in per capita income to planning for enhancement of human well being. The concept of human well being itself is more broadly conceived to include not only consumption of goods and services but also the accessibility of all sections of the population, to basic services such as education, health care etc.

Human development is the process of enlarging people's choice and expanding human capabilities and functioning – what people do and can do in their lives. At all levels of development, a few capabilities are essential for human development, without which many choices in life would not be available. These capabilities are: to lead long and healthy lives; to be knowledgeable; and to have access to the resources needed for a decent standard of living – and these are reflected in the human development index.

The new millennium has witnessed progressive integration of Indian economy with the global economy. The recent development experience has brought to focus the advantages of adaptation in economic policies and encompassing liberalization in trade and investment policies. It has been able to share dividends of globalization through establishing linkages between Indian economy and global economy in trade, investment and technology. The development outcome of these linkages has been extensively analyzed so far in this chapter. In the rest of the chapter, we examine to what extent, it has succeeded in giving a human face to development. Through the study of various social and economic indicators, we assess the progress in human and social development achieved by India.

STATUS OF POVERTY

An anti-poverty strategy has been integral to Indian development planning. As we have seen in chapter–IV that a number of developing countries in East and South East Asia succeeded in almost eliminating poverty because of fast economic growth and pattern of development. Economic growth can positively impact the reduction in poverty only when it is combined with a broad–based economic growth. In other words, high rate of economic growth and the choice of pro-poor pattern of economic development can lead to a significant decline in poverty in a developing economy.

The anti-poverty strategy of India is a combination of economic growth and specific programmes of employment generation which have led to decline in the incidence of poverty during the last 3 decades. The incidence of poverty is estimated by the Planning Commission on the basis of the large scale sample surveys on household consumer expenditure conducted by the National Sample Survey Organization (NSSO). The latest survey relates to the 55th round conducted in 1999-2000.

The Incidence of poverty declined from 55 percent in 1973-74 to 26 percent in 1999-2000. The reduction of proportion of people living below poverty line has been particularly sharp in the 1990s, when there has been a 10 percentage points decline between 1993-94 and 1999-2000. These trends indicate that India is on track with respect to the target of halving the proportion of people below poverty line. Please see table below.

Table 6.1: Indicators Relating to Poverty and Hunger

	Indicator	*1987-88*	*1993-94*	*1999-2000*
Poverty Headcount Ratio	Overall	38.9	36.0	26.1
	Rural	39.1	37.3	27.1
	Urban	38.2	32.4	23.6
Poverty Gap Ratio				
	Rural		8.5	5.3
	Urban		8.1	5.2
Share in Poorest Quintile in National Consumption	Overall		9.2	9.5
	Rural		9.6	10.1
	Urban		8.0	7.9

Source: Planning Commission and Ministry of Health & Family Welfare.

The Planning commission in the Tenth Plan (2002-07) has targeted the poverty ratio in reducing it by 5 percentage points by 2007 and 15 percentage points by 2012. It aims at achieving a poverty ratio of 19.3 percent for the country as a whole by 2007; 21.1 percent for the rural and 15.1 percent for the urban areas. In absolute terms the number of poor is projected to decline from 260 million in 1999–2000 to 220 million in 2007, with rural poor declining to 170 million and urban poor to 50 million.

It is important to mention that despite a reduction in the proportion of people living in poverty by over 50 percent between 1973-74 and 1999-2000, the absolute number of poor continued to be in excess of 260 million in 1999-2000 in view of India's large population. While there was a reduction in the total number of poor from 320 million in 1993-94 to 260 million in 1999-2000, yet the absolute member of poor people continue to remain high.

In a country as large and as diverse as India, the aggregates tend to obscure the fact that the proportion of those living below the poverty line is not uniform throughout the country. There are States like Bihar and Orissa in the eastern parts of the country, where the poverty ratio was estimated in 1999-2000 to be over 40 percent, while in States like Haryana, Himachal Pradesh and Punjab, the ratio is under 10 percent. The four States of Uttar Pradesh, Bihar, Madhya Pradesh, and Orissa accounted for nearly 39 percent of the total population of the people below poverty line.

At the national level, the incidence of poverty on the Head Count Ratio declined from 44.48 percent in 1983 to 26.10 percent in 1999-2000. It was a decline of nearly 8.5 percentage points in the ten years period between 1983 and 1993-94 followed by a further decline of nearly 10 percentage points in the period between 1993-94 and 1999-2000. In absolute terms, the number of poor declined from about 323 million in 1983 to 260 million in 1999-2000. The decline has not been uniform: poverty in the rural areas declined from 45.65 percent in 1983 to 27.09 percent in 1999-2000; in urban areas poverty declined from 40.79 percent to 23.62 percent during this period.

An analysis of the incidence of poverty among social and economic groups in India in 1990's indicates that among social groups, scheduled castes (SCs) and scheduled tribes (STs) continue to be mired in poverty (Table 6.2). These groups show higher incidence of poverty compared to the general population.

Table 6.2: Percentage of People Living below Poverty Line in Rural and Urban Areas of India by Social Groups in 1993-94 and 1999-2000

Year	*Poverty Rate (%)*					
	Rural			*Urban*		
	SCs	*STs*	*All*	*SCs*	*STs*	*All*
1993-94	48.1	51.9	37.3	49.5	41.1	32.4
1999-00	36.3	45.9	27.1	38.5	34.8	23.6

Source : Estimated by Planning Commission, India.

Though the incidence of rural poverty has marginally declined, it is getting increasingly concentrated in Central and Eastern parts of the country. The States of Bihar (including Jharkhand), Uttar Pradesh, Madhya Pradesh (including Chhattisgarh), West Bengal and Orissa accounted for 54.27 per cent of the rural poor in 1973-74. The accounted for 68.81 per cent of the rural poor in 1999-2000.

The share of the urban poor in total poor increased from 22 per cent 1993-94 per cent to 26 per cent in 1999-2000. The casual workers and self-employed in the urban areas constitute over 44 per cent of the total urban poor. They are engaged in informal, unorganized low paid activities. In most urban centers, they function in violation of outdated and archaic municipal laws, which prohibit these activities. Many have few linkages with the formal sector of the economy. They face higher transaction costs. Urban poverty is increasingly becoming a problem in countries like Bangladesh, India and Pakistan. The urban poor are generally unskilled casual workers, with high levels of illiteracy and low levels

Table 6.3: Percentage of People Living Below Poverty Line in Rural and Urban Areas by Occupation, India 1993-94 and 1999-2000

Rural	*1993-94*	*1999-2000*
1. Self Employed in non agriculture	32.31	22.59
2. Agricultural Labour	56.75	42.13
3. Other Labour	39.69	26.27
4. Self employed in agriculture	29.19	20.07
5. Others	17.57	13.86
6. Overall Rural	37.20	27.10
Urban	**1993-94**	**1999-2000**
1. Self Employed	36.91	26.47
2. Regular wage & salary earners	20.93	12.21
3. Casual Labourers	62.64	50.61
4. Others	26.48	16.81
5. Overall Urban	32.40	23.60

Source : **RPP** 2005 India Country Team.

of skills. Most of them live in shantytowns in unhygienic living conditions. Development of Small and Medium Enterprises (SMEs), creation of jobs for the unskilled through urban infrastructure development, access to micro-finance and skills training to the urban poor, and improvement of roads, housing, sewerage, sanitation and drinking water facilities in the shanty towns may greatly help reduce poverty.

A disturbing development in the last 20 years in India has been the fact that, though the incidence of poverty has declined, the intake of calories across States has gone down. One of the major targets, therefore, should be the elimination of hunger. Provision for balanced diets with special focus on nutritional status of women and the girl child also need to be made.

The analysis of incidence of poverty across Indian States indicates that poverty is very closely linked to the absence of economic and social infrastructure. The Eleventh Finance Commission had constructed an index of infrastructure, which included economic, social and administrative infrastructure. Eight major sectors, under these three broad heads were covered. These are: agriculture; banking; electricity; transport; communication; education; health; and civil administration. If we juxtapose the index of infrastructure with incidence of poverty, we find that States with a high value for the infrastructure index have low incidence of poverty.

EMPLOYMENT

The creation of adequate employment opportunities holds key to poverty alleviation and therefore, it is a priority area of policy for human and social development. The persistence of unemployment in a society deprives a nation not only of the potential income earned by employed persons but it also inflicts disgrace to the individual. The creation of employment opportunities in a developing economy is an economic necessity and also a vehicle for equitable development. Two recent NSSO surveys viz. 55th and 60th round bring out a disturbing trend in the employment scenario. According to 55th NSSO survey, the incidence of unemployment increased in 1994–2000 as compared with 1985–1989.

As part of the annual series in the 60th round of the NSSO, an all-India survey on the situation of employment and unemployment was conducted in January to June 2004 with a moderately large sample of households. The findings of the survey are as follows:

- According to the Survey, the unemployment rate went up between 1993-94 and 2004. On the basis of current daily status (unemployed on an average in the reference week), during the reference period, unemployment rate for males increased from 5.6 percent to 9.0 percent in rural areas, and from 6.7 percent to 8.1 percent in urban areas.

- It was also pointed out in the survey that unemployment rates on the basis of current daily status were much higher than those on the basis of usual status (unemployed on an average in the reference year) implying a high degree of intermittent unemployment.

- Urban unemployment (current daily status) was higher than rural unemployment rates for both males and females in 1993-94. However, in 2004, rural unemployment rates for males were higher than that of urban males.

Economic growth is a necessary condition for sustainable employment generation. However, growth alone will not create employment. State interventions are also required to ensure that growth is broad based and that the benefits are passed on to the poor through employment. Such policy measures and reforms should target improving the macroeconomic environment, labour market-related issues and institutional development. But labour-market policies by themselves cannot generate employment. A sufficient pull from the demand side is also necessary. Sound macroeconomic policies, a strong macroeconomic environment and a solid development agenda are imperative for the creation of

Table 6.4: Unemployment Status 2004

Status	Rural			Urban		
	Male	Female	Total	Male	Female	Urban
Un-usual principal status	24	22	23	46	89	53
Current weekly status	47	45	46	57	90	64
Current daily status	90	93	91	81	117	88

Source: NSSO's 60th Round Survey on Employment and Unemployment conducted In January – June 2004.

Table 6.5: Unemployment Rates 1993-94

Unemployment rates for 50th round (1993-94) and 60th round (January – June 2004) of the NSSO.							
	Males			*Rural*	*Females*		
Round	Usual	CWS	CDS		Usual	CWS	CDS
60th (2004)	24	47	90		22	45	93
50th (1993-94)	20	30	56		14	30	56
	Males			Urban	Females		
Round	Usual	CWS	CDS		Usual	CWS	CDS
60th (2004)	46	57	81		89	90	117
50th (1993-94)	45	52	67		83	84	105

Source: NSSO's 60th Round Survey on Employment and Unemployment conducted in January – June 2004.

adequate jobs. For example, macroeconomic policies need to accommodate wage-moderation policies to make room for private sector engagement in economic activities.

Benefiting from trade liberalization requires improving absorptive capacity. The stock of human capital plays a key role. Providing a supportive environment, through domestic reforms and greater access to global markets, is also required if any economy is to benefit from trade liberalization. Adequate protection, through social safety nets, capacity-building and opportunities for training, is also needed for those who lose out because of trade liberalization. Labour-market flexibility is a key determinant of the success of economic reforms. Long spells of unemployment signal a stagnant labour market, with limited chances of escaping unemployment. Reducing labour-market costs is another important reform. High labour-market costs impede the evolution of the private sector as a major force for employment generation in the formal and informal sectors, eroding the competitive edge of developing countries and constraining businesses expansion. There is need to vigorously pursue the development of the small and medium enterprises (SMEs) by facilitating provision of adequate bank credit and of clusters with adequate infrastructure; and through removal of limitations of scale by rapid removal of items from the ambit of small-scale reservation. There is a need for a paradigm shift to encourage the banks to look at provision of credit to SME and agriculture more as an opportunity for profit rather than as a social obligation under directed subsidized credit. The main reason that so many small and medium-sized enterprises remain in the informal sector is the high cost of entry and the strict regulatory environment in the formal sector. Reducing such costs is vital if the private sector is to contribute meaningfully to employment generation.

In many economies in transition there is a mismatch between educational content provided under planned economic systems and the skills demanded by a market economy, and those economies are lagging behind. In a globalized economy, technical knowledge needs to be adjusted to market demand and changing circumstances. Thus, while basic education remains a fundamental necessity, reforms in secondary and tertiary education to suit the changing demand would minimize the skills mismatch. Despite high returns to vocational training generally, in many developing countries of the region vocational training does not seem to provide the required technical and practical exposure. Reasons include a lack of recent industrial exposure by trainers, lack of regular technical and pedagogical upgrading and the absence of professionalism in curriculum development. Training programmes are most effective when they are tightly targeted and small-scale, with a strong on-the-job component and linked to industry.

The 'demographic dividend' will also pay off in terms of a larger and younger labour force gainfully employed in production, and generating a larger national income, particularly in a world where many countries are transiting to ageing societies. The suggestion by various empirical studies that, given its institutional strengths, India's per capita income should be four to five time of what it is now portends a bright outlook for growth over the medium term. The multi-pronged challenge lies in providing an appropriate policy framework to harness the dormant talent pool of Indian work-force and entrepreneurs to position the economy on a sustained high-growth trajectory. Interventions to enhance the employability of youth should be a key component of active labour-market policies and education reforms. Such programmes need to target youth early, before attitudes harden and aspirations are set. The extent that unemployment arises from prolonged searching for "good" jobs, credible reform of public sector recruitment and wage policies could arrest high unemployment by reducing incentives for people to queue for public sector jobs. Removing the artificial benefits associated with public sector jobs and creating the conditions for sustained improvements in the quality of other jobs would help to bring about important attitudinal changes. Non-agricultural employment in rural areas could be created through the development of small scale infrastructure, such as, rural roads, rural electrification, expansion of irrigation facilities, building of schools and health posts, watershed management, drinking water and sanitation programmes. Poverty could be reduced through the development of agricultural processing industries in the rural areas, access to micro-finance and basic life skills to the poor.

The development of entrepreneurship is a vital component of human resources development aimed at job creation. Lack of competence and the aptitude to initiate, nurture and expand industrial enterprises is a major reason why small and medium-sized enterprises and self-employment fail to become viable options for generating employment in the informal sector.

If countries are to mobilize the economic and political resources to stimulate reform, they will have to resolve issues of managing the demographic dividend or youth bulge. Youth issues by nature cut across sectors, while most policies that influence them are set within sectors. So the challenge of coordination looms large. Countries that have experienced success are those that have drawn up a coherent national frame-work for youth, supported by all ministries. Young people need to be encouraged to participate more fully in public life. Governments and other agencies need to learn to communicate with them make their programs attractive to them, and tap their immense talents as partners in service delivery.

The provision of employment opportunities is an important socio–economic objective. Without assuring full employment it is not possible to give a human face to development. The Special Group on Employment also expressed concern on the increase in the rate of unemployment during 1993-1994 and during 1999-2000 in spite of improvement in the over all growth performance of the country. According to projections in the 10th plan, it has been estimated that during the plan period a total of 50 million additional employment opportunities will need to be created to absorb the addition to the labour force. In working out an appropriate strategy for the creation of employment opportunities, India faces a number of challenges. Globalization has changed the contours of economic development in the 21st century in many ways. On the one hand, the creation of employment opportunities to a large extent depends on the application of labour intensive technique of production. On the other hand, the operation of global competition and the play of market forces call for competitive edge to be gained by India in its products. In most of the sectors it is the application of sophisticated technology in production that reduces the cost of production and raises the level of competitiveness for Indian products. There are, therefore, limitations on the choice of technique in production in an era of globalization.

Indian strategy to bring down unemployment intensity has duly recognized the limitation of economic growth to reduce unemployment. In most of the developing countries in East and South East Asia, who succeeded in tackling the problem of unemployment, the process of economic growth led to a large scale shift in the rural workforce to off–farm activities in industrial and tertiary sector. In India, the process of economic growth had very limited success in absorbing rural unemployed and hence the intensity of unemployment continued to rise in the 1990s and during initial years of 21st century. It has therefore, launched special employment generation programmes so that additional job opportunities in this country are created to absorb increasing work force. Some of the employment generation schemes include Pradhan Mantri Gram Sadak Yojana (PMGSY), Swaran Jayanti Swayam Rozgar Yojana (SJSRY), Sampoorna Grameen Rozgar Yojana (SGRY), National Food for Work Programme (NFFWP), Swaran Jayanti Sahari Rozgar Yojana (SJSRY).

These schemes are multi–purpose schemes through which, in addition to the generation of employment, rural infrastructure is also created. In some of theses schemes credit facilities are given to those who are self-employed. With a view to tackle the problem of rural unemployment on priority basis and in a more effective manner, the government has recently passed the National Rural Employment Guarantee Act (NREGA). This was notified on September 7, 2005 and the scheme was launched on February 2, 2006. The on-going programmes of SGRY and NFFWP will be subsumed within the NREGS in the 200 districts identified in the initial stage. All the districts in the country will be covered under the scheme within five years.

The objective of the Act is to enhance the livelihood security of the people in rural areas by generating wage employment through works that develop the infrastructure base of that area. The choice of work selected, addresses the causes of chronic poverty like drought, deforestation, and soil erosion. The objective behind selecting key activities/works is to rejuvenate the natural resources of the area to stimulate the local economy. Implementation of the Act calls for the formulation of NREGS by the State Governments. Section 4 provides that within six months from the date of commencement, every State Government shall, by notification, make a scheme for providing not less than 100 days of guaranteed employment in a financial year to every household in the rural areas covered under the scheme and whose adult members volunteer to do unskilled manual work subject to the conditions laid down in the Act.

Poverty is a multi-dimensional phenomenon and hence only reduction in the incidence of income-poverty does not address the problem of deprivation in terms of basic needs of people such as education, access to health care, drinking water etc. To address non-income dimensions of poverty, the anti–poverty strategy has laid emphasis on the promotion of human development and on targeted programmes of poverty alleviation. India has made significant progress in some of the social indicators, which determine the level of human and social development of its people. In giving a conceptual framework to human and social development, the UNDP has identified 3 criteria, which broadly determine human and social development of a country. These include income, education and health. The social indicators, which relate to education and health, determine the progress that a country has made in the alleviation of non-income poverty.

HEALTH

In the health sector, India's progress can be assessed from the indicators such as life expectancy, infant mortality rate, etc.

Life expectancy has increased from 59.7 years to 63.9 years from males and from 60.9 years to 66.9 years for females between 1991–95 and 2001-06. Under-Five Mortality Rate (U5MR) at the national level has declined during the last decade. It has come down from 125.1 per thousand (1988-92) to 98.1 per thousand during the period 1998-2002. A perceptible decline in the rate has taken place in rural areas. Please see Annexure **'I'-(b)** for a snapshot of the status of progress.

The country has been observing a continuous decline in infant mortality rate (IMR). It stood at 192 during 1971, which came down to 114 in 1980 and further declined in the last decade and reached the level of 60 in 2003. The decline in IMR has been noticed both for male and female during the period; however, the rate of decline is more pronounced in the case of males as compared to females. It is also observed that there is continuous decline both in rural as well as in urban areas observed from the following table.

Table 6.6: Infant Mortality Rate by Sex

(Per 1000 live births)			
Year	*Male*	*Female*	*Total*
1980	113	115	114
1985	96	98	97
1990	78	81	80
1993	73	75	74
1996	71	73	72
2000	67	69	68
2003	57	64	60

It has been realized that a faster pace of progress is needed if the stated goal in the National Population Policy of achieving an IMR of 30 per 1000 by the year 2010 is to be achieved.

The National Common Minimum Programme mandates health care as one of the seven thrust areas; it is proposed to increase the expenditure in health sector as a proportion of GDP from 0.9 percent to 2-3 percent over next five years. National Rural Health Mission was launched on April 12, 2005 for a period of 7 years (2005-2012). NRHM includes the second phase of Reproductive and Child Health (RCH) Programme. The RCH Programme Phase-II has been launched with effect from April 1, 2005 for a period of 5 years. It intends to improve the performance of the family welfare programme in reducing maternal and infant morbidity and mortality.

The fulfillment of basic needs is a necessary pre-requisite for eliminating poverty and for increasing the capabilities of the poor to be able to exercise choices in various aspects of life. India has adopted a basic-needs strategy as a major developmental goal in its over-all development strategy. Towards this end, the government has given priority to ensure access to drinking water and sanitation. Provision of safe drinking water to all rural habitations has been made in the Tenth Plan.

There are various areas of concern in India's performance in human and social development. The aggregative analysis of social indicators related to poverty alleviation employment, access to education and to health care conceals very marked variations in the performance of states in these sectors. These variations in social indicators have been shown in various tables at Annexure 'I'. Human and social development is integral to the process of economic development and the potential for globalization to act as a catalyst of development can be realized only when economic growth becomes all-inclusive and participatory. This objective can be fulfilled when basic needs of the masses are fulfilled. Human resources are an important input for economic growth and to harness this it is necessary to give sound health and education to all. Unless the entire population acquires capabilities to enjoy a decent standard of life and to be able to work and contribute to the process of economic growth, a large segment of society will remain marginalised. Global consensus on the need for improving economic and social indicators has been built up and has been manifested in various commitments by the international community too.

A major programme called the Accelerated Rural Water Supply Programme (ARWSP) is being implemented since 1972 – 73 to achieve this objective. With an investment of over Rs. 50,000 crore (up to March 31, 2005), considerable success has been achieved in meeting the drinking water needs of the rural population. More than 3.7 million hand pumps and 1.73 lakh piped water schemes have been installed in the rural areas. As on April 1, 2005, 96.1 percent of rural habitations were fully covered, leaving 0.3 percent not covered with drinking water facilities. As shown in the table below, 62% of the total households in the country could use safe drinking water in 1991. By 2001, this proportion had increased to 85%. There has been substantial increase in the rural India, the percentage having increased from 55.5% in 1991 to 86.6% in 2001 and to 90% in 2005.

The programme Bharat Nirman has been launched to be implemented in four years (2005-06 to 2008-09) for building rural infrastructure. Rural drinking water supply is one of the six components of the initiative. The coverage in respect of rural drinking water supply includes: coverage of all rural schools in coordination with the Ministry of Human Resource Development; coverage of 55,067 remaining uncovered habitations of the comprehensive Action Plan 1999; coverage of 2.16.968 water quality affected habitations; and coverage of slipped back habitations.

The Central Rural Sanitation Programme (CRSP) launched in 1986 was restructured in 1999 to introduce the Total Sanitation Campaign (TSC). TSC envisages interaction between Government, people and active NGOs. It also incorporates intensive information, education and communication (IEC) campaigns, provision of the alternative delivery system and more flexible, demand-oriented construction norms. The revised centrally sponsored scheme envisages a shift from allocation-based programme to a demand-based project, with greater household involvement, intensive IEC campaign and emphasis

Table 6.7: Proportion in Population with Access to an Improved Water Source and Sanitation

Indicator/Year	*1991*			*2001*		
	Rural	*Urban*	*Total*	*Rural*	*Urban*	*Total*
Proportion of the population with access to an improved water source	55.54	81.38	62.30	86.77	82.22	85.22
	1991		2001		2005	
Proportion of the population with access to sanitation	Rural 9.48	Urban 47.00	Rural 21.92	Urban 63.00	Rural 32.66	Urban N.A.

Source: Ministry of Rural Development, Ministry of Urban Development, Registrar General of India.

on school sanitation. Under TSC, projects in 540 districts covering 30 States / UTs have so far been sanctioned with an approved outlay of Rs. 5694.44 crore.

The analysis of various social indicators in this chapter brings to focus the challenges that India faces in improving the quality of life of its people. It lags behind many developing countries in attaining the right level of human and social development. The study of development experience of some of the developing countries in Asia and in Latin America shows that even with lower level of economic growth, a country can achieve much higher level of human and social development. The progress of selected developing countries improving their social indicators such as health, education etc. has been documented in chapter-IV and is also seen in the table at Annexure **'J'**.

The emphasis on contribution of human capital to economic development was also supported by the growth experience of the East Asian countries. Their experience demonstrated the important role of human capital in the process of growth. Human capital development as a part of development strategy to tackle the problem of poverty has a strong relationship with the problem of unemployment and this also contributed to the poverty alleviation in Malaysia, Indonesia and South Korea. The study of their policies shows that these countries followed a model in which the expansion of human capabilities reinforced economic growth. They invested in the development of skill of labour and at the same time the absorptive capacity of economy increased to utilize the skilled labour. This resulted in a virtuous spiral of economic growth, human capital development and reduction in poverty.

EDUCATION

In the Indian development strategy, education is one of the thrust areas and the government has taken several policies initiatives to spread literacy and promote education development. The National Policy on Education (NPE) was launched in 1986 and later modified in 1992. The policy aims at:

- Universal access and enrolment.

- Universal retention of children up to 14 years of age, and

- A substantial improvement in the quality of education to enable all children to achieve essential levels of charge.

For providing elementary education to all children, a programme called Sarva Siksha Abhiyan (SSA) was launched in 2001-02. Implemented in partnership with the States, it addresses the needs of 209 million children in the age group of 6-14 years. It covers 9.72 lakh existing primary and upper primary schools and 36.95 lakh teachers. The goals of SSA are:

- All children in school, education guarantee center, alternate school and back-to-school camp by 2005.

- Bridge all gender and social category gaps at the primary stage by 2007 and at elementary education level by 2010.

- Universal retention by 2010

- Focus on elementary education of satisfactory quality with emphasis on education for life.

The National Literacy Mission (NLM) was launched on 5th May, 1998 as a Technology Mission to impart functional literacy to non-literates in the country in the age group of 15-35 years in a time-bound manner. This age-group has been the focus of attention because they are in the productive and reproductive period of life. NLM's objective is to attain a sustainable literacy rate of 75 percent by 2007. The Total Literacy Campaign (TLC) has been the principal strategy of NLM for eradication of illiteracy in the target age-group, and it emphasises that education must play a positive and interventionist role in correcting social and regional imbalance, empowering women, and in securing a rightful place for the disadvantaged and the minorities. The priority areas include free and compulsory elementary education, covering children with special needs, and special focus on the education of SCs/STs and minorities.

Secondary education prepares students in the age group of 14-18 years for entry into higher education and employment. The number of secondary and senior secondary schools increased from 1,07,140 in 1997-98 to 1,45,899 in 2003-04 with a total student enrolment of 35.01 million (Classes IX to XII). There has been an impressive growth in the area of higher education with an increase in annual student enrolment from 7.26 million in 1997-98 to 9.95 million in 2003-04. Enrolment of women students rose from 2.45 million in 1997-98 to 4.03 million in 2004-05, constituting 40.22 percent of the total enrollment. (Please see Annexure **'I'- c&d**)

Gross enrolment ratio (GER) is one of important indicators of progress in education sector. This ratio indicates the proportion of children in the 6-14 age groups who are enrolled in elementary schools. According to Government of India educational statistics 2002–03, there has been significant progress in the ratio of GER between 1992–93 and 2002-03.

Not only has there has been an increase in GER, drop-out rates have also declined. Over the period of 10 years between 1990-91 and 2000-01, the all India drop-out rate for primary schools fell from 41.6 percent in 1991-92 to 39.03 percent in 2001-02. According to economic survey 2005-06, drop-out rate at the primary level further declined to 31.4 percent in 2003–04. As regards GER, it has pointed out that there has been a progressive increase in enrolment in elementary schools since 1950–51. The proportion of children in the age group 6 to 14 years enrolled in elementary schools was only 32.1 percent in 1950-51. This increased to 84.91 percent in 2003-04.

India has also achieved significant progress in literacy rate, which indicates the spread of education in mass. The literacy rate (age 7 and above) at all India level according to Census 1991 was 52.2 percent. The male literacy rate was 64.1 percent whereas the female literacy rate was much lower at 39.3 percent. The literacy rate increased to 64.84 percent in 2001 from 52.2 percent in 1991 at the national level. For males, it increased from 64.1

Table 6.8: Gross Enrolment Ratio Data

Indicator / Year		*1992-93*	*2000-01*	*2002-03*
Gross enrolment ratio in primary education		84.6	95.7	95.4
	Male	95.0	104.9	97.5
	Female	73.5	85.9	93.1
Proportion of children starting Grade 1 who reach Grade 5		55.0	59.3	65.1
	Male	56.2	60.3	64.1
	Female	53.3	58.1	66.3
Adult Literacy rate (7 year and above)		52.2	64.84	
	Male	64.1	75.26	
	Female	39.3	53.67	

Source: Selected Educational Statistics 2002-03, Government of India.

Table 6.9: Comparison of Literacy Status

Developing countries	*Adult Literacy % (15 yrs and above)*		*Youth Literacy % (15-24 yrs)*	
	1990	*2004*	*1990*	*2004*
LDCs	52.4	63.7	66.9	71.9
Arab States	49.8	69.9	66.4	85.3
E Asia/Pacific	79.7	90.7	95	97.8
Lat America	85.6	90.2	93.3	96.7
S Asia	49.1	60.9	62.7	75.1
China	78.3	90.9	95.3	98.9
Sri Lanka	88.7	90.7	95.1	95.6
India	49.3	64.3	64.3	76.4

Source: UNDP HDR 2006.

percent to 75.26 percent and for females from 39.3 percent to 53.67 percent. Higher literacy rate resulted in decline of illiterates from 329 million in 1991 to 304 Million in 2001.

Literacy rates in India have risen sharply from 18.3 percent in 1981 to 64.8 percent in 2001. However, India continues to lag behind several other developing countries in the region such as China. Please see Table 6.9 for a comparison.

Higher attainment in education calls for increasing investment in the sector. Through education, a developing economy harnesses its human resources in which they have comparative advantages. Educated and skilled manpower prepares all segments of population for creatively and constructively participating in nation–building. One of the contributory factors leading to sustained high rates of economic growth in East and South East Asia was their rich human resources in terms of skill and education. The table below compares the investment in education sector (Table 6.10).

India is committed to universalizing the access to basic quality education with greater emphasis on covering all the un-reached segments and social groups, including minorities. This commitment is reflected in a substantial increase in the allocation of funds for elementary education by 56 percent from Rs. 57.5 billion in 2003-04 to Rs. 89.8 billion during 2004-05, which had been further stepped up by 36 percent to Rs 122.4 billion in 2005-06. The levy of an education cess at the rate of 2 percent of major central taxes with the proceeds being paid into a non-lapsable fund (the Prarambhik Shiksha Kosh), is a concrete step towards providing assured funding for primary education. The long-term goal, as spelt out in the National Policy is to raise educational expenditure to 6 percent of gross domestic production. One of the most remarkable developments in policy perspectives on education was the passing of the Constitution 86th Amendment Act 2002, which makes free and compulsory education a fundamental right for all children in the age group of 6 to 14 years.

Table 6.10: Comparison of Investment in Education Sector

Country	*As % of GDP*		*As % of Total Govt Expenditure*	
	1990	*2002-04*	*1990*	*2002-04*
S Korea	3.8	4.6	25.6	16.1
Malaysia	5.1	8	18	28
Thailand	3.1	4.2	20	40
India	3.7	3.3	12.2	10.7

Source: UNDP HDR 2006.

Table 6.11: Rising Schooling in East Asia, 1960-90

	Proportion of the population over 25 years of age with no schooling (percent)	
Indonesia	75.5	32.0
Rep. Of Korea	56.9	11.0
Malaysia	58.5	25.6
The Philippines	33.5	9.1
Thailand	48.1	22.0

Source: Barro Lee 1994.

While India has made considerable progress in education sector, the attainment is much behind the comparable rates of literacy and GER achieved by some of the developing countries in Asia and also by developing countries outside Asia. Please see Table 6.11giving comparative education attainment in East Asia.

The other point of concern is the persistent gender disparity in the GER and the literacy rate, which needs to be removed on priority basis in order to attain a high level of human and social development. Table 6.12 shows the degree of gender disparity, which needs to be urgently addressed in India.

It is encouraging to note that there has been some progress towards gender parity. (Please see various tables at Annexure 'I'). Female literacy has gone up from 39.2 percent in 1991 to 53.67 percent in 2001. The growth rate in female literacy at 14.39 percent has been higher than for males at 11.13 percent. Gender gap in literacy has declined from 24.85% in 1991 to 21.59 percent in 2001. GER at Primary Level is 97.53 for boys and 93.07 for girls in 2002-03. At Elementary Level, the GER for boys is 85.43 and for girls is 79.33. Girl's enrolment to total enrolment has increased at the primary level from 42.6 percent in 1992-93 to 46.83 percent in 2002-03. At the middle school level, there is a significant jump in enrolment from 43.90 percent in 1992-93 to nearly 68.8 percent in 2002-03. At the primary level, the drop out rate among girls has come down from around 45.00 percent in 1992-93 to 34.99 percent in 2002-03 and the gender gap currently has been eliminated. At the elementary level, the drop out rate for girls has comedown from 61.1 percent in 1992-93 to 52.8 percent in 2002-03 and the gender gap is below 1 percent. The dropout rate has comedown by 41.1 percentage points in a single year between 2001-02 and 2002-03 from 39.0 percent to 34.9 percent. During the said period, dropout rate for girls has declined even more than for boys, the reduction being 6.2 percentage points for girls against 2.5 percentage point for boys.In addition to gender-disparity in education, another area of concern is states–disparity in educational attainment. The progress in education sector in Bihar,

Table 6.12: Gender Disparity in Indian Education

Indicator / Year	*1990-91*	*1996-97*	*2000-01*	
Female male ratio in primary education	0.71	0.76	0.78	
Female male ratio in secondary education	0.49	0.57	0.63	
Female male ratio in higher education	0.50	0.56	0.58	
Ratio of literate women to men (7 +)	0.61	NA	0.71	
Share of women in wage employment in the non-agricultural sector (1999-2000)	NA	NA	Rural 15.09	Urban 16.61

Source: Ministry of Human Resource Development and NSSO.

Assam, Uttar Pradesh, Madhya Pradesh, Orissa, Jharkhand, has been very slow as compared with Gujarat, Maharashtra, Tamil Nadu, Karnataka etc. As education is a state subject, primary responsibility for improving the performance in this sector lies with individual states. As we have seen earlier, the countries which succeeded in achieving high educational standards, had also invested a higher percentage of their public expenditure in education sector. The performance of the States in promoting literacy shows a varied pattern (Table 6.13).

India has recognized the importance of augmenting its human resources for economic development and has increased allocation for expenditure in education sector. Allocation for elementary education in the Tenth Five Year Plan period (2002-07) at Rs. 28,750 crore is 75 percent higher than the allocation in the Ninth Plan. Resources for elementary education have been augmented through imposition of the education cess at the rate of 2 percent on direct and indirect central taxes imposed. Budgetary outlay for elementary and adult education more than doubled from Rs. 6,000 crore in 2004-05 to Rs. 12,532 crore in 2005-06.

The NPE 1986 had set a goal of expenditure on education of 6 percent of the GDP. As against this target, the combined total expenditure on education by Central and State Governments was 3.49 percent of GDP in 2004-05 (BE) to Rs. 15.244 crore in 205-06 (BE), with Rs. 12,242 crore for elementary education, Rs. 290 crore for adult education and Rs. 2,712 crore for secondary and higher education.

INFRASTRUCTURE

Speedy provision of quality infrastructure through appropriate policy stimulus constitutes the first and foremost component of the growth challenge. India's growth prospects are intricately intertwined with the rapid development of physical infrastructure such as power, roads, ports, and airports, and efficient delivery of such services. India's economic growth is intertwined with its infrastructure development and there is a strong positive association between the two.

Table 6.13: Regional Dimensions of Literacy in India (%)

State	1991			2001		
	Male	*Female*	*Total*	*Male*	*Female*	*Total*
Andhra Pradesh	55.13	32.72	44.09	70.85	51.17	61.11
Bihar	52.49	22.89	38.48	60.32	33.57	47.53
Kerala	93.62	86.13	89.81	94.20	87.86	90.92
Rajasthan	54.99	20.44	38.55	76.46	44.34	61.03
Madhya Pradesh	58.42	28.85	44.20	76.50	50.35	64.08
Orissa	63.09	34.68	49.09	79.95	50.97	63.61
Tamil Nadu	73.75	51.33	62.66	82.33	64.55	73.47
Uttar Pradesh	55.73	25.31	41.06	70.23	42.97	54.36
All India	64.13	39.29	52.21	76.64	54.16	65.38

Source : *Educational Statistics of India, 2001.*

A rapidly expanding telecom sector and intense competition amongst the various service providers have resulted in improvement in quality of the services and their affordability. Competition and a growing economy will continue to raise the performance bar for the telecom sector in the medium term.

The completion of substantial portions of the Golden Quadrilateral is fuelling demand and facilitating the growth of productivity in the country. The model concession agreement (MCA), which has been finalized for the roads sector is expected to give a further impetus to the timely completion of the road projects. MCs are also being developed in the ports and airports sectors to facilitate Public Private Partnerships (PPPs). The existing infrastructure in ports and their rail connectivity with other regions has not kept pace with economic growth and rise in trade volumes. For example, containers account for over 50 per cent of world merchandise trade; nearly 80 per cent of the world's general cargo volumes are shipped in containers. World containerized trade more than doubled during the decade 1997-2006, to around one billion tones, with a compound annual growth rate (CAGR) of 9 per cent. Containers handled at India's major ports recorded a 14 per cent CAGR during 1992-2005. The National Maritime Development Programme expects the country to deal with 17.98 million TEU (twenty foot equivalent unit) at all its ports by 2013-14, against the current level of 5.5 million TEU. India's share in global containerized traffic is just about 1 per cent. Within India, containerization amounts to 70 per cent of the country's total export volumes, and 40 per cent of imports. Rail-based export-import container traffic is estimated to go up from 9, 94,140 TEU in 2005-06 to 19,61,3000 TEU by 2009-10, or more than double the current levels. Capacities need to be increased rapidly.

The total investment required in infrastructure is enormous. The Committee on infrastructure, headed by the Prime Minister, has estimated the investment requirements as: Rs. 1,72,000 crore in the National Highways sector by 2012; Rs. 40,000 crore for Airports by 2010; and Rs. 50,000 crore for Ports by 2012. A substantial share of this investment is expected to come from the private sector. India has an estimated potential to absorb US$ 150 billion of FDI in the next five years in the infrastructure sector alone. It is important that the India Infrastructure Finance Company Limited (IIFCL), incorporated on January 5, 2006, not only becomes operational but starts lending funds, especially debt of longer term maturity, directly to the eligible projects to supplement other resources from banks and financial institutions from an early date.

INDIA AND THE MDGS

In September 2000, the world's leaders adopted the UN millennium deceleration, committing their nations to global efforts to reduce poverty, to improve health and widen the access to education. The details of the millennium development goals that emerged from the declaration are at Annexure **'K'**. The progress in the achievement of these goals is being monitored through national reports on the progress in various social indicators. India's Country Report 2005 brings to focus the progress made by India in achieving the development goals specified in the MDG. The report also highlights the various tasks that lay ahead to achieve these time-bound goals. The progress made by India towards achieving these goals is at Annexure **'L'**.

In achieving MDG goal number **One** i.e. to halve the proportion of people below poverty line by 2015, India is on track. Incidence of poverty declined from 55 percent in 1973–74 to 26 percent in 1999–2000. In achieving MDG goal **Two**, i.e. universal primary education by 2015, India has to increase the primary school enrolment rate to 100 percent. The gross enrolment ratio in primary schools has remained 100 percent for boys. For Girls 100 percent enrolment is yet to be achieved.

To ensure gender parity under MDG-**Three**, India will have to promote female participation in education to reach parity by 2015. Under MDG –**Four**, child under-five mortality rate has to be reduced by 2/3 between 1990 and 2015. While there has been some progress in reducing under-five mortality rate during 1998–2002, further reduction is required to reach the MDG target. Similarly under MDG-**Five**, India may reduce maternal mortality from 437 deaths in 1991 to 109 by 2015.

It is evident that India has to intensify its efforts to reach MDG targets in health and education sector. As pointed out earlier, several policy initiatives have been under taken by India to reach MDG targets. These initiatives, inter alia, are the passage of National Rural Employment Guarantee Act 2005, National Rural Health Mission and Sarva Siksha Abhiyan etc. In meeting basic needs of the poor, lack of rural infrastructure has acted as a major constraint. The government has launched on a programme for the creation of rural infrastructure called "Bharat Nirman". This programme aims at enlarging the connectivity of rural areas; provide drinking water for all and to provide electricity to all.

ENVIRONMENTAL AND ENERGY ISSUES

Long-term climate changes due to greenhouse gas emissions portend global problems of great magnitude. It is estimated that greenhouse gas emission reductions on the order of 60 to 80 per cent will be needed by 2050 to avoid worse than predicted. Yet, the overriding interest of developing countries will be economic growth and poverty eradication. According to the International Energy Agency, India's carbon dioxide emissions increased by a third between 1992 and 2002, and greenhouse gas emissions are on the rise.

On the other hand, India is an example of a country that is making use of existing incentives for economies to grow along a greener path. For example, it already has 155 registered projects, with another 400 in the pipeline, which range from bio-mass to wind power projects. These are expected to generate about 300 million certified emissions reductions by the end of 2012, each representing a tonne of carbon dioxide equivalent that can be traded on the international carbon market. The Indian example shows that economic growth and environment protection need not be mutually exclusive. It should be noted that 75 percent of emissions is by the West, where the reductions should be the most.

The gases that are warming the earth have built up over hundreds of years. They do not disappear or dissipate easily. Even if the world adopted the most far-reaching plans to combat climate change, most scientists agree that the concentration of greenhouse gases will continue to rise for the next few decades. Global warming is already baked into earth's future. India and China are currently building 650 coal-fired power plants. The combined CO2 emissions of these new plants is five times the total savings of the Kyoto accords – that is, if the Kyoto targets were being adhered to by Western countries, which they are not. Even under the most optimistic scenarios the industrialized world will continue to burn substantial amounts of coal and oil. But even so, the earth would still warm substantially over the next few decades. So in additional to our efforts to prevent and mitigate climate change, we need to employ another strategy – adaptation.

Adaptation programmes could move forward fast. Unlike plans to slow down global warming, which required massive and simultaneous international efforts, adaptation strategies can be pursued by individual countries, states, cities and localities. The challenge of sustainable development requires integration of the quest for economic development with environmental concerns. Traditional energy and resource intensive and waste-generating models of industrialization not only impose a heavy cost on society in terms of pollution and deteriorating quality of life, but also are unsustainable in the medium to long run, particularly with exhaustible natural resources.

The Government has put in place necessary legislative and regulatory measures, both preventive and promotive, for protection, conservation and development of the environment, an effective implementation of which is expected to harmonize the demands of development and environment. Major thrust areas, ongoing and proposed, for abatement of pollution are summarized in the box below.

Environmental concerns gain significance in the light of three aspects that characterise the Indian energy sector – high-energy intensity, low per capita consumption and potential for rapid economic growth. While energy intensity in developed countries is less than one, India has energy intensities greater than one. This means that rate of consumption growth of primary energy in India is higher than the rate of growth of its GDP. Growth in demand for petroleum products over the last 20 years has increased at rates of above 6 per cent which is 4 times the world average.

Table 6.14: *Initiatives to Control Environmental Pollution.*

- Existing policy initiatives to improve environment like the National Conservation Strategy and Policy Statement for Environment and Development, 1992. Policy Statement for Abatement of Pollution, 1992 and National Forest Policy, 1988;
- Stipulation of ambient and industry specific emission and effluent standards;
- Setting up of clean technology mechanisms in polluting industries;
- Setting up of Common Effluent Treatment Plants (CETPs) in industrial estates;
- Establishing waste minimization circles 9WMC) in clusters of small scale industries;
- Implementing recommendations of Charter of Corporate Responsibility for Environmental Protection (CREP) in 17 categories of highly polluting industries;
- Prior environmental clearance of development projects based on impact assessment;
- Implementation of an Eco-mark scheme to encourage production / consumption of environment – friendly product;
- For controlling vehicular pollution, progressive emission norms at the manufacturing stage have been notified, cleaner fuels like unleaded petrol, low sulphur diesel and compressed natural gas (CNG) introduce;
- Promotion of economic instruments to internalize the costs of pollution and fiscal incentives for pollution control equipment, and
- Monitoring of ambient air and water quality, bio-monitoring of rivers / lakes and identification of hazardous wastes streams in various sectors / processes.

New Policy Initiatives :

- Formulation of National Environment Policy;

(Contd.)

(Contd. Table 6.14)

- Setting up of National Clean Development Mechanism (CDM) Authority as per Kyoto Protocol;
- Reengineering of environmental clearance process with a view to bring greater transparency and efficiency in the clearance process;
- Revisiting the Coastal Regulation Zone (CRZ) Notification to enable environmentally sustainable use of coastal resources; and
- Developing a National Chemical Management profile for the country.

India has expressed a strong commitment to pursue energy policies which take due account of environmental considerations. Adopting the recommendation of the expert committee on auto fuel policy, the country has adopted environmentally benign measures with regard to usage and quality of transportation fuels. Lead phasing-out and benzene reduction in gasoline, sulphur reduction and cetane improvement of diesel are amongst the prominent measures that are under implementation/consideration. Such quality upgradation of fuels will call for adopting latest/state-of-the-art technology requiring huge investments by the refineries of the order of US$ 2500 million by way of providing reformulated gasoline producing units, hydro crackers, hydro-treaters, hydro-desulphurisers, etc.

The Kirit Parikh headed Committee Report on an Integrated Energy Policy (2005) presents an integrated view of the projected demand and supply by various ministries of the energy sector. It is truly visionary and makes a wide range of policy proposals towards fulfilment of the county's future energy need. However, the document should have provided strategic planning and clear roadmaps for each sector and for cross cutting issues like R & D and efficiency. The GOI needs to, at a suitable time, prioritise the policies of each sector in an integrated fashion to avoid wastage of resources. The "renewables" vision could have been more focused and wholly based on the country's inherent strengths rather than emphasise on everything. A major issue is financing of the energy infrastructure. This issue reemphasises the need for prioritization and optimization. A focus on scientific and systematic data collection, research and analysis will provide tools to correctly hone policies in all sectors. The promotion of smaller distributed units across the country may lead to better energy availability and security to a larger population base. The section on energy efficiency is pertinent. The country now needs a definite roadmap besides efficiency targets to implement.

The suggestion that India would become energy independent and secure by 2050 is premised on the success of the three-stage thorium-based nuclear programme. The programme's success depends not only on adequate funding but also far greater accountability from the Department of Atomic Energy. Though the draft report plays down the issue of geopolitics and acquiring equity abroad, the analysis within the report clearly brings out dependencies outside the country for the next three decades in all energy scenarios for oil, gas and even coal.

In conclusion, there are several key obstacles in realizing India's quest for stable, secure and sustainable energy supplies at relatively stable prices. While these vary in kind and in degree from one energy source to another, they are essentially two fold in nature: The slow pace of sectoral reforms, internal problems of political/ bureaucratic inertia and entrenched resistance to outward looking liberalized trade and investment policies and; Built-in constraints of geology and geopolitics.

THE GLOBAL COMPACT IN INDIA

The United Nations Global Compact is an initiative to encourage businesses world-wide to adopt sustainable and socially responsible policies, and to report on them. Corporate Social Responsibility (CSR) is a concept that suggests that commercial corporations have a duty of care to the society. It is closely linked with the principles of sustainable development, which says that companies should be obliged to make decisions based not only on financial/economic factors but also on the social, environmental and other consequences of their activities. The Global Compact has two main objectives: mainstream its ten principles in business activities around the world; and catalyze actions in support of UN goals.

All major Indian Industry Associations have expressed full support to CSR and have committed to play a promotional role so as to encourage their members to engage in this initiative. By the end of 2005, there were 124 major Indian companies that were participating in the programme.

7

Addressing the Critique of Globalisation

It is important to keep cognizance of some of the criticism and alternative suggestions in order to make the globalization concept inclusive. Some of these are documented in the following paragraphs. Many are valid issues which have been stressed upon in the various chapters of the book.

In terms of its economic ramifications, globalization essentially means the breakdown of national barriers against trade and finance. Proponents of globalization would like to emphasise that the ongoing process of globalization is unprecedented. However, those who place a stronger emphasis on history argue that globalization has always been an abiding feature of capitalism. After all, colonization of nations was in some ways a globalization process.

As per critics, contrary to what neoliberal protagonists would like the world to believe, the phenomenon of contemporary globalization is neither "natural" nor "autonomous". Instead, it is shaped by complex and dynamic set of interactions between transnational capital and nation states. It is not surprising that globalization is such a divisive issue. Those who stand to gain from the free flow of trade and finance in a borderless world are obviously on one side of the divide, arguing passionately for "more" of the same set of policies. But the labour and popular movements across the world, which have lost a great deal from the opening up of national markets, see things differently. Economic growth has been sluggish; and, whatever growth has occurred has been at the expense of jobs; in other words, "jobless growth". Inequalities, both within and among nations, have risen sharply in the past two decades. This unevenness and asymmetry is best exemplified by the contrast between the mobility of capital vis-à-vis labour. While trillions of dollars move across a seamless world every day, labour mobility is severely restricted, except in the case of niche jobs for highly skilled professional workers in the advanced countries. On the other hand, several countries – notably India and China – have managed to attract sizeable amounts of foreign investment even while pursuing a more restrictive financial regime. Japan, China and South Korea are examples of countries that have managed to perform very well without following the liberal prescription for financial markets.

Neoliberal globalization is not merely an economic project. It has political ambitions as well. Realising that the diversity in economic, social, legal and administrative systems is a hindrance to the free play of markets, the Fund-Bank-WTO triumvirate is attempting "to create a uniform political, administrative and legal system at the global level". Multilateral agencies have taken upon themselves the task of promoting democracy. This project, according to critics, "has become an integral part of the emergent global economic order".

ASSESSMENTS BY UNDP

The UNDP had voiced concerns in its Human Development Report (1999) about the route globalization was taking. Some of these were:

- The new rules of globalization—and the players writing them—focus on integrating global markets, neglecting the needs of people that markets cannot meet. The process is concentrating power and marginalizing the poor, both countries and people.

- The top fifth of the world's people in the richest countries enjoy 82% of the expanding export trade and 68% of foreign direct investment—the bottom fifth, barely more than 1%.

- Today's flow of culture and cultural products is heavily weighted in one direction—from rich countries to poor. The rise of culture as an economic good has added to the identification of culture with commodities that can be sold and traded—crafts, tourism, music, books and films. Although the spread of ideas and images enriches the world, there is a risk of reducing cultural concerns to protecting what can be bought and sold, neglecting community, custom and tradition.

- An example of lack of a level playing field is the passage of the agreement on Trade-Related Aspects of Intellectual Property Rights (TRIPS). Almost all knowledge-based production is now subject to tight intellectual property protection, unified internationally. Further, the TRIPS agreement is unbalanced: it provides an enabling environment for multinationals, tightening their dominant ownership of technology, while impeding and increasing the cost of transfer to developing countries.

- Stronger policies for human development —more investment to equip people for the globally competitive economy, and to participate in the global network society—are needed to promote human development. But they are also needed to make globalization work. Ultimately, people and nations will reject global integration and global interdependence if they do not gain from it and if it increases their vulnerability. Pressures will mount to retreat to isolationism in economic policy, culture and political priorities. To pursue human development, globalization has to mean:

- Ethics—less, not more violation of human rights and disregard of human values.

- Development—less, not more poverty of countries and people.
- Equity—less, not more disparity between and within nations and generations.
- Inclusion—less, not more marginalization and exclusion of countries and people.
- Human security—less, not more vulnerability of countries and people.
- Sustainability—less, not more degradation of the environment.

Not much seems to have changed in the interim, as is exemplified in UNDP's 2006 Human Development Report, Trade on Human Terms: Transforming Trade for Human Development in Asia and the Pacific. In sum it says: Asia and the Pacific have embraced globalization, but globalization cannot embrace the region's poor without determined action on the part of governments. It notes that Asia's opening to the global market has propelled record economic growth and reduced income poverty in much of the region. Its cheap, labour-intensive manufacturing and high-tech goods have made it the factory of the world. East Asia's miracle economies, in particular, have used trade to boost exports and accelerate progress in other areas including education, health and gender equality.

Yet at the same time, trade has exacerbated inequalities, not only between countries but also within national borders. And some of the region's most open economies – particularly the East Asian success stories – are grappling with the challenge of "jobless growth," with job creation lagging far behind workforce expansion. The benefits of free trade have accrued more to highly-paid skilled workers than unskilled workers, while job opportunities and working conditions for women in textiles and clothing in the poorer countries are threatened by competition from China and the demise of global quotas. Overall, trade 'winners' and 'losers' are dependent on factors such as the pre-existing health, education and infrastructure development of a country, which then stimulates more balanced growth. In the miracle economies, for example, past human development achievements had positively influenced their ability to take advantage of trade opportunities.

Some parts of Asia-Pacific, especially the 14 LDCs and the Pacific Island countries, have been severely challenged by the lack of tangible human-development benefits from trade. These countries have been eager globalizers, but face tough conditions for membership of the WTO. Due to the tyranny of averages, the relatively poor performance of Asia's LDCs gets little attention. At the same time, they are being out-competed and overwhelmed by imports from China, while having little success selling their own goods in the region's largest market. The 14 Asia-Pacific LDCs include the SAARC states viz. Afghanistan, Bangladesh, Bhutan, Maldives, Myanmar and Nepal. The report makes eight key recommendations for them, which also are perfectly applicable to the Indian policy maker.

- Invest for competitiveness, including in technical or tertiary education as well as in research and development, especially for agriculture and trade-related infrastructure.

- Adopt strategic trade and industrial policies, by not opening up too early strategic industries and by introducing properly sequenced tariff barriers with a clear timeframe.

- Refocus on agriculture, emphasising investment in rural development, maintaining tariffs on food imports, and ensuring that global trade negotiations agree on special safeguard mechanisms.

- Combat "jobless growth," by recalibrating interest rates; phasing out fiscal incentives that artificially raise the return on capital and result in moves away from labour; and adopting labour-market policies to encourage flexibility and retraining.

- Prepare a new tax regime, ensuring that new taxes are equitable and protect the poor; develop income taxes and curb evasion, while exploring promising new areas such as real estate, capital gains and value-added tax to compensate for revenue losses from trade liberalization.

- Maintain stable exchange rates, providing realistic exchange-rate management that values a currency neither too high nor too low and maintains real stability.

- Persist with multilateralism, for more durable human-development outcomes, building up slower but ultimately more productive relationships under the multilateral global trade regime rather than seeking highly imbalanced bilateral agreements with rich nations

- Promote regional cooperation, strengthening regional trade agreements, pooling of foreign-exchange reserves and development of an Asian bond market.

MULTILATERAL TRADE REGIMES

The considerable, and still growing, degree of global interdependence in contemporary world economic relations provides a strong rationale for a well-structured system of global economic governance. The guiding principle of these arrangements would be to manage the interface between different national systems, rather than reducing national difference and establishing one omnipotent economic and legal structure.

Economic size and natural resource endowments will influence the depth of a country's trade integration, while the pattern of domestic support policies will vary with a country's level of industrial development at any level of economic development, the optimal degree of openness for benefiting a country is likely to differ across different spheres such as trade, investment, finance, labour and technology. For example, countries would be well-advised to postpone capital market integration until they have successfully integrated into other areas, notably trade. Such differences in the optimal degree of openness may extend beyond narrow economic areas to involve equity considerations or the preservation of national culture and national institutions.

In the Sao Paulo Consensus reached at UNCTAD XI in 2004, the international community recognized that "it is particularly important for developing countries, bearing in mind development goals and objectives which all countries take into account, the need for appropriate balance between national policy space and internationals disciplines and commitments." However, multilateral arrangements do not appear to move in that direction.

As per UNCTAD-Trade and Development Report 2006, the current system of global economic governance does not seem to be entirely satisfactory, largely because of the existence of two overlapping asymmetries. First, contrary to the existing institutional structure in international trade, current international monetary and financial arrangements are not organized around a multilateral rules-based system that applies a specific set of core principles to all participants. The asymmetry has particularly strong adverse effects on developing countries because self-centred national monetary and financial policies can have much more damaging effects that those caused by trade and trade-related policies. Second, the multilateral rules and commitments governing international economic relations are, in legal terms, equally binding for all participants, but in economic terms they are biased towards an accommodation of the requirements of the national development strategies of developed countries.

Taken together, these two asymmetries result in multilateral rules and practices that seek to deepen economic integration in a number of areas crucial to the interests and priorities of developed countries, and reduce the degrees of freedom for national economic policies in areas crucial for industrialization and economic catch-up. For instance, the institution that is in charge of promoting exchange-rate stability and of avoiding excessive and prolonged payments disequilibria is unable to impose meaningful disciplines on the policies of those economies that run the most significant external imbalances and whose exchange-rate volatility has the most significant negative impact on the international economy. The IMF's policy oversight is confined primarily to its poorest members, who need to draw on its resources because of their lack of access to private sources of finance and, occasionally, to emerging-market economies experiencing currency and financial crises.

The lack of a functioning financial framework in a globalized economy requires a new and multilateral approach to the management of the most important international price – the exchange rate. A new or reformed institution that promotes a system of stable exchange rates to ensure a predictable trading environment would need to provide more symmetrical treatment to all member countries. The main objective of such an institution would be the prevention of systemic financial crises based on a close monitoring of trade imbalances and global exchange-rate misalignments in both surplus and deficit countries.

The scope of market access and the volume of trade generated by the international trade regime are poor measures of how well it functions. As the preamble to the WTO agreement emphasizes, trade is useful only to the extent that it serves broader social and development goals. Developing countries should not be concerned with increasing their access to foreign markets at the cost of jeopardizing or overlooking more fundamental development challenges at home. Instead of asking what kind of multilateral trading system maximizes foreign trade and investment opportunities, analysts should ask what kind of multilateral system best enables all countries to pursue their own values and development objectives.

There is no single recipe for economic growth. Although market incentives, clear property rights, competition and macroeconomic stability are universal requirements, these can and have been embodied in diverse institutional forms. Rich and poor nations also have different needs for environmental standards and patent protection. Poor countries need space to follow development policies that rich countries no longer require. When countries use the trade system to impose their institutional preferences on others, it erodes the system's legitimacy and efficacy.

Developing nations complain that trade laws are too intrusive and leave little room for development-friendly policies. WTO advocates reply that its rules provide useful discipline to rein in harmful policies that would otherwise end up wasting resources and hampering development. One way to cut through this impasse is to accept that countries can uphold national standards and policies in these areas by withholding market access or suspending WTO obligations if trade undermines domestic practices that have broad popular support.

Industrial country governments, which hold the keys to the most important markets, have applied these measures more often and with a greater impact on international trade. Trade-related environmental measures have sometimes been used as a form of trade protectionism, choking off markets to products from countries with lower or merely different environmental standards. Producers in developing countries often find it difficult or impossible to meet these environmental standards.

Environmental control standards can affect trade patterns by raising production costs, if higher costs reduce a country's trade competitiveness. But this does not usually happen, especially since environmental control costs are an insignificant part of production costs. To encourage environment-friendly economic activities, governments can provide direct or indirect payments to producers who meet environmental standards and government agencies can use their purchasing power to support environment-friendly products.

Each country should be free to manage its domestic environmental problems consistent with its human development priorities. Trade measures designed to protect a country's consumers and its national environment from hazardous products are a legitimate part of its human development strategy. But trade measures designed to coerce the harmonization of domestic environmental standards by another country are fundamentally protectionist. A 'way forward' recommended by an independent UNDP study very succinctly captures the required ethos of multilateral trade regimes:

- Trade policy should allow countries to pursue locally appropriate solutions to their domestic environmental challenges without fear of facing trade sanctions by countries with different environmental priorities. This flexibility should include the ability to impose import restrictions to protect against health and environmental risks associated with specific products.

- The evolving relationship between global trade rules and multilateral environmental agreements should respect the principle of common but differentiated responsibilities. Domestic environmental standards aimed at achieving global environmental objectives must take into account differences between countries in economic development levels and financial and technical capacity.

- Efforts to liberalize trade in environmental goods and services should help identify products and sectors that will open new opportunities for developing country exporters, rather than constructing new conditions for market access.

- Developing country policy-makers and civil society should participate fully and effectively in assessing the potential environmental and development impact of any new trade rules negotiated.

- Negotiations on environment-related issues of agricultural reform and intellectual property rights reform should take into account the human development dimension. Initiative in this area should allow developing countries to retain trade policies that support food security and rural livelihoods and ensure respect for traditional knowledge.

THE CONCEPTUAL CRITIQUE

According to critics, the inhabitants of the 'Davos World' conceive of globalization as a very positive force both economically and culturally, in that the predicted economic growth and development resulting from a globalized world will also bring forth a modernized society that will enjoy a higher quality of life. The opposite view is that globalization undermines local culture and does not allow for personal autonomy. There is a lack of control over the process of globalization, especially on the part of ordinary people in developing countries. Developing countries' elites tend to maintain their connection to the global economic and cultural elite, thus reproducing the pathologies of inequality and poverty that are still seen in the developing world and are arguably exacerbated by the globalization process. A globalization 'from below' is the overall thematic nature of this alternate view.

Some criticize that a deeper examination of the development process is necessary for people to regain control of their globalized lives "from below" in a mass movement sense. Without that knowledge, a "global fatalism" sets in and forces not necessarily in their best interests remain privileged in their activities. Globalization becomes synonymous with neoliberal and economic rationalist theories, and in the end an utterly economic zeitgeist. Modern consumer demand power can be construed as an immediacy of desire in which the producer manipulates the consumer by adjusting their behavior to accommodate the new charming product. Therefore, it calls for education from below, with mass preferences playing a much larger role in educational decisions in order to avoid fatalism, as opposed to the highly technocratic perceived needs of the globalized world. Education should serve to better the quality of one's internal life, as opposed to enriching others' treasure.

One line of criticism underlines that underdevelopment is caused precisely by the incorporation of peripheral economies into the world capitalist system that has been dominated by the developed North, particularly the United States. To equate democratization with empowerment and emancipation is to ignore the ways in which democratization may not represent true self-determination. After all, corporate discussions about democracy have little to do with popular power. "Telecolonialism" is identified as a modern imperial frontier by which imperial powers maintain control over the developing world through technological hegemony. Continuing on this theme of threatened cultural annihilation, while the globalizing Western culture allows one to understand everything in terms of its practical ontology and metaphysics; it also constitutes a trace of a world that is not explicated. Every culture, even if it is framed in the modernizing notion of self-creation, elicits in the articulation of the self-creation a world that cannot be pointed to or signified. The contention is that every signification may cover a domain of presumed objectivities, yet at the same time such signification comprises a trace of a lived awareness of the universe.

Globalization continues to establish objectives that reflect primarily the interests of developed countries, while transnational capitalism overwhelms national economies. Critics are disturbed by the metric of globalization and its purported advances in political and economic freedom. However valuable these religious and moral bases of freedom may be, they must be replaced by more universal, historical and human categories. Human rights can supply this new basis; they constitute the most important expression of the contemporary world in the quest for a fundamental philosophical, axiological, and juridical basis for liberty and human dignity. The implication is that human rights can stand apart as a standard; and the challenge is to present this standard as being exogenous to other ideologies. There is a need to consider an expanded view of nationhood so that the multiplicity of existence in most developing countries, especially erstwhile colonised states, is taken in to account. In fact, it is this multiplicity which spans race and ethnicity, colonial and economic experiences "that binds the people together".

Though lacking quantitative data to back up claims or appeals to empirical political theory, overall the views serve as a cogent critique of globalization's themes. There is generally a return to the primacy of the individual and the individual's culture in controlling one's destiny, especially in the areas of the developing world that are vulnerable to the rising tide of globalization. The common refrain is that globalization does not, in the often used metaphor, raise all individual and cultural boats equally, and globalization must be monitored carefully in this regard. This is a valid point as much for the individual as for nations.

INDIA: THE ROAD AHEAD

India's strong and ancient civilisational foundation will not allow the indigenous cultural boat to be rocked around too much. Besides other components of soft power, the success of Yoga, a unique brand of spirituality, Bollywood and Indian TV serials all over the world are indicators of inherent strength and potential. However, this does require nurturing and a long-term vision to be employed as a strategic tool. India may in the long run prove to be a clearly distinct model of growth, where the best opportunities are availed of without compromising on identity or sovereignty.

Coming to reforms per se, the Indian Finance Minister recently said that good economics works for different times, and it falls upon good politics to moderate when any section of society gets left behind. As a corollary, in an age of coalition politics and rising regional aspirations, the success of economic reforms would require the centre to ensure calibrated political catalyst to channel voter pressure on state govts toward changes that may have short-term transition costs, but will ultimately improve governance and public services. A key issue is functional transparency, and the central govt must support all efforts towards this. The Right to Information Act (RTI) is a step in the right direction. Professional collection, analysis and dissemination of data of programme implementation would go a long way in providing accountability and effective monitoring. Efficient management and delivery of the social sector programmes necessitate adequate capacity building at all levels, decentralization of implementation and transparency in delivery and accountability of the agencies involved. Evaluation studies repeatedly indicate that only those programmes tend to succeed which have elements of the above critical success parameters.

With a promising economic outlook, the nation could ill afford to falter in its fiscal resolve without adverse consequences. The journey for sustained economic growth and stability is a long one and quick fix solutions for higher fiscal deficit to temporarily prop up growth through expansionary policies, albeit in increasing productive capacity, would prove to be counterproductive. Instead, there is much scope for better productivity in expenditure and greater growth dividend through deepening the reform process that could harness higher savings and investment.

India's greatest strength lies in its democratic polity, which with time will mature and demand genuine empowerment. One key enabler would be the genuine free flow of information through ever-growing links such as telephones, media, internet etc. As such, the centre is fully aware of the myriad of issues involved in propelling India to an equitable society; what is required is sustaining a dialogue to achieve a broader consensus on, among other things, the mechanics of **how to**:-

- Be a balanced and an egalitarian economic powerhouse (Superpower?); for which a pre-requisite is sustained high levels of economic growth, and therefore, more reforms, sound economic policies and fiscal prudence.

- Improve governance and bring in pragmatic transparency; including quality of implementation of various programmes, and efficiency and accountability of the public distribution system.

- Address internal vulnerabilities and fault lines, including the growing divide between haves and have-nots without curbing private entrepreneurship which is a main driver of the current Indian growth.

- Improve and drastically upgrade general literacy levels, public health and the country's infrastructure to power the engine of growth.

- Develop and project Indian soft power with a distinct identity, divorced from western value projections.

- Possess full spectrum military capability to safeguard interests around the country and the Indian Ocean Region.

- Achieve consistency of will and intent to shape India's future. This would necessitate an increasing focus on self-reliance, as also regional cooperation and multilateralism in all components of national security.

Commonly Used Abbreviations/ Acronyms

BPO	:	Business Processing Outsourcing
DAC	:	Development Assistance Committee
FDI	:	Foreign Direct Investment
FFEs	:	Foreign Funded Enterprises
FIIs	:	Foreign Institutional Investors
GATS	:	General Agreement on Trade in Services
GDRs	:	Global Depository Receipts
GOI	:	Govt of India
HIPC	:	Highly Indebted Poor Countries
ICT	:	Information and Communication Technology
ITES	:	Information Technology Enabled Services
LDCs	:	Least Developed Countries
MDGs	:	Millennium Development Goals
MNC	:	Multinational Corporation
MFN	:	Most Favoured Nation
NIEs	:	Newly Industrialised Economics
ODA	:	Official Development Assistance
SAFTA	:	South Asian Free Trade Area
SAARC	:	South Asian Association for Regional Cooperation

References

CHAPTER I

- D Greenway (ED 1987) "Economics Development and International Trade" Macmillan, London.
- WH Gruber and R Vernon (1970) "The Technology factor in a World Trade Matrix In R Varnon (ed); The Technology Factor in International Trade" Columbia University Press, New York.
- R Paul Krugman (1990) "Rethinking International Trade" The MIT Press, Cambridge.
- Gote Hansoon (ED 1993) "Trade, Growth and Development" Routelage, London and New York.
- Krueger Anne and W Jones Ronald (ED 1990) "The Political Economy of International Trade Basic Blackwell" Cambridge, Massachusetts,USA.
- IB Kravis (1970) Article "Trade as a handmaiden of growth" Economic Journal December 1970.
- WA Lewis (1980) Article "The slowing down of engine of growth "American Economic Review 70-5-564.
- IMD Little (1982) "Economic Development: Theory, Policies and International Relations" Basic Books, New York.
- G Myrdal (1962) "Economics Theory and Underdeveloped Regions" Duckworth , London.
- R Nurkse (1962) "Pattern of Trade and Development" Basil Blackwell, Oxford.
- R Prebisch (1950) "The Economics Development of Latin American and its Principal Problems" United Nation, New York.

- HB Chenery and H Syrquin (1975) "Pattern of Development 1950-75 "Oxford University Press , London.
- J Viner (1952) "International Trade and Economics Development " Glenoe Free Press.
- J Riedel (1984) "Trade as the engine of growth in Developing countries" Economic Journal March 1984.
- AP Thirlwall (1989) Article "Growth and Development "Macmillan Education, London.
- GK Helleiner "International Trade and Economic Development".
- H Myint (1964) "The Economics of Developing Countries" Hutchinson, London.
- AO Hirscman (1958) "The Strategy of Economic Development" Yale University Press, New Haven.
- BE LA Balassa "The Newly Industrializing countries in the World Economy "Pergmon Press, New York 1981.
- Colin Clark "The conditions of Economic Progress "Macmillan-London, London 1951.
- World Bank for Reconstruction and Development "World Development Report 1975-93".
- Anne O Krueger "Trade and Employment in Developing Countries "University of Chicago Press, Chicago 1981.
- Paul Bairoch "The Economic Development of the Third World since 1900" University of California Press 1975.
- G Lloyd Reynold "The Three Worlds of Economics" Yale University Press, New Haven 1971.
- ED Gustav Ranis"Comparative Development Perspectives" Westview Press 1983.
- B Hollis Chenery "Structural Change and Development Policy" Oxford University Press 1979, New York.
- W Hans Singer and A Javeda Ansari" Rich and Poor countries" UNWIN- Hyman, London 1988.
- UNCTAD" Trade and Development Report 1984-94.
- D Morawetz "Twenty five years of Economic Development-1959-1975" World book 1977, Washington DC.
- AO Hirschmen" The Strategy of Economics Development "Yale University Press, University Press 1958, New Haven.

- WA Lewis" Economics Development with unlimited supplies of labour" Manchester School Vol. 22 N.2 (1954).
- IMF" Economic Outlook, 1984-1995.
- United Nations "World Economics Survey- 1990, 1991, 1992, 1993".
- Anne Krueger "Trade and Employment in Developing Countries " University of Chicago Press, Chicago.
- Bairoch Paul (1975)" The Economic Development of the Third World since 1900 " University of California Press.
- The World Bank "World Development Report (1975-1993)" Oxford University, New York.
- UNCTAD "Document N.TD/281. Economic Cooperation among Developing countries: Review of activities in the major performance areas and proposals for the future work".
- UNCTAD – August1990 "Discussion papers on protection pressures in the 1990 and the coherence of North-South Trade Policies.
- R Malloch Theodre "Isuue in International Trade and Development Policy".
- Ohlin Havrylyshyn (1984) "The Issue of South – South Trade in Historical and Global Perspective in Ohlin Havrylyshyn (Ed) – South- South and South- North Trade".
- Stewart Frances "North-South and South-South "Macmillan, London.
- Steen Folke, Niels Fold, Thyge Eneroldsen-1993 "South-South Trade and Development" St Martin's Press, London.
- Institute of Developing Economies, Tokyo "Global adjustment and the future of Asian Pacific Community".
- South East Asian Studies. Vol.28- 4th March, 1991 "ASEAN – Prospects for NIC Status".
- T.Shin(1989)"The pacific Basin Community and Korean – Article Economy" in Trends of Economic Development in East Asia by W Clenner- Springer- Vering- Berlin-1989.
- Asia Development Bank Report (1992).UNCTAD" Revitalising Development Growth and International Trade" A Report to UNCTAD-VIII.

- World Bank" Trade and Development Report 1975-93. IMF-World Economy Outlook 1989-93"
- UNCTAD " Trade and Development Report 1987-93"
- WR Cline and Sydney Wentraub" Economic Stabilization in Developing Countries.
- Gustav Ranis and TR Schultz (Ed) " The State of Development Economics".
- GK Helleiner" Developing Countries in the New Global Economy".
- Jalan Bimal (1991) "India's Economic Crisis – The way ahead" Oxford University Press, New Delhi.
- Wolf Martin (1992) "India's Exports" A World Bank Publication.
- Krishnalekha Sood (1989) "Trade and Economic Development- India, Pakistan and Bangladesh" Sage Publications, New Delhi.
- Economic survey, Ministry of Finance (1989-93)
- The World Bank "World Development Report-1989-93"
- The World Bank "World Bank Report-1989-93"
- Asian Development Bank Report (1992-93)
- "The Challenge to the South"- The Reports of the South Commission, Oxford University Press, Bombay, Calcutta, Madras.

CHAPTER II

- Storm Servaas, Naastepad C.W.M. (2001 ed), "Globalization and Economic Development", Edward Elgar Publishing – USA.
- Chang Ha-Joon, "Globalization, Economic Development and the Role of the State", Zed Books Ltd. – London and New York.
- Mcgreed Anthony and Held David (2000), "The Global Transformation Reader", Polity Press – USA.
- Yusuf Shahid, Wu Weiping and Evenett Simon (2000 Ed), "Local Dynamics in an Era of Globalization: 21st Century Catalysts for Development", Oxford University Press.

- Das K.Dilip (2004), "The Economic Dimensions of Globalization", Palgrave & Macmillan.
- Aseem Prakash and Jefrey A.Hart (1999 ed), "Responding to Globalization", Routledge press – New York.
- Nayar Baldev Raj (2005), "The Geo-Politics of Globalization", Oxford University Press.
- Bhagwati Jagdish (2004), "In Defense of Globalization", Oxford University Press.
- World Trade Organization (2004), "World Trade Report – 2004: Exploring the Linkage between the Domestic Policy Environment and International Trade", WTO.
- Desai Y.B., "Thoughts on the New Global Economy", Tata McGraw- Hill Publishing Company Ltd. New Delhi.
- Adhikari Ramesh and Athukorala Prema-Chandra (2002 Ed), "Developing Countries in the World Trading System: The Uruguay Round and Beyond", Edward Elgar Publishing.
- Michie Jonathan (2003), "The Hand Book of Globalization" Edward Elgar – UK.
- Flexmoses Edoho (1997 Ed), "Globalization and the New World", Praeger Publishers Westport.
- James H. Mittelman (1997 Ed), "Globalization: Critical Reflections", Lynne Rienner Publishers – London.
- Jonathan Mischie, John Gieve Smith (1998 Ed), "Globalization: Growth and Governance", Oxford University Press – London.
- Charles E. Morrison, Hadi Soesastro (1998 Ed), "Domestic Adjustments to Globalization", Japan Centre for International Exchange, Tokyo, New York.
- Dean Baker, Gerald Epstein, Rolurt Pollin (1998 Ed), "Globalization and Progressive Economic Policy", Cambridge University Press.
- Peter Dicken (1998), "Global Shift: Transforming the World Economy", The Guilford Press – New Delhi.
- Horst Siebert (1999), "The World Economy", Routledge – London.
- D. Achi Kgi (1999 Ed), "Innovation Policy in the Global Economy", Cambridge University Press.

- John H. Dunning, Khabil A Hamdani (1997), "The New Globalism and Developing Countries" UN University Press.
- Nagrie Woods (2000 Ed), "The Political Economy of Globalization", Macmillan Press Ltd. London.
- Vincent Cavle (1999), "Globalization and Global Governance", The Royal Institute Of International Affairs.
- Ulrich Hiemenz (1999 Ed), "Growth and Competition in the New Global Economy", OECD 1999.
- John-Razin, Efraim Sadka (1999), "Economics of Globalization: Policy Perspectives from Public Economics", Cambridge University Press – New York.
- Jonathan Michie, Gohn Grieve Smith (1998), "Globalization and Technology", Oxford University Press – New York.
- Jan Knippers Black(1999), "Development in Theory and Practice" West View Press.
- Mats Lundale, Denno J. Ndulu (1996 Ed), "New Directions in Development Economics", Landa Routeleoge – London.
- George Macesich (1997), "World Economy at the Crossroads", Praeger Press – Westport, Connecticut, London.
- Akhtar Hussain and Anis Chowdhary (1998), "Open Economy: Macro Economies for Developing Countries", Edward Elgar Pub Ltd.
- H.W. Arndt and Hal Hill (1999 Ed), "Economic Crisis", Institute of Southeast Asian Studies.
- Shahid Yusuf, Weiping Wu, and Simon Everett (2000 Ed), "Local Dynamics in an Era of Globalization", Oxford University Press.
- Ulrich Hiemenz (1999 Ed), "Growth and Competition in the New Global Economy", OECD – 1999.
- C.Col. Clough, James Manor (1991), "State or Market", Clarendon Press – Oxford.
- Yujiro Hayami (1997), "Development Economics", Clarendon Press – Oxford.
- Malcolm Ruther Rofd (1994), "Institutions in Economics", Cambridge University Press.

- The World Bank (1999), "Annual World Conference on Development Economics", The World Bank.
- World Trade Organization, "WTO Report: 2000, 2001, 2002, 2003, 2004, 2005, 2006", WTO.
- UNCTAD, "World Investment Report: 1999, 2000, 2001, 2002, 2003, 2004, 2005", United Nations.
- The World Bank, "Global Economic Prospects and the Developing Countries: 2000, 2001, 2002, 2003, 2004, 2005, 2006", World Bank.
- Johanns Dragsback Schmidt and Jacque Hersh (2000 Ed), "Globalization and Social Change", Routeledge Press.
- Isabelle Grunberg (2000 Ed), "Globalization: The UN Development Dialogue", UN University Press.
- Zdenek Drebek (2001 Ed), "Globalization under Threat", Edward Elgar Publishing Ltd.
- Lioyd P.J. (2000), "International Trade Opening and the Formation of Global Economy", Edward Elgar Publishing Ltd.
- Mirngman Alian and Boyd Gavin (2001 Ed), "The WTO in the New Global Economy – 2001", Edward Elgar Publishing Ltd.

CHAPTER III

- Jha Veena (2006) "India & the Doha Work Programme": Opportunities and Challenges, a Co-Publication of UNCTAD and Macmillan India Ltd.
- UNCTAD (2005), "Trade and Development Report, 2005", United Nations Publication.
- UNCTAD (2006), "The Least Developed Countries Report – 2006", United Nations Publication.
- Storm Servaas, Naastepad C.W.M. (2001 Ed), "Globalization and Economic Development", Edward Elgar Publishing – USA.
- Sharma Kishor (2003 ed), "Trade Policy, Growth and Poverty in Asian Developing Countries", Routledge Press.
- Tseng Wanda (2003 ed), "China Competing in the Global Economy", International Monitory Fund.

- Sally Razeen and Sen Rahul (2005), "Asean Economic Bulletin: Revisiting Trade Policies in Southeast Asia Vol.22", ASEAN.
- WTO (2005), "Ministerial Conference Sixth Session Hong Kong, 13-18 Dec 2005", WTO.
- Chirathivat Suthipand and Montreevat Sakulrat (2004), "Asean Economic Bulletin: Thailand:-Economic Challenges and the Road Ahead. Vol.21", ASEAN.
- Economic and Social Commission for Asia and the Pacific, "Economic and Social Survey Of Asia and the Pacific – 2001, 2002, 2003, 2004, 2005 and 2006." United Nations ESCAP.
- The World Bank (2003, 2004, 2005, 2006), "Global Development Finance: Harnessing Cyclical Gains for Development", The World Bank.
- UNCTAD, "The Least Developed Countries Report – 2000, 2001, 2002, 2003, 2004, 2005 and 2006", United Nations.
- UNCTAD, "Trade and Development Report – 2000, 2001, 2002, 2003, 2004, 2005 and 2006", United Nations.
- The World Bank, "World Development Report – 2000, 2001, 2002, 2003, 2004 and 2005", World Bank and Oxford University Press.
- Govt of India –UNCTAD- DFID project (2005), "Stakeholders speak on India's negotiating options at the WTO", Govt of India –UNCTAD- DFID.
- The World Bank, "Global Economic Prospects: 2000, 2001, 2002, 2003, 2004, 2005 and 2006", World Bank – Washington.
- The World Bank, "World Development Indicators - 2000, 2001, 2002, 2003, 2004, 2005 and 2006", World Bank.
- UNCTAD, "World Investment Report: 2000, 2001, 2002, 2003, 2004, 2005 and 2006", United Nations.
- World Trade Organization, "World Trade Report –2004, 2005 and 2006", WTO.
- Morrison Charles E. And Soesastro Hadi (1998), "Domestic Adjustments to Globalization", Japan Center for International Exchange – Tokyo and New York.

- Adhikari Ramesh and Athukorala Prema-Chandra (2002 Ed), "Developing Countries in the World Trading System: The Uruguay Round and Beyond", Edward Elgar Publishing.
- Gangopadhyay Partha and Chatterji Manas (2005), "Economic Globalization in Asia", Ashgate Publishing Co., USA.
- Aseem Prakash and Jefrery A. Hart (1999 Ed), "Responding to Globalization", Routledge – New York.
- World Trade Organization, "WTO Report: 2000, 2001, 2002, 2003, 2004, 2005, 2006", WTO.
- United Nations, "Economic and Social Survey of Asia and the Pacific: 2000, 2001, 2002, 2003, 2004 and 2005", United Nations.
- UNCTAD, "World Investment Report: 1999, 2000, 2001, 2002, 2003, 2004, 2005", United Nations.
- UNCTAD, "Trade and Development Report: 2000, 2001, 2002, 2003, 2004, 2005", United Nations.
- The World Bank, "Global Economic Prospects and the Developing Countries: 2000, 2001, 2002, 2003, 2004, 2005, 2006", World Bank.
- Indian Council for Research on International Economic Relations, "Trade Liberalization and Food Security: Challenges to Indian Policy Makers-2000", ICRIER.
- Chanda Rupa, "Movement of Natural Persons and Trade in Services: Liberalizing Temporary Movement of Labour under the GATS: Working Paper No.51 Of 1999" ICRIER.
- Mukherjee Arpita, "Distribution Services: India and the GATS 2000 Negotiations: Working Paper No.80 of 2002" ICRIER.
- Chanda Rupa (2002), "Globalization of Services", Oxford University Press – New Delhi.
- Chandra Prema, Prasada D.S. and Shepherd W. (2002 Ed), "The Asian Economies in the Twentieth Century", Edward Elgar Publishing Ltd.
- Dunning H. John, Hamdani A. Khabil (1997), "The New Globalism and Developing Countries", UN University Press.
- Sinha Kamala (1999 Ed), "Globalization and Developing Countries", The New Age International Publishers.

- Kagami Mitsuhiro, Humphiery John And Piore Michael, "Learning Liberalization and Economic Adjustment", Institute of Developing Economies - Tokyo.
- Yusuf Shahid, Wu Weiping and Evenett Simon (2000 Ed), "Local Dynamics in An Era Of Globalization", Oxford University Press.
- The World Bank (1993), "The East Asian Miracle", The World Bank.
- Choudhary Anish and Islam Ineytal (1997 Ed), "Asia Pacific Economic Survey", Routeledge Press - Prajeri.
- Roy Chulpeper, Berry Alberty, Frances Stewart (1997), "Global Development Fifty Years after Bretten Woods", Macmillan Press Ltd, - London.
- Akyuz Yilmaz (1998 Ed), "East Asian Development", New Perspective Frank Cass Newbury House 900 Eastern Avenue, London IG2 7HH, UK.
- Martin Kurt (1991 Ed), "Strategies of Economic Development", Macmillan Academic and Professional Ltd.
- Renee Prendergast and Frances Steward (1994), "Market Forces and World Development", The Macmillan Press Ltd.
- Das Bhagirath Lal (1999), "The World Trade Organization: A Guide to the Framework for International Trade", Zed Books Ltd. – London.

CHAPTER IV

- Soz Saifuddin, Sahni S.K., Srivastava R.N. (2004 ed), "Towards South Asian Economic Integration and Unity", Foundation for Peace and Sustainable Development.
- SAARC Secretariat (2006),. "SAARC: Regional Poverty Profile – 2005", SAARC Secretariat.
- Jha Raghvender (2005 Ed), "Economic Growth, Economic Performance and Welfare in South Asia", Palgrave Macmillan.
- Mahmud Wahiduddin (2001 Ed), "Adjustment and Beyond: The Reform Experience in South Asia ", Palgrave Houndmills IEA Conference Vol.128.

- Babu R.Ramesh (1998 Ed), "Globalization and the South Asian State", South Asian Publishers Pvt Ltd. New Delhi.
- Ghosh R.N., Melotte Y.M. And Siddique M.A.B. (1996 Ed), "Economic Development and Change: South Asia and the Third World", New Age International Publishers.
- Williamson John (2001), "Financing for Development – The Implications of the Zedillo Report For South Asia", South Asia Network of Economic Research Institutes – New Delhi.
- RIS (2003), "Globalization and the Non-Aligned Movement: An Economic Agenda for Action", RIS for the Non Aligned and Other Developing Countries- New Delhi.
- Hossain Moazzem, Islam Iyanatul and Kibria Reza "South Asian Economic Development: Transformation, Opportunities and Challenges", Routledge Press.
- Karmacharya K. Binod (2001), "South Asia Economic Journal: Article: - Economic Reforms in Nepal and their Implications for Trade, Economic Growth, Inequality and Poverty", Sage Publications New Delhi and London.
- Srinivasan T.N. (2002 Ed), "Trade, Finance and Investment in South Asia", Social Science Press New Delhi.
- The World Bank (2002), "Poverty and Vulnerability in South Asia" World Bank.
- Asian Development Bank, "Asian Development Outlook: 1999, 2000, 2001, 2002, 2003, 2004, 2005 and 2006", ADB.
- United Nations, "Economic and Social Survey of Asia and the Pacific: 2000, 2001, 2002, 2003, 2004 and 2005", United Nations.
- United Nations Industrial Development Organization, "Industrial Development Report: 2002-03", United Nations.
- Research and Information System for the Non-Aligned and Other Developing Countries, "South Asia Development and Cooperation Report: 2001, 2002, 2004", RIS.
- Indian Council for Research on International Economic Relations, "Emerging Issues in Trade and Technology: Implications for South Asia- 2002", ICRIER.
- Indian Council for Research on International Economic Relations, "Trade Liberalization and Food Security: Challenges to Indian Policy Makers-2000", ICRIER.

- South Asia Network of Economic Research Institutes: Financing For Development, "The Implications of the Zedillo Report for South Asia – 2001", SANERI.
- Adhikari Ramesh, Chandra Prema Athukorala (2002 Ed), "Developing Countries in the World Trading System", Edward Elgar Publishing Limited U.K.
- Chandra Prema Athukorala (Ed), "The Economic Development of South Asia", Edward Elgar Publishing Limited U.K.
- Article by Karmacharya K. Binod, "Economic Reforms in Nepal and Their Implications for Trade, Economic Growth Inequality and Poverty", South Asia Economic Journal (Jan-June 2001).
- Regional Conference on Globalization and Agriculture: Challenges for South Asia – 4.5 December 2002, India Habitat Centre, New Delhi, Market Access in Agriculture in WTO Negotiations by Ministry Of Commerce and Consumer Affairs.
- Vanaik Achin (2004 Ed), "Globalization and South Asia", Manohar Publications.

CHAPTER V

- Independent South Asian Commission on Poverty Alleviation (SAARC-2003), "Our Future Our Responsibility", SAARC Secretariat.
- The World Bank, "World Development Report – 2000, 2001, 2002, 2003, 2004, 2005 and 2006", Oxford University press – New York.
- UNDP, "Human Development Report – 2000, 2001, 2002, 2003, 2004, 2005 and 2006", Palgrave Macmillan.
- SAARC Secretariat (2006), "SAARC: Regional Poverty Profile – 2005", SAARC Secretariat.
- UNCTAD, "The Least Developed Countries Report – 2000, 2001, 2002, 2003, 2004, 2005 and 2006", United Nations publication.
- UNDP (2005), "Voices of the Least Developed Countries of Asia and the Pacific", Elsevier.

- Chirathivat Suthipand and Montreevat Sakulrat (2004), "Asean Economic Bulletin: Thailand:-Economic Challenges and the Road Ahead. Vol.21", ASEAN.
- Jha Raghvender (2005 Ed), "Economic Growth, Economic Performance and Welfare in South Asia", Palgrave Macmillan.
- Mahmud Wahiduddin (2001 Ed), "Adjustment and Beyond: The Reform Experience in South Asia ", Palgrave Houndmills IEA Conference Vol.128.
- Kohli Atul, Moon Chung-In and Sorense George, "States, Markets, and Just Growth: Development in the Twenty – First Century", United Nations University Press.
- Sharma Kishor (2003 Ed), "Trade Policy, Growth and Poverty in Asian Developing Countries", Routledge Press.
- World Bank & IMF (2005), "Global Monitoring Report 2005", World Bank.
- Bhalla S Surjit, Imagine There's No Country: Poverty, Inequality and Growth in The Era of Globalization", Penguin Books – New York.
- Sach D Jeffrey (2005), "The End of Poverty", Penguin Press - New York.
- Haq Ul Mahbub (2003), "Human Development in South Asia 2003", Human Development Centre.
- Mehrotra Santosh and Jolly Richard (Ed), "Development with A Human Face: Experiences in Social Achievement and Economic Growth", Clarendon Press – Oxford.
- Economic and Social Commission for Asia and the Pacific, "Economic and Social Survey Of Asia and the Pacific – 2000, 2001, 2002, 2003, 2004, 2005 and 2006", United Nations ESCAP.
- The World Bank (2004), "Global Development Finance: Harnessing Cyclical Gains for Development", World Bank.
- Ministry Of Statistics and Programme Implementation CSO (2005), "Millennium Development Goals India Country Report – 2005", Government of India.
- Ministry of Statistics and Programme Implementation CSO (2005), "SAARC Social Charter India Country Report", Government of India.

- United Nations (2005), "Report on the World Social Situations 2005: The Inequality Predicament", United Nations – New York.
- Fields Gray S. and Pfeffermann Guy (2003 Ed), "Pathways Out of Poverty: Private Firms and Economic Mobility in Developing Countries", Kluwer Academic Publishers.
- Adams F.Gerard and James E. William (1996), "Public Policies in East Asian Development: Facing New Challenges" Praeger – Westport, Connecticut London.
- UNDP (2003), "Making Global Trade Work for People", Earthscan Publication – London, Virginia.
- UNCTAD (2004), "Economic Development in Africa: Debt Sustainability:- Oasis Or Mirage?" United Nations – New York and Geneva.
- Tanzi Vito, Chu Ke-Young and Gupta Sanjeev (1999), "Economic Policy and Equity", International Monetary Fund.
- White Howard and Killick Tony (2001), "African Poverty at the Millennium: Causes, Complexities, and Challenges", The World Bank – Washington.
- Mahbub Ul Haq Human Development Centre (2001 & 2002), "Human Development in South Asia 2001 2002 & 2003" Oxford University Press.
- Jugale V.B. (2004), " Globalisation, Growth and Poverty" Serials Publications.
- International Labour Organisation (2004), "World Employment Report 2004-05: Employment, Productivity and Poverty Reduction", ILO Geneva.
- UNCTAD (1996), "Globalization and Liberalization: Effects of International Economic Relations on Poverty", UNCTAD.
- Phillipe Aghion and Jeffrey G. Williamson (1998), "Growth, Inequality and Globalization: Theory, History and Policy", Cambridge University Press.
- Deepa Narayan (2000), "Voices of the Poor: Can Anyone Hear? ", Oxford University Press.
- Richard E. Mashomba (2000), "Africa in the Global Economy" Nynne Rienner Publishers - London.

- United Nations (2000), "Reports of the Secretary General – 54th Session: Agenda Item 49B – The Millennium Assembly of the United Nations", United Nations.
- UNCTAD (1999), "Report of the Secretary General UNCTAD To UNCTAD X-Tenth Session Bangkok Thailand 12-19 Feb'2000", UNCTAD.
- Michael Lipton (1997), "Why Poor People Stay Poor: Urban Bias in World Development", Temple Smith – London.
- John Cameron, Hans Ranbark and Ken Cole (1995), "Poverty and Power" Oxford University Press.
- Howard White and Tony Kellick (2001), "African Poverty at the Millennium", The World Bank.
- Vito Tanzi, Ke-Young Chu, Gupta Sanjeev (1999), "Economic Policy and Equity", International Monetary Fund.
- United Nations (2000), "United Nations Millennium Declaration", United Nations.
- International Monetary Fund (2000 To 2004), "World Economic Outlook", IMF.
- Jean Dreze and Amartya Sen and Athar Hussain (Ed), "The Political Economy of Hunger", Oxford University Press.
- Santosh Mehrotra, Richard Jolly, "Development with a Human Face", Clarendon Press Oxford.
- Center for International Relations Faculty for Social Sciences University of Ljubljano (1996), "Development and International Cooperation Vol.12, 22/06/1996" CIRFSS University of Ljubljana.
- UNDP (1998), "Combating Poverty: The Korean Experience" UNDP Seoul.
- Michael Bamberger Abdullahi M. George Matovu, "The Design and Management of Poverty Reduction Programs and Projects in Anglophone – Africa", Economic Development Institute Of The World Bank.
- African Development Bank (1998), "African Development Report" The African Development Bank – Oxford University Press.
- Can Africa Claim (1999), "The 21st Century? – Report by Africa Development Bank, African Economic Research

Consortium, United Nations, Economics for Africa and World Bank.

- Raundi Haldvorson – Quevedo and Hartmut Schnieder (2000 Ed), "Waging the Global War on Poverty" OECD.
- United Nations (1999), "Growth with Equity: Policy Lessons from the Experiences of Selected Asian Countries", United Nations.
- United Nations (2002), "International Conference on Financing for Development", United Nations.
- The World Bank (2002, 2003, 2004, 2005), "World Development Indicators", World Bank.
- Zwass (Adam) (2002), "Globalization of Unequal National Economies: Players and Controversies " Armonk, M.E., Sharpe.
- Nicholas Stern (2002), "A Strategy for Development", The World Bank.
- Layard Richard (1999), "Tackling Inequality", Macmillan Press Ltd. – London.
- OECD, "Participatory Development", O.E.C.D. Paris.
- Chen Ren, John (1999 Ed), "Economic Effects of Globalization: Policy Perspectives from Public Economics", Cambridge University Press - New York.
- Assaf Razin, Efraim Sadka (1999), "Economic Effects of Globalization: Policy Perspectives from Public Economics", Cambridge University Press - New York.

CHAPTER VI

- Govt. of India Planning Commission (2005), "Mid Term Appraisal of 10th Five Year Plan (2002-07)", Planning Commission of India.
- Gupta Des, Dahia Bhagwan (2005), "India in a Global Economy", Hope India Publications - Gurgaon.
- Virmani Arvind (2006), "Propelling India from Socialist Stagnation to Global Power", Academic Foundation - New Delhi.
- Dreze Jean and Sen Amartya (2005), "India: Development and Participation", Oxford University Press – New Delhi.

- Cassen Robert and Dyson Tim (2004 Ed), "Twenty-First Century India", Oxford University Press.
- Narsimhan Sushila And Balachandirane G., "India and East Asia: Learning from Each Other", Manak Publications Pvt. Ltd. Delhi.
- Rao C.H.H., Bhattacharya B.B. And Siddhartha N.S. (2005),"Indian Economy and Society in the Era of Globalisation and Liberalisation", Academic Foundation.
- The World Bank (2004), "Attaining the Millennium Development Goals in India: Role of Public Policy & Service Delivery", The World Bank.
- Srinivasan T.N. And Tendulkar D. Suresh (2003), "Reintegrating India with the World Economy", Oxford University Press.
- Kaliappa Kalirajan and Ulaganathan Sankar (2003), "Economic Reform and the Liberalization of the Indian Economy", Edward Elgar Publishing – U.K.
- Jaya Prakash Pradhan (2003), "RIS Discussion Papers: Rise of Service Sector Outward Foreign Direct Investment from India:- Trends, Patterns and Determinants", RIS Release.
- Joseph K.J. (2004), "RIS Discussion Papers: Transforming Digital Divide Into Digital Dividend:- The Role Of South-South Cooperation In ICTs", RIS Release.
- Sen Rahul and Asher G. Mukul (2005), "RIS Discussion Papers: India-East Asia Integration: - A Win-Win for Asia", RIS Release.
- Planning Commission, Govt. Of India, "India Vision 2020: Report + Background Papers", Planning Commission Govt. Of India.
- Dahlman Carl and Utz Anuja, "India and the Knowledge Economy: Leveraging Strengths and Opportunities", World Bank Institute.
- Ministry Of Statistics and Programme Implementation CSO (2005), "Millennium Development Goals India Country Report – 2005", Government of India.
- Ministry Of Statistics and Programme Implementation CSO (2005), "SAARC Social Charter India Country Report", Government Of India.

- Kapila Raj and Kapila Uma (2002 ed), "India's Economy in the 21st Century", Academic Foundation- New Delhi.
- All India Management Association (2003), "India's New Opportunity – 2020: 40 Million New Jobs, $200 Billion Annual Revenue" The Boston Consulting Group and Confederation of Indian Industry.
- Planning Commission (2002), "Tenth Five Year Plan 2002-07 Vol.1& 2" Planning Commission Govt Of India.
- The World Bank (2005), "India: Re-Energizing the Agricultural Sector to Sustain Growth and Reduce Poverty" Oxford University Press.
- The World Bank (2004), "India: Investment Climate Assessment 2004 Improving Manufacturing Competitiveness", World Bank.
- Joshi Vijay and Imd Little (1998), "India Macroeconomics and Political Economy (1964-91)", Oxford University Press – Delhi.
- International Monetary Fund, "Economic Adjustment and Reform in Low Income Countries", International Monetary Fund.
- The World Bank (1997), "India: Sustaining Rapid Economic Growth:- Country Study", The World Bank – Washington DC.
- Lal Deepak (1998), "India in the World Economy: Unfinished Business", Oxford University Press – Delhi.
- Kapila Uma (1997 Ed), "Indian Economy since Independence", Academic Foundations.
- Laure C. Steven (1997 Ed), "The India Handbook", Fitzroy Dearborn Publishers- Chicago & London.
- Gupta S.P. (1998), "Post Reform India: Emerging Trends", Allied Publishers – New Delhi.
- Government of India, "Five-Year Plans: New Delhi (4th To 10th Five Year Plan)", Planning Commission Govt. of India.
- Isher, Judge Ahluwalia and IMD Little (1998 Ed), "India's Economic Reforms and Development" Oxford University Press – Delhi.
- Panagariya Arvind, "India at Doha: Retrospect and Prospect" Article in Economic and Political Weekly January 26, 2002.

- Panth Ananth S., "Swarozgar Yojana; Old Wine, New Cocktail", Article in Economic and Political Weekly September 8, 2001.
- Rao C.H. Hanumantha, "WTO and Viability of Indian Agriculture", Article In Economic and Political Weekly September 8, 2001.
- Kaushik Basu, "India and the Global Economy", Article In Economic and Political Weekly October 6, 2001.
- Chaulia Shreeram, "Social Clause in WTO", Article in Economic and Political Weekly February 16, 2002.
- Kureger Anne O. (Ed), "Economic Policy Reforms and the India Economy" Oxford University Press – New Delhi.
- Srinivasan T.N. (2002), "Trade, Finance and Investment in South Asia", Social Science Press - New Delhi.
- Prema, Chandra Athukorala (Ed), "The Economic Development of South Asia", Edward Elgar Publisher.
- Federation of India Chambers of Commerce and Industries. "Indian Economic Profile March – 2003", FICCI.
- Sengupta Arjun (2001), "Reforms, Equity and the IMF" Har-Anand Publications Pvt. Ltd.
- Indian Investment Centre (2003, 04, 05), "Foreign Direct Investment Policy and Business Opportunities.
- Planning Commission of India, "Approach Paper to the Tenth Five Year Plan 2002-2007" Planning Commission of India.
- Research and Information System for the Non-Aligned and Other Developing Countries – RIS (2003), "Globalization and the Non-Aligned Movement", RIS - New Delhi.
- Mehta Rajesh (2001), "WTO: Liberalization and Industrial Sector", RIS.
- Planning Commission Of India (2002), "Report Of The Committee On India Vision: 2020.", Planning Commission Of India – New Delhi.
- Indian Investment Centre- A Govt. of India Organization (2003), "Foreign Direct Investment Policy and Business Opportunities", Govt. of India.
- Ministry of External Affairs (2001), "India: Business Opportunities", Govt. of India.

- Ministry of Finance, Government of India, "Economic Survey (1998-99, 1999-00, 2000-01, 2001-02, 2002-03, 2003-04, 2004-05, 2005-06)", Government of India.
- Planning Commission, Government of India, "National Human Development Report – 2001", Government of India.
- Planning Commission, Government of India, "Five Year Plan: 2002-07. Volume 1, 2, 3", Government of India.
- UNCTAD, "World Investment Report: 1999, 2000, 2001, 2002, 2003, 2004, 2005", United Nations.
- All India Management Association, "India's New Opportunity – 2020: High Level Strategic Group".
- Tendulkar Suresh D, "Indian Export and Economic Growth Performance in Asian Perspective: Working Paper No.54 of 2000", ICRIER.
- Dekajar Anil, "Attaining the M.D.G. In India 2004 ", The World Bank.
- Acharya Shankar, "India's Economy 2004", Academic Foundation – New Delhi.
- Dyson Tim, Cassen Robert and Visaria Leena (Ed), "Twenty-First Century India – Population, Economy, Human Development and the Environment", Oxford University Press.

CHAPTER VII

- "Human Development Report 1999", UNDP.
- "Trade on Human Terms: Transforming Trade for Human Development in Asia and the Pacific." 2006 Asia-Pacific Human Development Report, UNDP.
- Jung Min Choi, John Murphy & Manuel J Caro, "Globalisation with a Human Face". Praeger Publishers, 2004, Westport.
- "Making Global Trade Work for People", UNDP 2003.
- Trade and Development Report 2006, UNCTAD.

Annexure 'A' - (a)

Regional Distribution of FDI Inflows and Outflows, 1992-2003(Billion dollars)

Region Country	*1992-1997 Annual Average*	*1998*	*1999*	*2000*	*2001*	*2002*	*2003*
Developed countries	180.8	472.5	828.4	1108.0	571.5	489.9	366.6
Western Europe	100.8	263.0	500.0	697.4	368.8	380.2	310.2
Europe Union	95.8	249.9	479.4	671.4	357.4	374.0	295.2
Other Western Europe	5.0	13.1	20.7	26.0	11.4	6.2	15.1
Japan	1.2	3.2	12.7	8.3	6.2	9.2	6.3
United Status	60.3	174.4	283.4	314.0	159.5	62.9	29.8
Developing Countries	118.6	194.1	231.9	252.5	219.7	157.6	172.0
Africa	5.9	9.1	1.6	8.7	19.6	11.8	15.0

(Contd.)

(Contd. Annexure 'A'-(a))

Region Country	*1992-1997 Annual (Average)*	*1998*	*1999*	*2000*	*2001*	*2002*	*2003*
Developed countries	275.7	631.5	1014.3	1083.9	658.1	547.6	569.6
Western Europe	161.7	436.5	763.9	859.4	447.0	364.5	350.0
Europe Union	146.9	415.4	724.3	806.2	429.2	351.2	337.0
Other Western Europe	14.8	21.2	39.6	53.3	17.9	13.3	13.3
Japan	20.2	24.2	22.7	31.6	38.3	32.3	28.8
United Status	77.6	131.0	209.4	142.6	124.9	115.3	151.9
Developing Countries	51.4	53.4	75.5	98.9	59.9	44.0	35.0
Africa	2.2	2.0	2.6	1.3	-2.5	0.1	1.3

(Contd.)

(Contd. Annexure 'A'-(a))

Region Country	*1992-1997 Annual Average*	*1998*	*1999*	*2000*	*2001*	*2002*	*2003*
Latin America/ Caribbean	38.2	82.5	107.4	97.5	88.1	51.4	49.7
Asia and the Pacific	74.5	102.4	112.9	146.2	112.0	94.5	107.3
Asia	74.1	102.2	112.6	146.1	111.9	94.4	107.1
West Asia	2.9	7.1	1.0	1.5	6.1	3.6	4.1
Central Asia	1.6	3.0	2.5	1.9	3.5	4.5	6.1
South, East and South-East Asia	69.6	92.1	109.1	142.7	102.2	86.3	96.9
South Asia	2.5	3.5	3.1	3.1	4.0	4.5	6.1
The Pacific	0.4	0.2	0.3	0.1	0.1	0.1	0.2
Central and Eastern Europe	11.5	24.3	26.5	27.5	26.4	31.2	21.0
World	310.9	690.9	1086.8	1388.0	817.6	678.8	559.6

(Contd.)

(Contd. Annexure 'A'-(a))

Region Country	*1992-1997 Annual (Average)*	*1998*	*1999*	*2000*	*2001*	*2002*	*2003*
Latin America/ Caribbean	9.5	19.9	31.3	13.7	12.0	6.0	10.7
Asia and the Pacific	39.6	31.6	41.6	83.9	50.4	37.9	23.6
Asia	39.6	31.6	41.7	83.8	50.3	37.9	23.6
West Asia	0.5	-1.0	2.1	3.8	5.1	2.5	-0.7
Central Asia		0.2	0.4		0.1	0.8	0.8
South, East and South-East Asia	39.0	32.5	39.2	80.0	45.1	34.7	23.5
South Asia	0.1	0.1	0.1	0.5	1.4	1.2	0.9
The Pacific	0.1	-0.1		0.1	0.1		
Central and Eastern Europe	1.2	2.3	2.5	4.0	3.5	4.9	7.0
World	328.2	687.2	1092.3	1186.	721.5	596.5	612.2

Annexure 'A' - (b)

Regional Distribution FDI : 1970-97

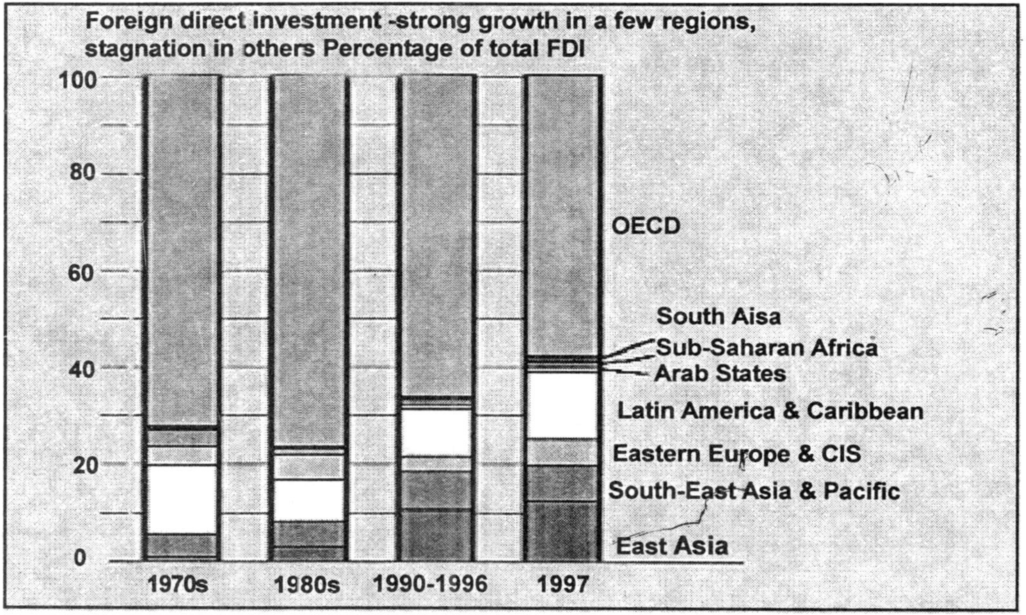

Source : Based on data from UNCTAD 1999.

Annexure 'B'

Regional Growth Performance

	GDP Growth (average annual %)		GDP Per Capita annual Growth Rate (%)
	1980 -1990	1990-2003	1990-2002
East Asia & Pacific	7.90	7.60	5.4
South Asia	5.50	5.40	3.2
Europe & Central Asia		0.60	-0.9
Latin America & Caribbean	1.50	2.70	1.3
Middle East & North Africa	1.30	3.20	-
Sub- Saharan Africa	1.70	2.80	-

Sources : World Bank, 2005, IMF, 2004.

Annexure 'C'

	Number of people living on less than $1 per day (Million)					
	GEP2004			*GEP2005*		
Region	*1990*	*2000*	*2015*	*1990*	*2001*	*2005*
East Asia and Pacific	470	261	44	472	271	19
China	361	204	41	375	212	16
Rest of East Asia and Pacific	110	57	3	97	60	2
Europe and Central Asia	6	20	6	2	17	2
Latin America and the Caribbean	48	56	46	49	52	43
Middle East and North Africa	5	8	4	6	7	4
South Asia	467	432	268	462	431	216
Sub-Saharan Africa	241	323	366	227	313	340
Total	1,237	1,100	734	1,218	1,089	622
Excluding China	877	896	692	844	877	606

(Contd.)

(Contd. Annexure 'C')

	$1 per day head count index (percent)					
	GEP2004			GEP2005		
Region	*1990*	*2000*	*2015*	*1990*	*2000*	*2015*
East Asia and Pacific	29.4	14.5	2.3	29.6	14.9	0.9
China	31.5	16.1	3.0	33.0	16.6	1.2
Rest of East Asia and Pacific	24.1	10.6	0.5	21.1	10.8	0.4
Europe and Central Asia	1.4	4.2	1.3	0.5	3.6	0.4
Latin America and the Caribbean	11.0	10.8	7.6	11.3	9.5	6.9
Middle East and North Africa	2.1	2.8	1.2	2.3	2.4	0.9
South Asia	41.5	31.9	16.4	41.3	31.3	12.8
Sub-Saharan Africa	47.4	49.0	42.3	44.6	46.4	38.4
Total	28.3	21.6	12.5	27.9	21.1	10.2
Excluding China	27.2	23.3	15.4	26.1	22.5	12.9

(Contd.)

Annexure 'D' - (a)

Average Annual Trade Growth Rate (per cent)

Country Group	*1991-95*	*1996-2000*	*2001-03*
Exports			
World	8.7	4.8	5.8
Developing Countries	12.2	7.7	7.4
Least Developed Countries	3.8	10.1	8.4
African Least Developed Countries	0.1	7.3	10.2
Low – Income Countries	8.7	9.6	8.1
African Low-Income Countries	2.8	12.6	4.2
Country Group	*1991-95*	*1996-2000*	*2001-03*
Imports			
World	8.1	5.2	6.0
Developing Countries	13.3	5.3	8.1
Least Developed Countries	5.8	3.3	12.0
African Least Developed Countries	3.1	1.9	13.3
Low-Income Countries	9.2	4.4	12.8
African Low Income Countries	5.2	0.9	16.1

Source : IMF, Direction of Trade Statistics.

Annexure 'D' - (b)

Share of Non-oil Exports (Percentage of total)

Country Group	*1975*	*1980*	*1990*	*1995*	*2000*	*2003*
Developed countries	80.3	78.9	76.5	70.6	65.1	62.6
Developing countries	19.7	21.1	23.5	29.4	34.9	37.4
Least developed countries	0.8	0.6	0.6	0.4	0.5	0.6
African least developed countries	0.6	0.4	0.4	0.2	0.3	0.3
Low – income countries	3.1	1.7	2.0	1.9	2.3	2.5
African low income countries	2.1	0.8	1.0	0.7	0.9	0.9

Source : IMF, Direction of Trade Statistics.

Annexure 'E'

Resource Flows to South Asia: 1985 & 1997

Country	*Net FDI US $ millions*		*Net Portfolio Investment US $ millions*		*Net Bank and Trade Related Lending US $ millions*		*Net ODA As % of GNP*	*Ext Debt As % of GNP*
	1985	*1997*	*1985*	*1997*	*1985*	*1997*	*1997*	*1997*
Bangladesh	1	145	-	11	-3	-28	2.3	35.1
Bhutan	-	-	-	-	-	-2	21.3	27.2
India	106	3,264	320	4,035	1,954	920	.4	24.9
Maldives	1	10	-	-	-3	5	8.4	48.6
Nepal	1	20	-	-	5	-11	8.4	48.6
Pakistan	131	800	-	627	-170	757	5	47.5
Sri Lanka	26	140	-	148	44	-4	2.3	51.2

Source : UNCTAD 1999 & World Bank 1999.

Annexure 'F'

Comparative Public Expenditure as % of GDP

Country	*Health*	*Education*		*Military*		*Debt Service*	
	2003-04	*1991*	*2002-04*	*1990*	*2004*	*1990*	*2004*
S Korea	2.8	3.8	4.6	3.7	2.4	–	–
Malaysia	2.2	5.1	8.0	2.6	2.3	9.8	7.8
Thailand	2.0	3.1	4.2	2.6	1.2	6.2	7.7
China	2.0	2.2	–	2.7	2.4	2.0	1.2
Philippines	1.4	3.0	3.2	1.4	0.9	8.1	13.7
Indonesia	1.1	1.0	0.9	1.8	1.1	8.7	7.9
Sri Lanka	1.6	3.2	–	2.1	2.8	4.8	3.8
Maldives	5.5	7.0	8.1	–	–	4.1	4.3
India	1.2	3.7	3.3	3.2	3.0	2.6	2.8
Pakistan	0.7	2.6	2.0	5.8	3.4	4.8	4.5
Bhutan	2.6	–	–	–	–	1.8	1.8
Bangladesh	1.1	1.5	2.2	1.0	1.2	2.5	1.2
Nepal	1.5	2.0	3.4	0.9	1.7	1.9	1.7

Source : Human Development Report 2006, UNDP.

Annexure 'G'

Comparative Public Expenditure as % of GDP

MDG	*LDC*	*SOUTH ASIA*	*EAST ASIA & PACIFIC*
GDP Per Capita US $ 2004	355	697	1,921
GDP Per Capita US $ PPP 2004	1,350	3,072	5,872
Growth rate 1990-2004	1.6%	3.3%	5.8%
Import of goods & services(% of GDP)1990	22	13	33
Import of goods & service(% of GDP) 2004	32	23	52
Export of goods & services(% of GDP) 1990	13	11	34
Export of goods & service(% of GDP) 2004	23	21	56
Primary Exports (as % of Merchandise) 1990	84	27	23
Primary Exports (as % of Merchandise) 2004	66	24	11
Manufactured Exports (as % of Merchandise) 1990	-	71	73
Manufactured Exports (as % of Merchandise) 2004	-	76	86
Life Expectancy at birth 2004	52.4	63.7	70.8
Adult Literacy	63.7	60.9	90.7
GER	45	56	69
Population Growth Rate 1975-2004	2.5	2.1	1.4

(Contd.)

(Contd. Annexure 'G')

MDG	*LDC*	*SOUTH ASIA*	*EAST ASIA & PACIFIC*
Population Growth Rate 2004-2015	2.3	1.5	0.7
Population % with Access to Sustainable Sanitation 1990	22	18	30
Population % with Access to Sustainable Sanitation 2004	37	37	50
Population % with Access to Sustainable Water 1990	51	72	72
Population % with Access to Sustainable Water 2004	59	85	79
Population % Undernourished 1990	34	25	17
Population % Undernourished 2004	33	20	12

(Contd.)

(Contd. Annexure 'G')

MDG	*LDC*	*SOUTH ASIA*	*EAST ASIA & PACIFIC*
IMR(per 1000 births)1970	148	128	84
IMR(per 1000 births)2004	94	62	28
U-5 MR 1970	240	203	122
U-5 MR 2004	147	84	34
Life expectancy at birth 1970-1975	44.5	50.1	60.5
Life expectancy at birth 2000-2005	52	63.2	70.4
Telephones/1000 1990	3	7	18
Telephones/1000 2004	9	35	199
Cell Subscripton/1000 1990	0	-	-
CellSubscription/1000 2004	28	42	262
Internet Connections /1000 1990	0	0	-
Internet Connections /1000 2004	8	29	91

Annexure 'H'-(a)

Selected Indicators of External Sector

								April-(Sept.)	
	1990-91	*1999-00*	*2000-01*	*2001-02*	*2002-03*	*2003-04*	*2004-05*	*2004-05*	*2005-06*
1. Growth of Exports – BOP (%)	9.0	9.5	21.1	-1.6	20.3	23.3	23.9	29.5	21.9
2. Growth of Imports – BOP (%)	14.4	16.5	4.6	-2.8	14.5	24.1	48.5	38.3	48.4
Of which , POL (%)	60.0	97.1	24.1	-10.5	26.0	16.6	45.1	58.2	42.9
3. Exports / Imports – BOP (%)	66.2	67.8	78.5	79.4	83.4	82.9	69.2	71.3	58.6
4. Import cover of FER (No. of months)	2.5	8.2	8.8	11.5	14.2	16.9	14.3	13.9	11.2
5.External assistance (net)/TC (%)	26.2	8.2	4.8	13.4	-29.4	-16.5	6.1	4.7	2.2
6.ECB (net)/TC (%)	26.8	3.1	50.6	-19.0	-15.9	-16.9	16.0	20.6	14.1
7. NR deposits /TC (%)	18.3	14.2	27.2	33.0	28.0	21.0	-3.1	-18.0	0.9

(Contd. ')

(Contd. Annexure 'H'-(a))

							April-(Sept.)	
	1990-91	*1999-00*	*2000-01*	*2001-02*	*2002-03*	*2003-04*	*2004-05*	*2004-05*	*2005-06*
As % of GDP at current market price									
8. Exports	5.8	8.3	9.9	9.4	10.6	11.0	11.8		
9. Imports	8.8	12.3	12.6	11.8	12.7	13.3	17.1		
10.Trade Balance	-3.0	-3.9	-2.7	-2.4	-2.1	-2.3	-5.3		
11. Invisibles balance	-0.1	2.9	2.1	3.1	3.4	4.6	4.5		
12. Current account balance	-3.1	-1.0	-0.6	0.7	1.3	2.3	-0.8		
13. External debt	28.7	21.9	22.4	21.1	20.4	17.8	17.3		

Annexure 'H'-(b)

Balance of Payments : Summary

Balance of Payments : Summary(In US $ million)1990-91 1998-99 1999-00 2000-01 2001-02 2002-03 2003-04 2004-05					
1. Exports	18477	34298	37542	45452	44703
2.Imports	27915	47544	55383	57912	56277
Of which. POL	6028	6399	12611	15650	14000
3, Trade balance	-9438	-13246	-17841	-12460	-11574
4. Invisibles (net0	242	9208	13143	9794	14974
Non factor services	980	2165	4064	1692	3324
Income	-3752	-3544	-3559	-5004	-4206
Pvt. Transfers	2069	10280	12256	12254	15398
Official transfers	461	307	382	252	458
5. Current Account Balance	-9680	-4038	-4698	-2666	3400
6. External assistance (net)	2204	799	891	410	1117

(Contd.)

(Contd. Annexure 'H'-(b))

Balance of Payments : Summary(In US $ million)1990-91 1998-99 1999-00 2000-01 2001-02 2002-03 2003-04 2004-05				*April-(Sept.)*	
				2004-05	*2005-06*
1. Exports	53774	66285	82150	36715	44761
2.Imports	64464	80003	118779	51483	76396
Of which. POL	17640	20569	29844	14578	20834
3, Trade balance	-10690	-13718	-36629	-14768	-31635
4. Invisibles (net0	17035	27801	31229	14283	18679
Non factor services	3643	10144	14199	5980	9512
Income	-3446	-4505	-3814	-1917	-3078
Pvt. Transfers	16387	21608	20253	9968	12043
Official transfers	451	554	591	252	202
5. Current Account Balance	6345	14083	-5400	-485	-12956
6. External assistance (net)	-3128	-2858	1923	346	436

(Contd.')

(Contd. Annexure 'H'-(b))

Balance of Payments : Summary(In US $ million)1990-91 1998-99 1999-00 2000-01 2001-02 2002-03 2003-04 2004-05					
7. Commercial borrowing net (net) @	2254	4367	333	4303	-1585
8. IMF (net)	1214	-393	-260	-26	0
9. NR deposits (net)	1536	961	1540	2316	2754
10. Rupee debt. Service	-1192	-802	-711	-617	-519
11.Foreign investment (net)	101	2312	5117	5862	6686
Of which (I) FDI (net)	96	2380	2093	3272	4734
(ii) FIIs	0	-390	2135	1847	1505
(iii) Euro equities & others	5	322	889	743	447
12.Other flows (net)	2284	623	3930	-3739	-96
13. Capital account total (net)	8401	7867	10840	8509	8357
14. Reserve use (-increase)	1279	-3829	-6142	-5842	-11757

(Contd.)

(Contd. Annexure 'H'-(b))

Balance of Payments : Summary(In US $ million)1990-91 1998-99 1999-00 2000-01 2001-02 2002-03 2003-04 2004-05				*April-(Sept.)*	
7. Commercial borrowing net (net) @	-1692	-2925	5040	1526	2752
8. IMF (net)	0	0	0	0	0
9. NR deposits (net)	2978	3642	-964	-1334	174
10. Rupee debt. Service	-474	-376	-417	-279	-142
11.Foreign investment (net)	4161	13744	12147	2490	7411
Of which (I) FDI (net)	3217	2388	3240	1979	2304
(ii) FIIs	377	10918	8280	339	4227
(iii) Euro equities & others	567	438	627	172	880
12.Other flows (net)	8795	6111	13830	4672	8827
13. Capital account total (net)	10640	17338	31559	7421	19458
14. Reserve use (-increase)	-16985	-31421	-26159	-6936	-6502

(Contd.)

Annexure 'I'-(a)

Trends of Social Sector Expenditure by General Government (Centre and State Government Combined)

ITEMS	2001-01	2001-02	2002-03	2003-04	2004-05	2005-2006
	Actual	Actual	Actual	Actual	RE	RE
Centre & States	(In Billions of Rupees)					
Total expenditure	5913	6447	7049	7964	9045	9798
Expenditure on social sector	1318	1378	1452	1569	1869	2052
Education	670	681	725	769	898	992
Health	280	286	315	348	415	477
Others	368	412	412	452	556	582
As a proportion of GDP	(In per Cent)					
Total expenditure	28.05	28.26	28.77	32.37	28.97	27.76
Expenditure on social sector	6.25	6.04	5.92	5.68	5.98	5.81
Education	3.17	2.98	2.95	2.78	2.87	2.81
Health	1.32	1.25	1.28	1.26	1.32	1.35
Others	1.74	1.80	1.68	1.63	1.78	1.64

(Contd.)

(Contd. Annexure 'I'-(a))

ITEMS	*2001-01*	*2001-02*	*2002-03*	*2003-04*	*2004-05*	*2005-2006*
	Actual	*Actual*	*Actual*	*Actual*	*RE*	*RE*
As a Proportion of total Expenditure						
Expenditure on social sector	22.3	21.4	20.6	19.7	20.7	20.9
Education	11.3	10.6	10.3	9.7	9.9	10.1
Health	4.7	4.4	4.5	4.4	4.6	4.9
Others	6.2	6.4	5.8	5.7	6.1	5.9
As a proportion of social sector expenditure						
Education	51	49	50	49	48	48
Health	21	21	22	22	22	23
Others	28	30	28	29	30	28

Source : Budget documents of union and State Governments.

Annexure 'I'-(b)

Selected Indicators of Human Development for Major States

Sl. No.	State	Life expectancy at birth (1998-2002)			Infant Mortality Rate per 1000 live births (2003			Birth rate (per 1000)	Death rate (per 1000)
		Male	Female	Total	Male	Female	Total	2003*	2003*
1	2	3	4	5	6	7	8	9	10
1.	Andhra Pradesh	62.0	64.6	63.5	59	59	59	20.4	80.0
2.	Assam	57.7	58.1	57.9	69	65	67	26.3	9.1
3.	Bihar	61.4	59.5	60.8	59	62	60	30.7	7.9
4.	Gujarat	62.4	64.4	63.4	54	61	57	24.6	7.6
5.	Haryana	64.7	65.4	65.2	54	65	59	26.3	7.1
6.	Karnataka	62.8	66.2	64.5	51	52	52	21.8	7.2
7.	Kerala	70.8	75.9	73.5	11	12	11	16.7	6.3

(Contd.)

(Contd. Annexure 'I'-(b))

Sl. No.	*State*	*Life expectancy at birth (1998-2002)*			*Infant Mortality Rate per 1000 live births (2003*			*Birth rate (per 1000)*	*Death rate (per 1000)*
8.	Madhya Pradesh	57.0	56.7	56.9	77	86	82	30.2	9.8
9.	Maharashtra	65.0	67.4	66.2	32	54	42	19.9	7.2
10.	Orissa	58.4	58.5	58.5	82	83	83	23.0	9.7
11.	Punjab	67.4	69.5	68.5	49	52	49	20.6	7.0
12.	Rajasthan	60.5	61.6	61.1	70	81	75	30.3	7.6
13.	Tamil Nadu	64.2	66.3	65.2	44	41	43	18.3	7.6
14.	Uttar Pradesh	59.4	58.5	59.1	69	84	76	31.3	9.5
15.	West Bengal	63.3	64.8	63.9	45	46	46	20.3	6.6
	INDIA	61.6	63.3	62.5	57	64	60	24.8	8.0

Source : Office of the Register General of India, Ministry of Home Affairs.

Annexure 'I'-(c)

Gross Enrolment Ratio in Classes I-V ABD VI-VIII and I-VIII

		2003-2004								
		Classes I-V (6-11 years)			Classes VI-VIII(11-14 yrs)			Classes I-VIII (6-14 YRS)		
Sl. No.	States / Uts	Boys	Girls	Boys	Girls	Boys	Girls	Boys	Girls	TOTAL
1	2	3	4	5	6	7	8	9	10	11
1.	Andhra Pradesh	87.42	88.03	87.72	67.10	62.49	64.86	79.80	78.58	79.20
2.	Arunachal Pradesh	115.35	103.47	109.56	67.99	59.06	63.60	98.68	87.64	93.29
3.	Assam	88.22	88.09	88.16	66.02	61.15	63.65	80.10	78.32	79.23
4.	Bihar	80.20	64.20	72.57	30.64	19.21	25.33	62.37	48.50	55.82
5.	Chattisgarh	123.69	122.86	123.29	78.51	62.21	70.52	106.99	99.97	103.58
6.	Goa	100.30	95.50	97.96	104.77	97.55	101.23	102.07	96.31	99.26
7.	Gujarat	117.67	108.62	113.41	81.88	57.40	70.40	104.19	89.38	97.23
8.	Haryana	73.53	77.31	75.25	68.24	62.40	65.51	71.53	71.49	71.51
9.	Himachal Pradesh	106.10	106.88	106.47	99.91	96.49	98.24	103.62	102.61	103.13
10.	Jammu & Kashmir	87.47	76.42	82.10	65.20	52.95	59.28	78.77	67.31	73.21

(Contd.)

(Contd. Annexure 'I'-(c))

	2003-2004									
		Classes I-V (6-11 years)			Classes VI-VIII(11-14 yrs)			Classes I-VIII (6-14 YRS)		
Sl. No.	States / Uts	Boys	Girls	Boys	Girls	Boys	Girls	Boys	Girls	TOTAL
11.	Jharkhand	86.70	71.10	79.09	42.47	32.19	37.54	70.51	57.15	64.04
12.	Karnataka	110.53	107.23	108.91	78.95	73.32	76.20	97.95	93.76	95.89
13.	Kerala	97.25	96.59	96.92	95.69	91.49	93.64	96.61	94.51	95.58
14.	Madhya Pradesh	112.11	100.68	106.59	71.78	53.88	63.30	96.89	83.43	90.44
15.	Maharashtra	108.32	106.84	107.60	89.41	85.52	87.55	100.71	98.31	99.56
16.	Manipur	139.30	135.64	137.51	86.95	81.57	84.33	118.85	114.60	116.77
17.	Meghalaya	104.19	106.88	105.51	60.27	62.05	61.14	88.01	90.34	89.16
18.	Mizoram	122.54	117.71	120.17	77.25	76.70	76.98	105.10	101.86	103.51
19.	Nagaland	80.95	79.97	80.48	43.56	45.85	44.66	66.11	66.50	66.30
20.	Orissa	114.23	107.44	110.91	58.13	49.69	54.01	93.28	85.86	89.65
21.	Punjab	71.04	76.38	73.45	59.31	60.93	60.06	66.52	70.25	68.22
22.	Rajasthan	120.18	109.41	115.07	74.30	47.22	61.54	103.65	87.19	95.87
23.	Sikkim	116.54	116.48	116.51	52.02	61.63	56.75	90.63	94.77	92.68

(Contd.)

(Contd. Annexure 'I'-(c))

		2003-2004								
		Classes I-V (6-11 years)			*Classes VI-VIII(11-14 yrs)*			*Classes I-VIII (6-14 YRS)*		
Sl. No.	*States / Uts*	*Boys*	*Girls*	*Boys*	*Girls*	*Boys*	*Girls*	*Boys*	*Girls*	*TOTAL*
24.	Tamil Nadu	117.47	115.49	116.51	102.28	98.44	100.41	111.57	108.88	110.26
25.	Tripura	125.73	119.68	122.76	75.34	70.23	72.84	105.01	99.41	102.27
26.	Uttar Pradesh	96.69	92.58	94.75	53.61	42.97	48.64	81.09	74.86	78.16
27.	Uttaranchal	106.10	107.66	106.85	81.08	79.59	80.36	96.57	96.88	96.72
28.	West Bengal	107.45	107.21	107.33	65.90	62.57	64.28	91.57	90.20	90.90
29.	A&N Islands	118.78	113.23	116.05	100.13	91.41	95.85	111.27	104.47	107.92
30.	Chandigarh	72.00	70.77	71.44	69.19	69.85	69.50	70.95	70.42	70.71
31.	D & N Haveli	133.92	117.88	126.06	95.75	66.08	81.64	120.14	99.86	110.30
32.	Daman & Diu	111.66	111.01	111.35	100.85	94.11	97.62	107.76	104.81	106.36
33.	Delhi	90.34	89.81	90.10	84.83	85.91	85.34	88.26	88.33	88.30
34.	Lakshadweep	111.65	100.93	106.37	104.04	89.77	97.09	108.51	96.38	102.56
35.	Pondicherry	121.94	118.72	120.37	121.89	117.37	119.68	121.92	118.18	120.09
	INDIA	100.75	95.67	98.31	66.87	57.69	62.49	88.02	81.51	84.91

Source : Selected Educational Statistics, 2003-04, Ministry of Human Resource Development, Government of India.

Annexure 'I'-(d)

Total Number of Recognized Educational Institutions in India 2003-04 (Provisional)

S.No.	*State / Uts*	*Primary / Junior Basic School*	*Middle / Senior Basic School*	*High Sch/ Hr. Sec./ Intermediate / Jr. College*
1.	Andhra Pradesh	63897	15215	3267
2.	Arunachal Pradesh	1364	449	74
3.	Assam	30068	8143	731
4.	Bihar	40337	9922	685
5	Chattisgarh	32556	9350	1439
6	Goa	1009	79	80
7.	Gujarat	7233	30646	2427
8.	Haryana	11500	2171	1776
8.	Haryana	11500	2171	1776
9.	Himachal Pradesh	11013	2076	820
10.	Jammu & Kashmir	10488	3975	380
11.	Jharkhand	16417	4324	122
12.	Karnataka	26163	25612	2237
13.	Kerala	6717	2975	1286
14.	Madhya Pradesh	66648	30592	4211
15.	Maharashtra	41258	26033	4212
16.	Manipur	2552	832	112

(Contd.)

(Contd. Annexure 'I'-(d))

S.No.	State / Uts	College for General Education	Professional Education	Universities / Deemed Univ./ Instt. Of National Importance/ Research Instt.
1.	Andhra Pradesh	1330	238	28
2.	Arunachal Pradesh	10	1	4
3.	Assam	317	3	7
4.	Bihar	743	7	23
5	Chattisgarh	213	2	9
6	Goa	24	4	1
7.	Gujarat	422	32	28
8.	Haryana	163	41	7
8.	Haryana	163	41	7
9.	Himachal Pradesh	69	2	7
10.	Jammu & Kashmir	73	4	5
11.	Jharkhand	146	5	7
12.	Karnataka	930	120	20
13.	Kerala	186	66	10
14.	Madhya Pradesh	513	56	17
15.	Maharashtra	1208	177	54
16.	Manipur	58	1	2

(Contd.)

(Contd. Annexure 'I'-(d))

S.No.	State / Uts	Primary / Junior Basic School	Middle / Senior Basic School	High Sch/ Hr. Sec./ Intermediate / Jr. College
17.	Meghalaya	5851	1559	80
18.	Mizoram	1504	908	71
19.	Nagaland	1495	480	52
20.	Orissa	42104	11510	744
21.	Punjab	13265	2493	1695
22.	Rajasthan	55757	23942	3159
23.	Sikkim	497	126	41
24.	Tamil Nadu	32242	6825	4136
25.	Tripura	2075	453	242
26.	Uttar Pradesh	119404	35427	7369
27.	Uttaranchal	14304	3557	1071
28.	West Bengal	49865	1984	2868
29.	A & N Islands	209	56	49
30.	Chandigarh	24	9	52
31.	D & N Haveli	127	91	9
32.	Daman & Diu	53	24	6
33.	Delhi	2126	681	1212
34.	Lakshadweep	20	4	4
35.	Pondicherry	329	125	77

(Contd.)

(Contd. Annexure 'I'-(d))

S.No.	State / Uts	College for General Education	Professional Education	Universities / Deemed Univ./ Instt. of National Importance/ Research Instt.
17.	Meghalaya	48	0	1
18.	Mizoram	26	0	1
19.	Nagaland	36	0	1
20.	Orissa	567	19	9
21.	Punjab	209	16	8
22.	Rajasthan	456	39	15
23.	Sikkim	2	1	2
24.	Tamil Nadu	441	96	28
25.	Tripura	14	1	1
26.	Uttar Pradesh	733	69	40
27.	Uttaranchal	47	2	7
28.	West Bengal	354	43	28
29.	A & N Islands	2	0	0
30.	Chandigarh	42	2	2
31.	D & N Haveli	0	0	0
32.	Daman & Diu	1	0	0
33.	Delhi	63	16	16
34.	Lakshadweep	0	0	0
35.	Pondicherry	11	5	1

Source : Selected Educational Statistics 2003-04, Ministry of Human Resource Development.

Annexure 'J'-(a)

India's Global Position on Human and Gender Development

Country	*Human Development Index (HDI)*		*HDI Rank*		*Gender Development Index (GDI)*		*GDI Rank*	
	2000	*2003*	*2000*	*2003*	*2000*	*2003*	*2000*	*2003*
Norway	0.942	0.963	1	1	0.941	0.960	3	1
Australia	0.939	0.955	5	3	0.956	0.954	1	2
Sri Lanka	0.741	0.751	89	93	0.737	0.747	70	66
China	0.726	0.755	96	85	0.724	0.754	77	64
Indonesia	0.684	0.697	110	110	0.678	0.691	91	87
India	0.577	0.602	124	127	0.560	0.586	105	98
Pakistan	0.499	0.527	138	135	0.468	0.508	120	107
Bangladesh	0.478	0.520	145	139	0.468	0.514	121	105
Nepal	0.490	0.526	142	136	0.470	0.511	119	106
Mozambique	0.322	0.379	170	168	0.307	0.365	144	133
Niger	0.277	0.281	172	177	0.263	0.271	146	140

Source : Human Development Report (HDR) 2002 & 2005.

Annexure 'J'-(b)

India's Global Position in Terms of Socio-demographic Parameters

Country	*Life expectancy at birth (years)*	*Under-five mortality rate (per 1,000 live births)*		*Infant mortality rate (per 1,000 live births*		*Maternal mortality ratio (per 100,000 live births)*
	2000-05	*1990*	*2003*	*1990*	*2003*	*2005*
China	71	49	37	38	30	45
India	63	123	87	80	63	540
Nepal	61	145	82	100	61	740
Pakistan	63	128	103	96	81	500
Sri Lanka	74	23	15	19	13	96
Bangladesh	63	144	69	96	46	380
South Asia	63	129	91	84	66	NA

Source : UNDP, Human Development Report 2005.

Annexure 'J'-(c)

Selected Health Indicators

Sl.No	Parameter	1951	1981	1991	Current Level
1.	Crude birth rate (per 1000 population	40.8	33.9	29.5	24.8 (2003)
2.	Crude Death Rate (Per 1000 population)	25.1	12.5	9.8	8.0 (2003)
3.	Total fertility rate (TFR) (per woman)	6.0	4.5	3.6	3.0 (2001)
4.	Maternal Mortality ratio (MMR)(per 100,000 live births)	146(1951-61)	110	80	60(2003)
5.	Infant mortality rate (IMR) (per1000 live births)	146(1951-61)	110	80	60 (2003)
6.	Chind (0.4) mortality rate (per 1000 chindren)	57.3(1972)	41.2	26.5	17.8 (2002)
7.	Couple protection rate %	10.4(1971)	22.8	44.1	48.2(1998-99)
8.	Life expectancy at birth				
8.1	Male	37.2	54.1	59.7	63.9 (2001-06)
8.2	Female	36.2	54.7	60.9(1991-95)	66.9(2001-06)

Source : Ministry of Health & Family Welfare and office of the Registrar General, India.

Annexure 'K'

Millennium Development Goal Indicators

Goal	*Target*	*Indicators*
Eradicate extreme poverty and hunger	* Halve, between 1990and 2015, the proportion of people whose income is less than $ 1 a day.	* Proportion of population below $ 1 (PPP) a day. * Poverty gap ratio (incidence x depth of poverty) * Share of poorest quintile in nation consumption.
	* Halve, between 1990and 2015, the proportion of people who suffer from hunger.	* Prevalence of underweight children under five years of age. * Proportion of population below minimum level of dietary energy consumption.
Achieve universal primary education	* Ensure that, by 2015 children everywhere, boys and girls alike, will be able to complete a full course of primary schooling.	* Net enrolment ratio in primary education. * Proportion of pupils starting grade 1 who reach grade 5. * Literacy rate of 15-to 24 –year-olds.
Promote gender equality and empower women	* Eliminate gender disparity in primary and secondary education, preferably by 2005, and in all level of education no later than 2015.	* Ratio of girls to boys in primary, secondary and tertiary education. * Ratio of literate women to men ages 15-24. * Share of women in wage employment in the non-agricultural sector. * Proportion of seats held by the women in national parliament.

(Contd.)

(Contd. Annexure 'K')

Goal	*Target*	*Indicators*
Reduce child mortality	* Reduce by two- thirds, between 1990 and 2015, the under –five mortality rate.	* Under- five mortality rate. * Infant mortality rate. * Proportion of one-year-old children immunized against measles.
Improve mental health	* Reduce by three-quarters, between 1990 and 2015, the maternal mortality ratio.	* Maternal mortality ratio. * Proportion of births attended by skilled heath personnel.
Combat HIV/AIDS, malaria and other diseases	* Have halted by 2015 and begun to reverse the spared of HIV/AIDS	* HIV prevalence among pregnant women 15-24. * Condom use rate of the contraceptive prevalence rate. * Condom use at last high-risk sex. * Percentage of 15-to 24- year-olds with comprehensive correct knowledge of HIV/AIDS. * Contraceptive prevalence rate. * Ration of school attendance of orphans to school attendance of non-orphans ages 10-14.
	* Have halted by 2015 and begun to reverse the incidence of malaria and other major diseases.	* Prevalence and death rates associated with malaria. * Proportion in malaria-risk area using effective malaria prevention and treatment measures. * Prevalence and death rates associated with tuberculosis. * Proportion of tuberculosis cases detected and cured under directly observed treatment short course (DOTS)

(Contd.)

(Contd. Annexure 'K')

Goal	*Target*	*Indicators*
Ensure environmental sustainability	* Integrate the principal of sustainable development into country policies and programmes and reverse the loss of environmental resources.	* Proportion of land area converted by forest. * Ratio of area Protected to maintain biological diversity to surface area. * Energy use (kilogram of oil equivalent) per $ 1 GDP (PPP) * Carbon dioxide emission per capita and consumption of ozone-depleting chlorofluorocarbons (CFCs). * Proportion of population using solid fuels.
	* Halve, by 2015, the proportion of people without sustainable access to safe drinking water and sanitation.	* Proportion of population with sustainable access to an improved water source, urban and rural. * Proportion of population with access to improved sanitation, urban and rural.
	* By 2020, to have achieved a significant improvement in the lives of at least 100 million slum dwellers.	* Proportion with households with access to secure tenure.

(Contd.)

(Contd. Annexure 'K')

Goal	*Target*	*Indicators*
Develop a global partnership for development	* Develop further and open, rule-based, predictable, non-discriminatory trading and financial system. Include a commitment to good governance, development, and poverty reduction-both nationally and internationally. * Address the special needs of the least developed countries. Includes: tariff-and quota access for least-developed countries' exports; enhanced programme of debt relief for HIPCs and cancellation of official bilateral debt; and more generous ODA for committed to poverty reduction.	<u>*Official development assistance (ODA).*</u> * Net ODA, total and to least developed countries, as a percentage of OECD/DAC donors' gross national income (GN) * Proportion of total bilateral, sector-allocable ODA of OECD/DAC donors to basis social services(basis education, primary health care, nutrition, safe water and sanitation) * Proportion of bilateral ODA of OECD/DAC donors that is untied. * ODA received in landlocked countries as proportion of their gross national incomes. * ODA received in small island developing states as proportion of their gross national incomes. <u>*Market access*</u> * Proportion of total developed country imports(by value and excluding arms) from developing countries and from the least developed countries, admitted free of duties. * Average tariff imposed by developed countries on agricultural products and textiles and clothing from developing countries.

(Contd. ')

(Contd. Annexure 'K')

Goal	Target	Indicators
	* Address the special needs of landlocked countries and small island developing states. * Deal comprehensively with the debt problems of developing countries through national and international measures in orders to make debt sustainable in the long term.	* Agricultural support estimate for OECD countries as per a percentage of their gross domestic product. * Proportion of ODA provided to help built trade capacity. <u>*Debt sustainability.*</u> * Total number of countries that have reached their HIPC decision point and number that have reached their HIPC completion point (cumulative). * Debt their relief committed under HIPC debt initiative * Debt service as a percentage of export of goods and services.
	* In cooperation with developing countries, develop and implement strategies for decent and productive work for youth.	* Unemployment rate of 15-to 24-year-olds, male and female and total.

(Contd.')

(Contd. Annexure 'K')

Goal	*Target*	*Indicators*
	* In cooperation with pharmaceutical companies, provide access to affordable essential drugs in developing countries.	* Proportion of population with access to affordable essential drugs on a sustainable basis.
	* In cooperation with the private sector, made available the benefits of new technologies, especially information and communications.	* Telephone line and cellular subscribers per 100 people. * Personal computers in use per 100 people. * Internet users per 100 people.

Annexure 'L'

Progress Towards Achieving MDGs in India

Indicator	*Year*	*Value*	*Year*	*Value*	*MDG target Value*
Proportion of population below poverty line (%)	1990	37.5	1999-2000	26.1	18.75
Undernourished people as % of total population	1990	62.2	1999-2000	53	31.1
Proportion of under-nourished children	1990	54.8	1998	47	27.4
Literacy rate of 15-24 year olds	1990	64.3	2001	73.3	1000
Ratio of girls to boys in primary education	1990-91	0.71	2000-01	0.78	1
Ratio of girls to boys in secondary education	1990-91	0.49	2000-01	0.63	1
Under five mortality rate (per 1000 live births)	1998-92	125	1998-2002	98	41
Infant Mortality rate (per 1000 live births)	1990	80	2003	60	27

(Contd.')

(Contd. Annexure 'L')

Indicator	*Year*	*Value*	*Year*	*Value*	*MDG target Value*
Maternal mortality rate (per 100,000 live births)	1991	437	1998	407	109
Population with sustainable access to an improved water source, urban (%)	1991	55.54	2005	90	80.5
Population with sustainable access to an improved water source, urban (%)	1991	81.38	2001	82.22	94
Population with access to sanitation urban (%)	1991	47	2001	63	72
Population with access to sanitation rural (%)	1991	9.48	2005	32.36	72
Deaths due to malaria per 100,000	1994	0.13	2004	0.09	-
Deaths due to TB per 10,000	1999	56	2003	33	-
Deaths due to HIV/AIDS	2000	471	2004	1114	-

Annexure 'M'

Tracking Growth of Select Countries Over Three Decades

Rates of	*Growth m'facture export volumes*		*Growth to total export volumes*		*Growth of GDP volumes*	
Country / territory	*1980-88*	*1970-80*	*1980-88*	*1970-80*	*1980-88*	*1970-80*
Indonesia	30.3	20.8	2.8	6.9	3.8	7.3
Turkey	23.3	13.2	14.3	4.3	5.3	5.5
Mauritius	19.8	33.2	11.4	3.7	5.9	6.2
Mexico	19.1	6.3	5.4	12.6	0.4	6.0
Thailand	17.6	16.2	10.7	9.6	5.7	6.7
Malaysia	14.8	15.1	9.0	4.7	4.1	7.4
Sir Lanka	14.1	20.8	5.7	1.9	4.2	4.7
S Korea	13.7	23.4	13.7	21.1	9.7	8.7
Taiwan	13.1	16.1	12.6	14.5	-	9.4
China	12.5	8.3	11.2	8.3	9.8	5.0
Morocco	11.3	13.7	4.8	3.8	4.0	5.2
Hong Kong	11.2	10.5	11.6	10.3	5.8	8.8
Pakistan	10.1	-0.4	8.1	0.6	6.1	4.5
Tunisia	8.3	19.3	2.9	7.2	3.1	6.5
Chile	8.1	20.3	4.4	9.6	1.6	1.2
Egypt	7.7	-10.4	6.0	1.5	5.3	6.5

(Contd.)

(Contd. Annexure 'M')

Rates of *Country / territory*	*Growth of manufactured value added*		*Investment to GDP*		
	1980-88	*1970-80*	*1970*	*1980*	*1988*
Indonesia	8.4	13.1	1.44	25.4	28.5
Turkey	7.6	5.9	20.6	22.3	19.6
Mauritius	10.8	6.9	15.4	20.9	38.1
Mexico	0.2	6.8	22.2	28.0	17.4
Thailand	6.5	10.0	28.7	26.6	26.5
Malaysia	7.0	11.0	23.5	31.6	27.6
Sir Lanka	6.1	1.9	15.4	34.0	23.3
S Korea	12.7	15.7	25.2	32.8	33.1
Taiwan	-	12.3	26.2	32.6	-
China	16.3	7.0	26.3	32.2	37.6
Morocco	4.1	5.8	21.3	25.0	25.5
Hong Kong	-	10.6	25.8	36.0	27.1
Pakistan	7.7	5.3	20.9	18.7	18.0
Tunisia	5.8	9.8	33.0	30.3	14.6
Chile	1.9	-0.8	21.0	21.6	16.9
Egypt	5.5	-4.4	14.2	29.4	22.0

(Contd.)

(Contd. Annexure 'M')

Rates of Country / territory	Growth m'facture export volumes		Growth to total export volumes		Growth of GDP volumes	
	1980-88	1970-80	1980-88	1970-80	1980-88	1970-80
Singapore	7.3	18.2	7.0	4.2	6.8	7.8
Bangladesh	6.8	2.5	5.9	3.6	3.5	3.5
Brazil	6.0	18.8	5.9	8.1	2.9	7.5
Jordan	5.6	20.1	6.3	18.6	3.0	7.8
Zimbabwe	4.8	7.4	1.5	2.8	2.5	3.5
Senegal	4.8	-2.6	6.8	1.8	3.1	2.0
India	4.5	7.5	4.6	5.4	5.5	3.3
Costa Rica	4.5	10.6	2.9	5.0	2.3	5.3
Trinidad	4.1	0.7	-6.2	-7.6	-5.8	4.9
Philippines	3.0	25.6	0.4	5.8	0.0	6.4
Uruguay	2.0	14.9	2.0	6.3	-0.7	3.2
Ecuador	1.4	22.5	5.5	11.8	1.9	8.9
Yugoslavia	0.5	7.2	0.9	5.2	0.5	5.8
Kenya	0.3	6.8	0.1	-1.9	3.0	5.4
Colombia	0.3	12.8	7.9	1.9	3.0	5.4
Guatemala	0.1	4.8	-2.0	5.5	-0.3	5.8
Ivory Coast	-1.0	12.4	1.5	4.7	0.4	5.6
Argentina	-1.3	9.1	0.1	6.9	-0.3	2.3

(Contd.')

(Contd. Annexure 'M')

Rates of *Country / territory*	*Growth of manufactured value added*		*Investment to GDP*		
	1980-88	*1970-80*	*1970*	*1980*	*1988*
Singapore	4.7	9.3	43.3	41.8	35.3
Bangladesh	2.4	14.2	14.2	15.0	14.5
Brazii	4.2	2.9	20.9	23.6	17.4
Jordan	3.4	12.0	12.0	41.4	25.0
Zimbabwe	2.0	26.5	26.5	19.1	15.2
Senegal	3.3	17.5	17.5	15.8	15.0
India	7.9	19.3	19.3	22.8	21.7
Costa Rica	2.3	19.0	19.0	27.9	25.8
Trinidad	-10.0	12.4	12.4	32.2	9.7
Philippines	-0.3	23.6	23.6	30.7	16.9
Uruguay	-0.5	10.1	10.1	17.5	9.4
Ecuador	0.6	24.0	24.0	27.5	16.7
Yugoslavia	1.3	38.0	38.0	40.3	38.3
Kenya	2.9	20.3	20.3	19.1	17.9
Colombia	2.9	20.3	20.3	19.1	17.9
Guatemala	1.1	12.3	12.3	11.6	10.3
Ivory Coast	7.5	19.3	19.3	29.8	12.9
Argentina	-0.2	20.0	20.0	22.4	12.2

(Contd.)

Index

F

V

W